Community and Change in the North Carolina Mountains

CONTRIBUTIONS TO
SOUTHERN APPALACHIAN STUDIES, 13

Contributions to Southern Appalachian Studies

1. *Memoirs of Grassy Creek: Growing Up in the Mountains on the Virginia–North Carolina Line.* Zetta Barker Hamby. 1997

2. *The Pond Mountain Chronicle: Self-Portrait of a Southern Appalachian Community.* Leland R. Cooper and Mary Lee Cooper. 1997

3. *Traditional Musicians of the Central Blue Ridge: Old Time, Early Country, Folk and Bluegrass Label Recording Artists, with Discographies.* Marty McGee. 2000

4. *W.R. Trivett, Appalachian Pictureman: Photographs of a Bygone Time.* Ralph E. Lentz. 2001

5. *The People of the New River: Oral Histories from the Ashe, Alleghany and Watauga Counties of North Carolina.* Leland R. Cooper and Mary Lee Cooper. 2001

6. *John Fox, Jr., Appalachian Author.* Bill York. 2003

7. *The Thistle and the Brier: Historical Links and Cultural Parallels Between Scotland and Appalachia.* Richard Blaustein. 2003

8. *Tales from Sacred Wind: Coming of Age in Appalachia. The Cratis Williams Chronicles.* Cratis D. Williams. 2003

9. *Willard Gayheart, Appalachian Artist.* Willard Gayheart and Donia S. Eley. 2003

10. *The Forest City Lynching of 1900: Populism, Racism, and White Supremacy in Rutherford County, North Carolina.* J. Timothy Cole. 2003

11. *The Brevard Rosenwald School: Black Education and Community Building in a Southern Appalachian Town, 1920–1966* Betty Jamerson Reed. 2004

12. *The Bristol Sessions: Writings About the Big Bang of Country Music* Edited by Charles K. Wolfe and Ted Olson. 2005

Community and Change in the North Carolina Mountains

Oral Histories and Profiles of People from Western Watauga County

Compiled by Nannie Greene *and*
Catherine Stokes Sheppard

Research Assistant Sarah Jean Joslin

Contributions to Southern Appalachian Studies, 13

McFarland & Company, Inc., Publishers
Jefferson, North Carolina, and London

Library of Congress Cataloguing-in-Publication Data

Greene, Nannie.
Community and change in the North Carolina mountains : oral histories and profiles of people from western Watauga County / compiled [and edited] by Nannie Greene and Catherine Stokes Sheppard ; research assistant, Sarah Jean Joslin.
p. cm.—(Contributions to southern Appalachian studies ; 13)
Includes index.

ISBN-13: 978-0-7864-2593-8
(softcover : 50# alkaline paper) ♾

1. Watauga County (N.C.)—Social life and customs—20th century—Anecdotes. 2. Mountain life—North Carolina—Watauga County—History—20th century—Anecdotes. 3. Community life—North Carolina—Watauga County—History—20th century—Anecdotes. 4. Social change—North Carolina—Watauga County—History—20th century—Anecdotes. 5. Mountain people—North Carolina—Watauga County—Biography—Anecdotes. 6. Watauga County (N.C.)—Biography—Anecdotes. 7. Interviews—North Carolina—Watauga County. 8. Watauga County (N.C.)—History—20th century—Anecdotes. I. Greene, Nannie, 1928– II. Sheppard, Catherine Stokes, 1929– III. Joslin, Sarah Jean. IV. Series.
F262.W34C66 2006
975.6'843043—dc22 2006011170

British Library cataloguing data are available

On the front cover: Grace, Catherine, Genevieve, Ralph, Helen and Jack Sherwood posing on a horse, circa 1930s *(courtesy of Genevieve Henson); (inset)* Newton Banner of George's Gap Road *(courtesy of the Banner family)*

Manufactured in the United States of America

McFarland & Company, Inc., Publishers
Box 611, Jefferson, North Carolina 28640
www.mcfarlandpub.com

Dedicated to the memory
of those who have gone before
to forge and to maintain our heritage.
From the pioneer days through the
Great Depression, they sacrificed, and fought
to make western Watauga County a good
place to live. In the years since, others
have worked to keep this heritage alive.
It is our hope that future
generations will pass the torch.

Contents

Preface and Acknowledgments

Our oral history project began after hearing Elie Wiesel give the fall convocation address at Appalachian State University in Boone, N.C., in 1998. Dr. Wiesel is a Nobel Peace Prize winner and a Holocaust survivor. He entered a concentration camp at age 15, and knew the horror of losing his family at such an early age. His emphasis that day was for his listeners to get a tape recorder and make older people talk.

Oral history is simply memories recorded. Our memories tell more than a story; they also tell something about the time period in which the story takes place. To understand our culture today, we need to know our past. What better way than to read first-person tales of the past?

Western Watauga County, North Carolina, was chosen because we have deep roots here. This is where we grew up. As far as we know there has been no oral history compiled from our communities. Furthermore, we knew there were stories that should be saved.

We sent out flyers asking people to think about events in their lives that they would like to share in a book, and we also published this request in the *Watauga Democrat*. We contacted individuals who we knew were good storytellers and asked them to tape or write their stories. Two people may not always remember events the same way. An oral history is not intended to be entirely factual or exact, so we do not vouch for their authenticity. Wherever possible, we have used the exact words of the speaker or writer. At times it was necessary to edit material for clarity or to prevent embarrassment to another person. Brevity had to be considered. However, we tried hard never to change the meaning of a story.

Most of the stories given to us were from the 1930s, 1940s, or 1950s—the Great Depression years, the war years, the recession years, and the Cold War years. Those who contributed to this book provide a clear picture of how people back then built upon the foundations laid by their forebears.

Elie Wiesel told us to pass on our history before it is lost. He said, "You are the bridge." We believe that everyone who submitted a story is a bridge in this narrative. Each has saved a piece of history.

To everyone who contributed written stories or gave us information for stories or who lent us photographs, we say a sincere thank you. This is your book, you wrote it; we merely compiled it. We are so grateful that because of this book we have made new friends and renewed friendships with several people with whom we had lost contact. We feel rewarded and grateful.

The first person to encourage us was Tommy Walsh of the Sustainable Development program at Appalachian State University in Boone, North Carolina. He sent us to Patricia D. Beaver of the Appalachian Studies department at ASU; she convinced us, "Yes, we can do this book." She has been our advisor and cheerleader each step of the journey.

Mr. Walsh also suggested that we ask the Cove Creek Preservation and Development, Inc. to endorse this project. They did just that, and paid for flyers to be printed for the initial venture. With this assistance we were on our way!

Sarah Joslin, our graduate assistant from the Appalachian Studies program, spent many hours untangling our errors and helping us to come up with a respectable format. Her work has been invaluable and we cannot thank her enough. Martha Farrell also typed much of the rough copy and deserves our appreciation. Another thank you goes to Anne Burgess for her assistance with proofreading.

Jerry Adams and Leo Mast searched their memories and their photo collections, as well as their files, to give us information regarding activities that have been instrumental in preserving the Cove Creek community. We are indebted to others who reached back in time to share information on their respective communities: Cove Creek, Sugar Grove, Vilas, Amantha, Mabel, Zionville, Timbered Ridge, Beaver Dams, Bethel, Watauga River, Valle Crucis, Oak Grove, Foscoe, Pottertown, and others. Thank you for the variety of subjects you introduced.

The Watauga County Historical Society offered their help in letting the public know about our book of oral history. We appreciate their interest.

There were times when we became discouraged and wondered if we would ever finish this book. Then a note or e-mail thanking us for doing this project would arrive. The writers cannot possibly know how encouraging those messages were. Thanks for keeping us going.

Introduction

If one is to believe the mass media's version of the so-called typical mountaineer, then he will come away with a sordid and contorted picture of Appalachia. Even before the days of television, Hollywood did a pretty good job of showing mountain people as ignorant, lazy, and often dimwitted. Al Capp's Li'l Abner came into homes in the funny papers to reinforce the images introduced by the movie industry. Following this came television with shows such as *The Beverly Hillbillies* and *The Dukes of Hazzard*.

There is no such thing as a *typical* mountaineer. People from the North Carolina mountains are as diverse as those in other areas. There are no physical characteristics that set us apart, nor does our intellect distinguish us. Our speech may vary from one family to another, but no more than occurs in communities in other locales. While we might want to claim the character of Jed Clampett, who was wise, patient and kind, he does not represent us any more than does Jethro.

Perhaps the word *unique* is more appropriate to describe Western Watauga County than *typical.* Yes, we have poverty. Yes, we have uneducated people. Yes, there is crime. We are not without the problems that face all areas. However, these factors do not dominate our culture. Since there has never been manufacturing on a large scale in this area, income has been derived from agriculture. Consequently, our populace has never been predominately affluent. Yet by hard work, thrift and good management, we have kept pace with the outside world.

No doubt our proximity to Appalachian State University has contributed much to our uniqueness. This institution has made it possible for our children to get a college education. It has provided our public schools with outstanding teachers. Not all of our benefits, however, derived from academics. Since the university is the largest employer in Watauga County, it has provided employment with benefits to many of our citizens. This is especially true of women who have worked in the housekeeping department and college offices. Job opportunities for non–college educated women have otherwise been limited. When women can supplement the income of their husbands, the quality of life for the family is greatly improved.

The academic environment provided by the university has also been a drawing card to retirees and other people who wish to relocate. Many of these newcomers have contributed greatly to the quality of life in Western Watauga County.

It is our desire that in reading this book one will see that Western Watauga County has been progressive on par with other regions of our country. The stories told by local citizens and the photographs of W.R. Trivette show that we were in step with the times from the 1930s forward. Our Law and Order section does not suggest we were involved in feuding or lynching, but rather ordinary crimes of the times. Many young men from our area went to war and achieved the ranks of leaders, not to mention those non-commissioned who did heroic deeds simply because they were in the position to perform a needed action. Western Watauga has produced medical doctors, lawyers, statesmen, a renowned neurosurgeon, teachers, musicians, and many fine citizens. We are a proud people.

Part 1: Everyday Life of the People

As we go about our mundane chores every day, it is difficult to regard them as having any historical significance. Yet when we compare them to the corresponding chores of our parents and grandparents, we are able to grasp the changes in our culture that have been brought about by technology. It is then that these changes seem very important to us.

Few people today under the age of sixty would recognize a bed bug, a head louse, a leaf of galax, or lye soap. This same group cannot imagine scalding the interior walls of their house, playing basketball in a gym heated with a wood heater, or seeing gasoline pumps showing the price of 14 cents per gallon. Other changes revealed here are items such as preparing at home a body for burial, having the shoemaker come to a private home to make the family's winter shoes, sleeping on a mattress made of straw, or having the mail delivered by a carrier on horseback. Yet the numerous stories here indicate that this was our every day life and we felt no deprivation.

Our stories show that recreation as well as work has also undergone dramatic change. What young man today would walk several miles for the pleasure of sitting in a parlor with his sweetie and her family? Who today would get excited about riding a boat 100 yards on Cove Creek? Who can imagine boarding in a private home for a three-week vacation?

While these and many more examples of everyday life in the past are shocking revelations to younger generations, they simply bring nostalgic memories to those of us who experienced them.

At Home on Timbered Ridge

Mary Faye Tester

Catherine Sheppard's first visit to Timbered Ridge was on a crisp October afternoon. The purpose of the trip to interview Mary Faye Tester. Catherine was mesmerized by the natural beauty of the area. The leaves were at their peak and the entire landscape seemed so vibrant. Then Catherine met Mary Faye, who is such a charming lady and such a tribute to her heritage. Her home is fairly new and modern in every way, yet it captures the past perfectly. Interwoven with new things are pieces that have been handed down from the past. A butter churn, a flax wheel complete with a weasel, and a pedal organ all remind the observer that past generations are revered. As they chatted, Catherine noticed two deer came out of the woods behind her house. Mary Faye was unperturbed by these visitors. She told Catherine they come often into her yard and bother nothing, not even her vegetable garden. No wonder Mary Faye never wants to move away.

Timbered Ridge has always been my home. Although I have lived in other places, I have always thought of Timbered Ridge as home. I was born and raised here, went to school here, married here, moved away two times, but always yearned to come back, because this is home.

My mother, Susie Hagaman Trivette, attended Appalachian Training School and was a teacher when she met and married my father, Eldridge Trivette. She continued to teach until her first child was born. She saved her salary and she and my father were able to buy their own farm. In those days, most women were not able to earn money, so this gave my parents an edge financially because they did not have to come up with cash for land payments. But I remember how Mama would sit and figure where the money would come from for taxes. Even so, farming was a hard life in these mountains, but I wouldn't take anything for the lessons in hard work and thrift that I learned early in life. It certainly prepared me for the life that lay ahead.

I was born during the Great Depression, but people in the mountains did not see a great deal of change from the way they had always lived. Most mountain farmers had always grown their own food, recycled everything (although we did not know what the word *recycled* meant), worshipped near home and made-do. Dad raised cattle and chickens. He loved chickens and we always had lots of chickens and eggs to sell. We always had plenty to eat. We butchered two hogs every winter. We sold some cattle, but now and then we butchered a cow. Daddy cured the hams and sides and Mama canned beef and pork. Today I sometimes see a good special on certain cuts of pork and I buy it, come home, and can it. It is so much better than frozen pork. It seems like we canned everything in the garden. There was a cannery built at Cove Creek in the early '40s and some neighbors would take meat, vegetables and fruit over there and put their stuff up in tin cans, but we did not have any transportation so we continued to can in fruit jars. Mama always made cheese. We always had lots of milk and Mama would make both cottage cheese and pressed cheese. I suppose the cheese would be more like cheddar in taste. It was the color of Swiss but we usually put color in it. It was good.

Today I still use many of the old recipes my mother used. She always made her own lye soap. We saved all our grease drippings to go in soap. When we killed hogs, we saved the fat off the intestines and cooked it for our soap. That fat was too strong and not fit for lard. Occasionally we bought a bar of soap but we kept that back for Sunday use. We used the homemade soap for washing clothes, bathing and even washed our hair with it. It never hurt us. We made soap one time a year, usually after we killed hogs, but we saved the waste grease all year long. Mama did not put ashes in her soap, but Grandma Hagaman did. That was called soft soap. I still make soap now and then just like Mama did. In fact, I have a pan making now.

There was not much we bought from the store. We did have to buy flour, but we grew corn and had our meal ground. We bought coffee but very little. Mama liked coffee and she would sift the corn meal, save the husks, and parch it to make something similar to coffee. The rest of us drank milk, three times a day. We never thought about tea. We also bought sugar but we sweetened a lot of things with molasses and honey. We bought salt and pepper. The Watkins man and the Rawleigh man used to come around peddling things like salt, pepper, vanilla flavoring and spices.

Another means of shopping that is interesting to young people now is the rolling store. A man would come in a truck from Tennessee and sell things similar to the Watkins and Rawleigh products. He came every Monday and we would go up to the road to meet him. He would take chicken, eggs, butter and cream for payment. You could get the biggest bag of candy for a nickel! Then he would go to the next house where he might sell the produce he had bought from you. Remember, in those days there was not much money around, especially in the hands of the housewife.

At one time, my daddy had a store and so did my uncle. Clyde Perry had a store on up the road. That was the main source of getting our groceries if we had to buy them. We would walk to the store unless we had to get kerosene for the lamps. Then Mr. Perry would deliver that, and pick up chickens and eggs. He would bring the kerosene in 5-gallon cans and he would put a piece of wax candy (gumdrop) over the spout of the can to seal it. We kids would fight over that candy!

Mother never did any weaving, but she did a lot of sewing and mend-

Timbered Ridge is "home" to Mary Faye Trivette Tester. She moved away twice and broadened her life experiences. She worked with ASU students for 20 years. Mary Faye always yearned to go back home. After retiring, she built a house near her brother, who lives in the family homeplace, and she moved back to her beloved Timbered Ridge. Mary Faye loves to can and freeze fresh vegetables and has plenty for winter use (photograph by Catherine Sheppard).

ing. I remember how she would darn socks. (You never threw away any sock just because it had a hole in it!) At night, she would darn socks by the light of an oil lamp. I do not know how she could see. Of course our eyes then were not used to bright lights. We got an Aladdin lamp and we thought that was really bright. We never made candles, but we always used kerosene lamps.

Another farm chore was making the straw ticks for the beds. We did not have mattresses when I was small; we slept on straw ticks or feather beds. Straw was good for the summer and feathers for the winter but really poor people did not have feather beds. The ticks were like a bed-sized pillowcase, often made from flour sacks. The farmer would thrash the wheat and his wife would save enough straw for bedding. When they were new the straw smelled so good. I remember how I'd wiggle out a place in the straw to fit my body. Mama would come to make up my bed and she'd put her hand under the straw tick, shake it up, and just ruin where I had made my body nest! Every year Mama would spring-clean and throw out the old straw, to be put in the stable for bedding there, and put in fresh straw. We never dreamed of a heated bedroom and I remember how I would stand by the fireplace or heater and get really warm and run upstairs and crawl in between two feather beds. Since we always had chickens, it was easy to get feathers.

Somewhere in the late 30s or early 40s a government agency decided we needed better beds. This was probably one of the New Deal programs. Anyhow they introduced us to the cotton mattress. I think the place we went to was Doc Mast's store in Vilas. We all went and made mattresses and thought we had arrived! There were no inner springs or nothing. We tacked them. They had a pretty striped cover and were smooth on the beds, unlike straw ticks, and we thought we were up-town. They lasted for years and years. We could also make quilts at this place. They had bolts of pretty cloth we could have for quilts but Mama already had plenty of quilts so we didn't make any there.

Spring-cleaning also meant washing the walls. Lots of people didn't have painted walls and they had to scrub them down with lye soap and hot water. We had painted walls and still scrubbed them down with hot water and lye. You see, bed bugs, which we called chinches, were a problem. If you got them about the only way you could get rid of them was to paint or scrub with hot lye water. They liked to nest in the cracks of the wall. They would bite and cause you to itch. If a traveler came by and one crawled off his clothes, it would hide in the cracks of the wall and soon you were infested. Another reason to scrub the walls was that we heated with a fireplace and at the very best, walls would get smoked.

Walls were not the only thing scrubbed with lye soap. Mama would boil our clothes in lye soap water in a big pot. I remember when I was little, one thing Mama would not let me help with was the wash because of the lye. Lye could really hurt you, because it would burn you. I think one reason we have so many germs today is that our clothes aren't really sterilized. So many fabrics cannot take that much heat. Back then washing was an all day job. You sorted the clothes, boiled the white clothes, then the colored. Work clothes boiled last and always with lye soap. Then everything had to be rinsed through two waters, wrung out and hung in the sun to dry. In the winter, things would freeze on the line but when they thawed, they would be dry, but stiffer than you would know now.

If a woman ever had any hired help it likely was when she was sick and then to do the wash. Usually if there was serious sickness, neighbor women would come in and help with cooking and washing. The men would come and cut firewood or help out with whatever was needed. Of course, now we don't need the help we once did. We have automatic washing machines and dryers. Usually some family member can put in a load of wash. In addition, we have ways of heating our houses that don't require labor. When I was eleven our mother had to go to Winston for surgery. There was a hospital in Boone but no surgeon. I knew how to cook some things but I remember that neighbor women came in and did the washing and the heavy work. Later we children got measles and gave it to our dad. He was so sick he nearly died. Neighbors came in, did the heavy work, and brought in wood. He was in the process of covering a barn with wood shingles and they helped do that.

Neighbors were also our entertainment. We used to visit our neighbors and that is how we became close to them. In good weather, we would visit after supper. The grown folks would sit on the porch and swap stories and the children would play games around the yard. Now neighbors visit on the phone.

Mama was a good manager. She could sew and re-do. She had a cousin Ruth who lived in New Jersey. She found out that Mama made beautiful quilts. She would send us huge boxes of clothes and money, and Mama would make quilts for her. It seemed she was a rather well to do lady and because of those boxes my brothers and I had better clothes than lots of our schoolmates. We would be so excited when those boxes came in the mail and we always referred to our clothes as Cousin Ruth clothes.

We had a very big kitchen and cooked on a wood stove. The stove sat in a sort of recessed space so that no heat from it came into the room. We had a fireplace in the living room and Daddy built an iron arm to hang an iron kettle on. In really cold weather we cooked in that fireplace and did not go into the kitchen unless it was absolutely necessary. We would boil potatoes over the fire and Mama would bake cornbread in an old-timey baker in the coals. We would eat potatoes, cornbread, and milk right in the living room for supper. I can remember wiping off the kitchen table in the winter and ice would freeze on the table. Now that is cold! Later Daddy built a flue in the kitchen and we had a wood-burning heater. Then the kitchen became the main living space. The kitchen table became the center of life. We ate there and did our homework there and often sat there to talk. We always had plenty of apples and that was our snack while we did homework.

Change came slow to Timbered Ridge. So slow in fact, I never noticed. Since no big military camps were close by and no main roads went past our door, about all we knew about the war of the '40s was radio news. Several boys in our area did go into service and of course, we were concerned about their safety. I guess we never doubted the USA would win the war eventually. One of the boys I had known in school was Clyde Tester. He was a few years older than me. After he finished at Bethel High School, he went into the Army. When he came back we started dating. Our dates were mostly going to church and he would walk me home. On Saturday night, he would come to our house and we would sit in the parlor, talk, and carry on. My parents liked him. He liked my parents too. My mother, like all mothers, was never ready for any of us to leave home. I had to finish high school and had no desire to go to college. My younger brother graduated from ASU and later in life I wished I had gone too. Anyway, I married Clyde when I was 19. We had a happy marriage; it just did not last long enough.

After we were married, Clyde went into the Highway Patrol and we lived in Mars Hill for 5 years. Every time he had a day off we'd come home. I always loved home. I loved my Mama and Daddy. Clyde was good to bring me back and he enjoyed being here too. Besides, if he was in Mars Hill on his day off he would always be called back to work. We solved that by getting out of town. Then he got a transfer to Nags Head. In 1953 or '54 we thought Nags Head was plumb out of the world. Today it would be a nice place to live. Our only child was 6 months old and neither of us wanted to be that far from home. He left the Highway Patrol and came back here and we put in a grade-A dairy. Later he got on as a security guard at ASU and after that he got a job in the ASU bookstore.

Clyde had developed diabetes and his eyesight had become so poor he could not see to drive after dark. We had to get closer to his job in Boone. We found out about a man who needed someone to care for ten apartments in Boone and who would provide a nice rock house for us. We took the job and moved to Boone. I really hated moving because we had only lived in our new house for two years. The man was so good to us and soon became like family. When our daughter started to high school, I had time on my hands so I found myself a job. I had worked in the kitchen at the hospital for about two years when my daddy came to live with us. I guess he was in early Alzheimer's because he got to wandering off so I quit my job to care for him. After he died, I went back to the hospital and worked another year. By this time, Clyde was real sick and I quit to take care of him. When he got better I went to work at Shadowline for a year. I was still on their payroll when Clyde died but I could not face working there anymore. I needed to be outside to deal with my grief. Later I went to ASU and worked as a housekeeper for six months in Lovill dorm. I loved it! When a job opened for housekeeping supervisor, I applied and got it. I was in charge of 34 people. In the summer, there were more than 34 because they hired extra people to thoroughly clean the buildings. There were seventeen dorms then. I dearly loved the job. This is what took me through Clyde's death. I needed something to keep me busy and that did. It didn't give me much time to sit around and think. The pay was not much at first but I worked my way up and I was able to build up retirement. It is not a big retirement but it pays my insurance. ASU was a good place and I am so thankful for being able to work there.

The time at ASU was the period in my life that I really grew. I had been pretty much a homebody before then. I learned so much about other cultures. The first day I was there, I felt like I could not face the world but I knew I had to. I was 45 years old and there was no Social Security or anything for me. It was hard work, keeping those dorms clean, but soon I dearly loved it. When I went there those dorms were in bad condition, but I had good supervisors and they furnished me with whatever I needed to get the job done. We cleaned those buildings up and made them look a lot better. I loved the students! As I said, it was there I learned to work with different colors, different types of people and know that no matter how you dress or what you look like, inside is what you are. Living out here, not communicating with different people, I'd never had a chance to learn that. Even working in the hospital, I didn't come in contact with many people. I considered working at the university such a blessing. I got along well with the students. There were good kids, bad kids, and all kinds. They would come to me with their problems. They sort of made me their mama, especially the boys. One day I went into the laundry room in a dorm and a boy was sitting on top of a washing machine. When I asked him why he was up there, he said it was because the lid would not close. I told him he had too much for one load. I often had to show the boys how much washing powder to use. Sometimes I would do mending for them. I not only grew, I enjoyed my twenty years at ASU. It was during this period in my life that I found time to take several courses at Caldwell Community College. I took courses in communications and other things that would help me with my job. I met so many nice people that my life was very full.

Sometimes people ask me why I never remarried. I guess one reason I never wanted to remarry was that I was married to my job. I was often called out at night when problems came up in a building. Besides, I just figured I never could find anybody who could take the place of Clyde. After his death, I moved back here. A few years ago I built this house which was a dream fulfilled. My brother lives in the old home place and I see him often. My daughter and grandchildren are in Boone. I am happy to be here and to be able to count my blessings every day.

The Cannery

Nannie Greene

Thanks to Robert Shipley for the information furnished here. Mr. Shipley succeeded Ernest Hillard as vocational agriculture teacher and continued the cannery project.

In an effort to help rural people safely preserve as much food as possible, a federal project funded seed money to build a cannery in areas where agricultural education was offered. This department was to manage and maintain such a facility. Ernest Hillard was the vocational agriculture teacher at Cove Creek at that time and he saw this as a golden opportunity for Western Watauga County.

In the mid-forties a cannery was built on the grounds of the Cove Creek High School campus to assist the community in food preservation. The cannery was to be self-supporting, but not a profit-making project. Farm families from anywhere in the county could take their meat and vegetables that had been prepared for canning to the cannery. An employee of the cannery would operate the machines that put the vegetables, or meat, in tin cans, seal them, and cook them under pressure for a specified time. A small per can fee was charged. This was wonderful for the housewife who no longer had to stand over a hot stove for hours to can in the conventional manner. Three sizes of cans were available: pints, quarts, and gallons.

The cannery was very successful until home freezing came into being. One staple in the Watauga homes was green beans. Even after many owned freezers, they still canned their beans. Robert Shipley recalls that one family from Bethel every year brought eight bushels of green beans, snapped, washed and ready for canning. This type canning was also a boost for preserving homegrown meat.

Several years prior to the cannery the federal government had sought to improve home canning by introducing the use of the pressure cooker. This was done through the Home Demonstration clubs. However, many people did not feel secure using the pressure cooker. The old method of open kettle canning often resulted in spoiled food.

Through vocational agriculture and home economics education, both sponsored by the federal government, an improved quality of life came to Western Watauga County.

Growing Up in Bethel

Genevieve Sherwood Henson

The original material for this piece was from an interview with Mrs. Henson conducted by Jo Harris in October 1999. The following year we again visited and recorded additional details that Mrs. Henson related. She and her siblings are depicted on the front cover of this book. Genevieve Sherwood Henson still lives in her home at Cove Creek, near her son's family.

I was raised in the Bethel section of Watauga County, over the hill from my home here about five miles. My mother was Nannie Farthing; she married Jim Sherwood, who was the son of Wiley Sherwood. My mother was born, married, and bore nine of her children in the same house. The house is still there; it is up on the side of Spoon Mountain. The Needle family from South Carolina bought the house and they named it Needle Point Farm.

My great-great grandfather, William Farthing, was the first Farthing to come to this area. He was a Baptist preacher and he came as a missionary to the people who lived in this area. He bought 487 acres of land for $2000 in the Bethel community. That was in 1826. He built a cabin and lived there. When William came to Watauga County, some of his 14 children were grown but they came with him. That proved to be good because he had only lived here a month when he died. He was buried in the little cemetery near the present Bethel Fire Department. Many Baptist preachers descended from him.

One of William's sons was Dudley, who married Nancy Mast, daughter of John Mast of Cove Creek. They built a log cabin near William's cabin. The story goes that they baked their bread on a flat rock in the fireplace. This was in the early 1800s. They had 13 children, I think, one of whom was Henry Farthing.

I am glad that I know something about my family history. I think it is important that people know who their relatives are and where their ancestors came from. I suppose I know more about the Farthings than the Sherwoods because I grew up among them. As you can see, there were so many Farthings I was kin to about everybody! Not really. Some of Dudley's children died young. Another died in the Civil War, some of the girls never married. One son went to Texas and died there. But that still left plenty of relatives. Dr. Perry once told us that all the Farthings were related but some were far enough off that we didn't have to claim them if we didn't want to.

Aunt Florence, who was 21 years older than Mama, was grown and married before Mama was born. Neither Aunt Florence nor Aunt Laura had any children. But, Mama had enough for all the rest of them; she had ten. By today's standards, that was a big family, but back then, that was not unusual.

We mostly grew everything we ate, because during the Depression money was scarcer than hens' teeth. We never had two nickels to rub together, but we were never, never hungry. Our grandfather Farthing had a lot of land and he had set out a tremendous lot of fruit trees. We had peaches, apples and gallons upon gallons of cherries. People used to come from everywhere to pick cherries. We had an old cherry seeder that you could crank. I have seeded cherries until my fingers were blistered. We dried apples; we canned apples; we picked blackberries and strawberries. We had an abundance of food, but to say we had money, forget it! We did not. We had cows and plenty of milk and plenty of butter. We always had at least two hogs to kill. We had chickens and eggs. We just didn't have money. Everybody was in the same boat. I was talking to a friend once and she said, "Well, we were poor as a church mouse, but we didn't know it. We would have been embarrassed if we had known." We ate good, healthy food. Our mother was a good cook.

Back then, I suppose about everybody I knew would have been classified as farmers because we grew our own food. Our father had a store, also he clerked for Clyde Perry. But our family owned a sawmill and gristmill. They ground corn, wheat and so forth. I don't remember when they ground wheat but my mother said they did. We used to pass the mill on our way to school. We never went to the store to buy a bag of meal. In those days, you shelled your own white corn, took it to the mill to be ground, and made it into cornbread. It was so much better than what you have today. The Winebargers also had a mill and they ground buckwheat into flour. Our mother made the best buckwheat pancakes! Besides the gristmill, our father had a little country store near our house. That building is still standing.

In our family everybody worked. Children these days don't work and I think that is a problem. Since I was next to the oldest, there was plenty for me to do. I can't remember not taking care of somebody's children. I took care of a lot of my brothers and sisters. One of my brothers said the saddest day of his life was the day I got married, because he was positive he would starve to death. My sisters didn't like to cook very much and our mother was sick a good deal of the time in later years. He just knew that they would starve when I left.

My family set a high value on education. I suppose they knew we didn't have much of a chance to get ahead if we did not have education. My brother, Jack, became a medical doctor. My brother, Harry, has a Ph.D. and has retired as the head of public relations at Wingate College. My sisters, Catherine, Helen, Grace and Carolyn, are all retired schoolteachers. Our early education was at Bethel School. I don't know how many children were in the school but I do remember it had four rooms. One large room had a sliding door in the middle that could be opened up to make a bigger room for plays and such. I went all the way from first grade through high school in that little building. The beautiful rock building was a WPA project, built about two years after I graduated in 1936. We had a hard time getting a high school over there. Once a woman said to me, "It's almost impossible to get into college if you graduated from Bethel School." I said, "That's where you are wrong, ma'am, because a larger percentage of children who went to Bethel School went on to college, I bet, than they did from any other school in the county." And some very smart people went on to get doctorates. For the most part, we had good teachers in that little school. They cared whether we learned or whether we didn't. Our parents cared also. It makes me furious that people think we were so backward and lived in the backwoods. Of course, not everybody went to college; I didn't because I let my husband outtalk me.

My sister, Catherine, is one year older than I. The first year we went to school, she was seven and I was six. Our daddy bought a little white pony for us to ride to school. My mother would put us on that pony and start us to school two miles away. We went down through the woods, not a house through there. That pony was real mean and he would stub up and go back home with us. Mama would take us off, whip the hide off the pony, put us back on and start us again; and he took us! We rode ponies to school up until about the time we went to high school or until we were old enough to walk the distance. Later Dad had a little pony wagon built and we had two ponies that we would harness to that wagon. We would go by the gristmill every morning on our way to school and leave the corn to be ground for cattle feed and some for cornmeal. We would put our pony (or later ponies) in a neighbor's barn near the school. In the afternoon, we would saddle or harness the pony for the return trip. Can you imagine a seven-year-old and a six-year-old today being able to do all that? There was no such thing as a lunchroom back then. Mama would pack our lunch in a little basket, one of us would carry the basket, and the other would drive the pony. Catherine was supposed to ride in the saddle going and I was to ride in the saddle coming home. But, nine times out of ten, Catherine would outtalk me and I would ride behind the saddle both ways. As we got older, we got bigger ponies or horses to ride to school. Many years later I remarked to my mother that I thought I would have let my children grow up not knowing how to read and write before I would have sent them off to school the way she did. She said, "No, you wouldn't!" Nothing was going to stop her children from an education.

Before cars were plentiful, riding horses was a necessity because it was the main mode of transportation. Nannie and Jim Sherwood got their children acquainted with animals at an early age. They watched as three of them, Catherine, Genevieve, and Ralph, sat on a cow, practicing for a riding lesson (photograph furnished by Genevieve Sherwood Henson).

Our social life was primarily centered around our school or church. My family went to the Bethel Baptist Church. There were several churches in the area but they were all Baptist. If people of a different faith moved into the area, they just went to the Baptist Church. Everyone was welcomed. That included the black people in the community. They mostly came to the revivals. The Timbered Ridge, Mountain Dale, and Forest Grove churches all branched out from the Bethel Baptist. If there was a night service or a program at school at night, young folks would walk home. If you had a sweetheart, he would walk home with you.

I met my husband at a pie or box supper. I don't remember if I made pies or a box. He didn't buy my box. I don't remember who bought my box that night. (The school often had box suppers to raise money to buy library books.) Anyhow, every now and then boys would take a notion to get a little whiskey and I noticed this night that some were drunk. Anyhow, after the supper was over we started home. Ernest Henson came up to me and said, "Can I take you home?" I said, "I don't know, are you drunk too?" And, he said, "No ma'am, I have not drinked." So, he took me home. I was 16 and he was 22. We dated for about four years. You must understand that

Catherine and Genevieve Sherwood Henson rode a pony to school when they were in the primary grades. Their parents prepared all their children for riding while they were young. Six of the Sherwood children posed for this picture in the 1930s. They are Grace, Catherine, Genevieve, Ralph, Helen and Jack (photograph furnished by Genevieve Sherwood Henson).

dating then was not like dating today. My daddy was very strict, and I guess I could count on the fingers of my hands and not use all of them the number of times we went anywhere by ourselves. Now he had an old A-model, rather his daddy had an old A-model car, which sometimes he would get it to come over there to see me. But he didn't get it every time, and he would walk from where he used to live about a mile up this road here and he walked down Forest Grove, down through Bethel and up the side of Stone Mountain. That must have been six or eight miles. I suppose all that walking was good for him because he was in good shape until he died. I mean he was 76 years old and he had never spent a night in the hospital and had not been to the doctor very many times. He had a stroke and it affected the left side of his body, his left hand never did quite get back to him. After a month he began to recover and he was determined he was going to walk. His determination paid off and he did get so he could walk and also drive his tractor.

As I said before, we dated for four years. I was twenty but nearer twenty-one when we got married in 1939. I never regretted marrying Ernest Henson. I loved him deeply and he loved me till the day he died. We were married in my daddy's home. I wore a navy blue and pink dress that I had ordered from Sears for $6.98. (Actually, that was rather expensive. Most of my dresses were from cloth that cost fifteen cents a yard. I was fourteen years old before I had a ready-made dress. Mama made our clothes and we had pretty clothes).

At the time we were married very few people were married in the church. It was much more customary to be married at home. I remember the first wedding I ever went to. The bride was Bessie Cook and she married Eli Farthing. They were married in Bethel Church right after the service one Sunday morning. It was wintertime and she had on a beautiful blue coat with a white fur collar. Her face was pale as death and his was just as red as a pickled beet. The preacher asked, "Will you take this man..." She said, "I w-w-i-l -l." And when Eli was asked he said, "*I will in deed and in truth.*" He really belted it out. I was just a child, but that made a big impression on me.

When we were first married, Ernest was working with the power company. Our first home was a trailer. That allowed me to move wherever the power company sent him. He was working in South Carolina when our first child was born and when the baby was six weeks old we joined Ernest. My mother felt this was not wise since I had had such a rough time having the baby. She thought I should stay with her for a while, but Ernest wanted me to be with him. And as long as he lived he wanted me to be wherever he was. I am thankful to this day that the good Lord gave me the strength to look after him as long as he lived because he wanted me to. I had to do a lot of things for him that he wouldn't ever have wanted anybody else to do. And I'm thankful, so thankful!

We had three sons and a daughter; Jim, Les, Linda and Joe. Since Joe is ten years younger than his sister, people used to think he was an only child. When he was small he came home from school one day and said, "Mom, how do you go about asking a girl to be your girlfriend?" And I said, "I really don't know. You'd better wait and ask your brother when he comes home. But, tell me about her. Is she pretty? Just what sort of girl is she?" He thought a minute and said, "Oh, I really don't know. I'm not much of a judge about whether a girl is pretty or not. But she is awfully nice and good. Come to think of it, I guess that is why Daddy married you, isn't it?

Cause you are so nice and good ... unless you was a whole lot prettier a long time ago than you are now." Well, you don't punish a child for telling the truth!

You asked about the changes I've seen in my life: mercy, there have been so many. Electricity has changed life a lot. We got electricity in the house in 1939. I still have Ernest's lantern that he used to carry to the barn. In later years we got current in the barn too. Then medicine has changed greatly. The doctor used to come to the house. Old doctor Perry was about as gruff as anybody could be, but he was a good doctor. He came out to the house, delivered all of my mother's babies and doctored us when we got sick. I never had been to a doctor but about once or twice until after I was married, but Dr. Perry came. Dr. Len Hagaman came and delivered my first baby. He was a wonderful doctor. We still have good doctors and medicine has advanced so much. Today we do not pay attention to a simple disease, like high blood pressure, that used to kill people.

Not much has changed more than entertainment. We made our own. Occasionally a family would have a party. We'd have cookies and grape juice or something; we did not serve cokes because we did not have cokes. I never drank a soda pop until after I was married. We had what we made at home. We would play games and we read an awful lot. We did not have a radio for years and years. It was great when we got a radio; my mother was tickled to death. We played checkers and Rook. When we were young, neighbor children would gather and play games like Hide and Seek or Ante-Over.

I think I went to my first movie when I was 14 or 15. I was at my Grandfather Sherwood's at Cove Creek and I went with Ruth Sherwood and her boyfriend to the movie in Boone. I knew good and well they didn't want me but my grandfather made them take me because I was there. It was a silent movie. I saw one other silent movie when my husband and I lived in Virginia. I think it was called "King of Kings." My Aunt Nora used to oppose movies. (Many people thought movies were sinful when they were a new thing.) I told her I learned a lot from that movie. She said, "Just what did you learn?" I told her about how a woman, accused of adultery, was brought to Jesus. The movie showed how she was on the ground and all the people had rocks in their hands ready to stone her to death. Jesus stopped and wrote in the sand. Now the Bible does not say what He wrote but in this picture, He wrote the name of different sins: prejudice, jealousy and things we don't think of as being sins. It made me think about that.

Communication certainly has changed in my lifetime. I mentioned how pleased we were to get a radio. Now we turn a knob and get a movie in our own home. I know my Aunt Nora would think some of these are sinful! Telephones have changed our lives. Now we can call up people, chat, and maybe not see that person for weeks. It keeps our families in touch.

That is good since families no longer live near each other. I don't know much about e-mail but it certainly has changed letter writing I am told.

Another tremendous change is the price of things. You used to could get a loaf of bread for a dime, a pound box of crackers for a dime. You could get a 25-pound bag of flour for a dollar. My daddy would get a man to work for him and at quitting time, he would pay him with a 25 pound bag of flour. Today if you get somebody to work for an hour it is $10 or $12, and sometimes they work and sometimes they don't. It is so different!

A yard of cloth cost a nickel, a dime, fifteen cents, or a quarter. The other day I was at my daughter's house in Tennessee, I found a piece of white wool, and it was $12 and something a yard. And the very idea! And the patterns cost $10 or $12. I wanted to make my little great-grandchildren little red jumpers for Christmas. Well, the pattern cost $8 or $9. I told my daughter I was not paying that price for a bunch of paper. And I didn't. My mama used to cut her own pattern, using newspaper.

When my children were at Cove Creek School I used to take tomatoes, fresh corn and other fresh vegetables down there and they would give me so many tickets for the children's lunches. We would take canned stuff too. Lots of times the lunchroom would make big pots of soup. It was hot, nourishing and good.

I have to say, some of the changes I have seen in my lifetime are for better and some are for worse. I don't think all entertainment is for a better way of life but some things are. Of my mama's nine children, we are still alive except one. He died in April of 2000. I doubt that could have been said without modern medicine.

Although we are all getting older the telephone lets us visit even if we don't live close together. Social Security checks and Medicare help pay some of these high bills. When I look around me I am reminded that I have come a long ways from that little girl who rode a pony to Bethel School but in my heart, many things have not changed.

A Boy from Beaver Dams

Dennis Creed

In August 2000, Catherine Sheppard visited Dennis Creed with her recorder in hand. She asked Dennis to tell her things that he remembered about growing up in Beaver Dams. It was a delightful afternoon spent listening and recording. Here are his memories as he shared them.

I was born at Beaver Dams in 1938 and lived all my early life there, as had my parents before me. I recall many stories my dad used to tell about his growing up in Beaver Dams and I recall lots of things that are really different from today.

One story I remember is that before there were paved roads or for that matter, good gravel roads, there was a road that went across Stone Mountain by Locust Gap, down through Mill Creek, past Buzzard Roost, and into Neva, Tennessee. This road was little more than a dirt path and in wet weather it had deep ruts that made travel pretty rough. Lots of the farmers would haul their turkeys and chickens and even lambs to Neva, Tennessee, because the train came there. Neva was the nearest market. Only a horse-drawn wagon could use this road.

One tale I recall is there was an old farmer who loaded up his turkeys and went to Neva. He had heard of bananas but had never seen any. He told his neighbors that when he sold his turkeys he was going to buy himself some bananas. When he got back home the neighbor asked him how he liked the bananas. He said, "Well, I thought it was tough and awful bitter and there was just too much cob."

About everybody in Beaver Dams farmed. A lot of what was raised was for the family use but there were some cash crops. I mentioned the lambs, chickens and turkeys. Another cash crop was cattle, but getting them to market was a problem. When I was just a small boy I remember a man from Cove Creek used to go to Frank Wilson's barn and all the farmers around who had anything to sell would bring their stock there and sell to the man who had a large truck. I don't know where he took the stock to market, maybe Shouns, Tennessee. This was a big help to the farmers who did not have a truck. By this time, the roads were better, of course, but few people had a car or truck.

Another thing I remember about Stone Mountain was the rattlesnakes. They were plenty. I remember my dad putting a joint of stove pipe on each of my legs when we went to pick huckleberries. I also remember that Mary Helen Davis, a young girl in our neighborhood, was doing a farm chore (I don't remember what, maybe gathering the eggs) and she was bit on the hand by a rattlesnake. My dad had one of the first cars in our neighborhood and the girl's dad ran all the way to our house to get Dad to take her to Boone to Dr. Hagaman. But she got there too late and died.

There was a Dr. Greer who lived over on North Fork. He went to your house in a horse and buggy. But if it was a real emergency you tried to get to Boone. There was a horse doctor, Dr. Thompson, who doctored the livestock. He lived on Vanderpool. Another time my dad took a neighbor to Boone to the doctor and heard the doctor tell the patient, "You must stop riding your horse." That afternoon here came Uncle Jake riding his mule all saddled up. Dad said, "Uncle Jake, I heard the doctor tell you not to ride your horse any more." Uncle Jake said, "He did not say anything about riding a mule."

Things have changed so much. I remember when the mailman carried the mail on horseback. I also remember that Preacher Roby Eggers rode a horse from Zionville to Beaver Dams Baptist Church to preach. In the winter, I've known his shoes to be frozen to the stirrup of his saddle. I don't know what he was paid for preaching, but I'd say it was very little.

[Dennis showed us a ledger his father kept of the Sunday school records. This ledger shows that in May 1962, 81 people were present for Sunday school and the offering that day was $6.47. In December of 1967, there were 45 present and the offering was $18.24. You can see that as times got better financially, people did not attend church as much.]

Dennis Creed recalls some stories of his early life in the 1940s that are different from his life today. He told about farming, cash crops, and rattlesnakes. He also remembers when doctors used to travel by horse and buggy and the church used a pot-bellied stove for heat. Things have changed today, even the way we talk, but his feelings for Beaver Dams are still the same, changes and all (photograph furnished by Dennis Creed).

I remember when we had a pot-bellied stove to heat the church, then we put in a coal furnace and today there is an oil furnace. When we burned coal, the men in the church took turns going in early and firing up the furnace. When we had the pot-bellied stove (I was very small, but I remember) it sat in a bed of sand. The men and women both came in and if they had a chew of tobacco or a dip of snuff they would spit in the sand. If the men smoked, they would come in church, roll a cigarette from Prince Albert or Velvet and smoke. When it was time for the service to start they would put the cigarette, snuff, or chew of tobacco in a barrel of sand and the service would go on. You see, people would get up at five A.M. on Sunday to get ready to leave home at eight A.M. in order to get to church in time for the service; usually Sunday school would be at ten A.M. Lots of times the women would cook a big meal before they left because you never knew who would come home with you from the church.

Since everybody walked, some arrived earlier than others did and it was a time of fellowship. Then the church would be full. Now we have all the modern conveniences available and people cannot get to church on time. They have all sorts of excuses for not going. Of course then the church was the gathering place. A lot of people went because that was their social life. However, people at Beaver Dams did visit each other. I remember how after supper we would sit on the porch and neighbors would come and visit. My dad bought one of the first TV sets in the community and neighbors would come and stay till midnight to watch the snow fly on the TV. Of course, that was in the '50s.

At one time our church used oil lamps and the ladies took turns keeping them clean and the wicks trimmed. REA brought electricity to Beaver Dams in the mid '40s. I don't know what changed our lives more, the electricity or cars.

When I graduated from Bethel High School in 1956, there were no jobs in Watauga County to be had. A few men went to Lenoir or Wilkesboro to work in the furniture factories. They made maybe 75 cents an hour. I had a chance to go to Delaware to work in the Chrysler plant. I made $7.50 an hour. That was big money then. I was a paint man. I bought a new car and in 1957, Ruth and I got married. I could come home on $4 or $5 a trip. Gas was 15 cents or 16 cents a gallon. If there was a gas war on, the price fell to 14 cents. Rent was $35 a month and the light bill was around $3, the phone bill was $2.65. I would bring home over $100. Boy! That was big money to us. We would go to the grocery store and fill the trunk of the car with groceries that cost maybe $12. We lived in Pennsylvania for 10 years (I worked in Delaware but we lived in Pennsylvania). We moved back to North Carolina to be near our families again. Ruth and I both went to work at the Blue Ridge Shoe factory. After taxes, the two of us brought home $60. Some things had not changed in Watauga County.

Another thing that has changed is the way we talk. Not many people in my community spoke correct English ... but some tried, and a lot of times ended up on the wrong side of a joke. I remember once an old farmer went in the country store and asked the clerk the price of shoestrings that were on a cardboard display. The clerk said, "Those are 10 cents." The farmer replied, "Those can stay right there." I remember the most shocking language I heard when I was a young'un. We had been to church and decided to visit some neighbors who lived up the road from the church. On our way we saw the preacher's car had broke down. He was very upset. He said, "I reckon I need to go back there and kick the thing in the tail end." Back then, I thought that was really coarse language for our preacher to use. Yes, times have really changed. If I had used some of the language that I hear young folks use today, my daddy would have tanned my hide and I would still be standing.

My father's mother died when he was six years old. He was raised by a couple who had no children. When he was grown, he joined the Army and served in Panama. After his discharge, he caught the train to Abingdon, Virginia. Someone gave him a ride to Mountain City in a Model-A Ford. He got there at 3:00 A.M. and walked from there to Beaver Dams. I am sure he saw a lot of things change in his time in Beaver Dams. But, I wonder if my children and grandchildren will see as much change in their lifetime as I or my dad saw. I look at Beaver Dams today and see all kinds of change. Where I used to see cattle grazing, now there are elk. Where everybody used to have kinfolks, now there are people from other states living. Strangers have bought land and built fine homes. I am sure they will bring their ways of doing things. Things always change, but Beaver Dams was, and still is, a good place to live.

Good Neighbors, Good Friends

Nannie Greene

Like many others, my family lost our home during the Depression years. As renters we moved often, but we lived on George's Gap for ten years. Since those were my pre-teen years, I cherish my childhood memories from those years.

We lived in the last house "at the top of the Gap." There were only a few houses in the area, but all the families had children. We could name all eleven families that lived between our house and the lane where we turned to go to the Cove Creek Schools we all attended. If one took the road, our house was 3 miles from the school, but one could take a shortcut and walk down the hollar, as we did most of the time. I started to first grade in 1935 and we walked to school. We became acquainted with all the children, but the Bill Banner family was the most prominent and there was a reason for that.

Mr. Bill and Mrs. Alice Banner had 17 children. The first girl died when she was 5 years old and the 13th child lived only a few months. The other 15 grew up to have families of their own. All 15 of them never lived at home at the same time. As the older children graduated from high school, they went on to college, got married or went to work. Five were already gone when I first recall the family. Blanche had married and moved to Mountain City. Because of her asthma, her activities were limited, but she did beautiful handwork. Jim became an excellent carpenter. Susie was talented in art and she was an elementary teacher at Cove Creek School. Joe became a

The Banner home was always filled with children. Bill and Alice Banner had 17 children in all; 15 of them lived to have families of their own. Their friends were always welcome, too. Mrs. Alice never knew how many would show up at the table for a meal, and Mr. Bill wanted all children to enjoy swimming in their pool. They were good neighbors. The Banner family: First row, Eva Nell, Martin, Johnny, Mack, and Charlotte; second row, Susie, Ruth, Bill Banner, and Billy on Mrs. Alice's lap; third row, Bob, Blanche, Josephine, Tony, and Helen; fourth row, Jim and Joe (photograph furnished by Charlotte Banner Martin).

teacher of agriculture in high school. Helen, a high school valedictorian and an accomplished musician, chose love over a professional career. She enjoyed about 40 years of married life, but has been a widow for over 25 years. She was 87 in 2005.

In my family there were five children, and in the Banner family there was at least one child close to the age of each of us. My closest friend was Charlotte, the 12th child. One summer we stayed together for three straight weeks. We always had a good time wherever we were, but I loved spending time at the Banner home. There was always a game of some sort going on. Kick-the-can, red rover, jump rope, or ballgames of some kind were all favorites. Inside games included Monopoly, Chinese checkers, checkers, dominoes, or a card game such as Old Maid, Rook, Go Fish, Hearts, etc. Several participants made the games more fun.

Frieda Campbell Long remarked that she thought the big house was like a hotel because it had so many rooms. She and Eva Nell were friends and they liked to play the big upright piano that was in the parlor. Eva Nell only played the hymn "Calvary," but they both sang along. Frieda also recalls, "Mrs. Alice made the best rabbit stew and gravy I ever tasted." Mrs.

Banner was a great cook. I'll never forget the huge bread pan she used to bake those delicious biscuits and she would make homemade syrup to eat on them for breakfast. Louise Greene Baird sometimes stopped by their house after school and would have a leftover biscuit with jam, jelly or honey for a snack. They always had plenty of food on the table and it was well prepared. Mrs. Alice never knew how many would be there to eat. She told Odenia Miller Rowe that there was always room for one more at her table. The older girls learned to cook and helped their mother when she needed them. I never heard her complain about having to cook. Tony and Charlotte became outstanding cooks, just like their mother. What a legacy!

Who can imagine finding a way to meet the needs of a family that size? The Banners, like the rest of us, raised most of their own food. They just needed more of it than we did. Usually on a cold November day, Bob would butcher a hog or two. The hams, fatback, and side meat for bacon were readied for curing. Tenderloin and sausage were canned. Lard was rendered and liver mush was made. It was a full day's work and it took several people to get the job done in one day. But it was worth all the trouble when it was put on the table. Um-Um! Several milk cows were kept at all times to provide milk to drink, cream, butter, buttermilk and even cottage cheese. Chickens and turkeys furnished eggs and fresh meat for the table. Bob would occasionally kill a beef and there would be steak to eat for a while and beef stew to can. Beef roasts were good, too!

The biggest chore by far was raising enough vegetables and preserving enough for the winter months. Helen remembers that just below the barn they had a hot bed where they raised tomato plants and pepper plants and maybe more. She said they had three plots for gardening and that took lots of hoeing and weeding by all the children to keep the weeds out. They raised potatoes, tomatoes, beans, cabbage, lettuce, onions, greens, cucumbers, sweet corn, beets, peas, carrots, peppers, pumpkins, and more. Sometimes they would trade something like apples for sweet potatoes raised below the mountain, because they are not as sweet as if grown up here. Lots of canning went on in the summer and fall and all had to help gather and string or shell beans or peas, shuck corn, pickle beets, cucumbers, corn or beans, or make kraut, etc. Extra fields of corn were grown for food for animals and for making corn meal for the family. Wheat and oats were also raised. The corn and wheat were taken to the gristmill to be ground and oats were for the animals.

Their fruits came mostly from apple, pear, or cherry trees. There were plenty of blackberries, strawberries, and raspberries if one knew where to find them. The Banners had the only mulberries I knew about. Grapes were used for juice and for making jam or jelly. Molasses was made from sugar cane and was used in cooking as a sugar substitute and was it good to eat on those good biscuits!

When lunchrooms began at Cove Creek School, canned goods or potatoes could be exchanged for lunch tickets. This is how most lunches were paid for and it was how many of the Banner children got a hot lunch. Never did they ask for free lunches.

Mr. Bill carried the mail during the 1920s and 1930s. His route was long and the roads were rough. Lora Greene Hollar wished she could give me the picture she had in her head of Mr. Bill as he came riding up Phillip's Branch Road on his horse in snow almost up to his horse's knees. His route began at the little Sugar Grove Post Office at the foot of George's Gap. It went down the Watauga River Road, and on to Beaver Dams, then back across George's Gap to the post office. The roads frequently were impassable and snow, wind, or mud made travel almost impossible. What a daily ride on a horse, come rain, or hail, or sleet, or snow or sun! Mr. Banner did upgrade to a horse and buggy and later to a Model-T Ford.

Mr. Banner was an adventurer. He took his son Bob, Bob's cousin Johnny Sherwood, and a neighbor, Ronald Palmer, to the World's Fair in Chicago. Each boy had to save all year to have his spending money ready. Mr. Bill asked each child to save $10 to spend on his trip. Along the way they cooked most of their meals because of his careful planning. They took sugar, salt, potatoes, eggs, bacon, apples, etc. and would sometimes trade some of their vittles with other fellow campers for cantaloupes or melons. The boys loved this camping experience and the variety of food they could obtain. One of the Banner sons has the little book Mr. Bill used to keep track of the money they spent on the trip. He was quite a record keeper.

Mr. Bill came home with a couple of ideas he got from one of his visits to the World's Fair. He built an icehouse near his house. In the winter when the milldam on Cove Creek froze over, they would cut out chunks of ice to store in the icehouse to keep it cool. It worked. But the second idea was more popular. At the fair he had learned to make ice cream. Of course he shared this unusual treat with his kids and many of his neighbors. For most of us mountain kids, ice cream was a new experience and a treat we greatly enjoyed. Ruth always enjoyed telling the story about giving a lady and her children cones of ice cream. The lady instructed her kids to eat the ice cream and return the little cups. I can just see Mr. Bill laughing about that. He had a wonderful sense of humor.

Another of Mr. Banner's innovative ideas was to build a swimming pool near his house. I watched that idea become a reality in the late 1930s. It had two sections, a shallow pool for smaller children and a deeper pool for swimmers. I believe every child in the area had a fun time in that pool learning how to dog paddle. Dressing rooms for boys and one for girls were built with one shower for each. These rooms were destroyed by a big storm in the 1940s, but both pools are still standing today. Mrs. Banner didn't care

Mr. Bill Banner took his son, Bob, and some friends to the World's Fair in Chicago. They camped along the way. From the left, Johnny Sherwood, Bob Banner, and Ronald Palmer are standing in front of the car they traveled in to get to the fair. Mr. Bill came back with some new ideas to try at home. The children in the neighborhood particularly enjoyed a treat he learned how to make—ice cream. He loved to share with others (photograph furnished by Charlotte Banner Martin).

for the pool. She didn't swim and was scared for those who did. But I never heard of anyone getting hurt in that pool.

I knew the last 10 children well. Bob chose to be a plumber. He lived near the Cove Creek Baptist Church and was available to help his mother. Ruth married and lived in Mountain City, where she worked in a school near her home. Josephine and her husband owned and operated a furniture store in Boone. Tony and her husband were in the dairy business. Mac was in the Air Force for 20 years and returned to George's Gap to rear his children. Charlotte and her husband built and owned a family insurance business in Boone. Eva Nell taught in Avery County Schools. Martin taught, too, and became dean of men at Gardner-Webb College. John was in finance and Billy was in management and auto parts. Billy and his wife still live in the big house on George's Gap where they reared their family.

Most Cove Creek people remember the winning basketball teams of the 1950s. John and Martin Banner were leaders on these teams and both were awarded athletic scholarships for their efforts. Bill and Tony were good players, too, as were Joe and Ruth before them. Mr. and Mrs. Banner must have been proud parents. All of their children have made meaningful contributions to their communities. Six couples have celebrated over 50 years of marriage. They must have had good role models to follow.

Mr. and Mrs. Bill Banner were outstanding parents who nurtured and supported all of their children. As overseers of their daily needs, I'm not sure how they gave each one the special care he or she needed, but they did. Helen and Charlotte both stressed the fact that the older children were always there to support the younger ones and to help their parents. Together they created a memorable legacy in our community.

Life at Amantha

Pearl Henson Greene

From an interview by Jo Harris, accompanied by Nannie Greene, with Mrs. Pearle Henson Greene on September 6, 1999.

Amantha is a community about a mile north of the Cove Creek Baptist Church on old Highway 421. That is where I was born and raised. My maiden name was Henson and my parents were Ed and Essie McBride Henson. Henson was a well-known name in the community. There was Henson Hollar, and, of course, the Henson's Chapel Methodist Church.

We lived on a dirt road about three-quarters of a mile from Henson's Chapel. The original Methodist church was located in the same place as the present one, which was built in 1925. The old church was moved across the creek and has been a private residence ever since. We walked or rode a buggy to Henson's Chapel in our early days. My mother was a Baptist and when we got our first car we started going to the Cove Creek Baptist Church. There wasn't much difference between the Methodist and Baptists back then; the churches were a place of gathering and entertainment as well as spiritual training.

There wasn't much to do for entertainment except to go to church and visit our neighbors. I remember very well the first time we tried to go to Boone. Uncle Newt Mast had a truck and the road was so bad with rain that they pushed the truck all the way to get to Doc Mast's Store; by the time we got there, the 4th of July celebration was over. I was in my young teens then. Our family did not play music but I can just barely remember about 81 or 82 years ago Father and Mother bringing home an Edison talking machine. Mama held it in her lap in the buggy. That was a big time in the community; they all came in to hear the talking machine. The machine played cylinder records.

We had to walk about three miles to school. We had a school across the hill from home, the Mast School. Then they consolidated and we went to the Cove Creek Elementary School. I was maybe in third or fourth grade.

Miss McNewel was my teacher and my sister's teacher was Miss Winnie Thornburg, who just recently died. Miss Thornburg never married. I remember how she would go to the churches and take part in the community. If the teachers came from away they would board in the community in walking distance of the school. A lot of teachers boarded with Mae Payne. The elementary school was a two-story building (with an auditorium on the top floor). Later a high school building was built. The high school building was about where the Western Watauga Community Center sits now. In the early '40s a new high school building was erected across the creek. I graduated in 1929 and there were 20 or 30 in my graduating class.

I went on to Appalachian College and got my one-year certificate to teach. I taught one year before I got married and after I married, I went back to teaching. The first school where I taught was over on Meat Camp and then I taught at Pottertown, Elk Knob now. As I recall, my salary was fifty dollars a month. I rode with Thelma Perry and we taught together for about five years.

I married a local, Herman Greene. We were raised within a mile of each other, graduated from high school together, joined the church together and lived together for fifty-six years. Our courting was mostly walking to church together and then back home. I guess I knew that was "it" even then. He has been dead for fourteen years. Back then, 86 years ago, you didn't spread out too much. I was eighteen years old when I got married. I do not remember why everybody went to Mountain City unless it was easier to get a license there. It was considered a big treat to be married in Mountain City. I had a pretty blue dress; I had taught school so I had the dress. I remember that very well. The snow was about knee deep; it was the 14th of January. Don and Blanche Perry spent the night with us up at Mama and Daddy's after we came back from getting married. We lived with Mama and Daddy until we got our first house built.

Just about everybody in our part of the county farmed a little even if it was just a garden. But, most of Herman's income came from house moving and carpentry. My father and his brother had moved buildings for years and soon Herman joined in. When roads were widened or rebuilt, lots of times houses had to be moved. Then came the flood of 1940 and down in Stony Fork lots of houses had to be moved. That community was hit hard. Herman's father was considered one of the better carpenters in the county and Herman learned from him. Although Herman was young, he spent many hours building the new Henson's Chapel. I suppose he got good lessons in building there too. We built our present home in 1940. In 1966, we added on the den and this room is very special to me. It is built from material salvaged from the old Cove Creek Baptist Church, the brick, the paneling, all of it.

Herman and I have three sons: Herman Carlock, Ned Patterson, and Jimmy. Carlock and Pat were born at home and delivered by Dr. Ottie Bingham. Jimmy was born in the old Watauga Hospital. Remember, we were married during the Depression and times were very hard. But, our children have turned out well. Our oldest son, Herman Carlock Greene, played baseball for the Milwaukee Braves for 14 years and then he was a scout. He was inducted to the Scout's Hall of Fame in October 1998. Baseball was all he ever thought about doing in high school. On the night he graduated from high school in 1949, we sat up all night with the scouts. He had offers from eight of the major teams. Carlock was known as a fireball pitcher. Jimmy also played ball. He played with the Washington Senators. He was as good as Carlock but he got a shoulder separation and only played two years. He, too, was a pitcher. The boys all played ball at school, and I passed the ball many an hour to them. I could catch that ball!

Mrs. Pearl Greene lived her entire life of more than 90 years within a radius of five miles. She was a wife, mother, teacher, gardener, a good neighbor, a Sunday school teacher, and a caregiver to her parents. She was devoted to her family and was truly a pillar in her community of upper Cove Creek (photograph furnished by Pearl Greene).

My boys also served their country. Carlock and Pat were in the Navy for four years each during the Korean War. Jimmy went to Vietnam where he was wounded when he stepped on a mine. He still suffers from that injury.

I am blessed that my sons live close enough by me and that I can see them often. Carlock lives about two miles away, Pat lives in Mountain City, and Jimmy lives in North Wilkesboro. I was also blessed that I could live near my parents and grandparents. When my parents were old and needed help I am glad I lived near them and could help. I suppose that was the tradition in our family.

I can just barely remember my Grandpa Henson; he'd had a stroke and my father had to lift him out of a chair and put him in the bed. He had fought in the Civil War for the South. He lived to be almost 100 years old. My Grandma Henson was a Farmer whose family came from Yadkinville. She was the prissiest old woman you ever saw. She always wore black after Grandpa died. We lived at the head of the hollar and if she saw anybody coming, she would reach for her apron hanging behind the door. She would put on that starched apron that my mother had fixed for her. She was always ready for company when they got there. Her apron was white and starched real stiff. She always went dressed just like she was going to church. That was most unusual back then.

Grandma and Grandpa McBride lived up the road from here. It is sad that their beautiful old house burned. It had five bedrooms downstairs and four up. I thought Grandma's parlor was the prettiest room I ever saw. She had red velvet furniture, marble top tables and, of course, an organ. Grandpa had the ceiling painted in a design. (I bought marble top tables for my living room because of Grandma's!) My sister and I loved to look into Grandma's parlor but we were not allowed to play in it very often. My mother and her brother Smith were both artists. I guess they had that flair from their mother. I also remember that Grandpa McBride kept bees and we always had such good honey. I might add, Grandpa and Grandma Henson also had a large, beautiful house and it, too, burned.

Herman's grandfather Greene was Lemuel Greene. He also fought in the Civil War and lived to be 95 years old. The family referred to him as "Big Grandpa." He was Watauga County's last surviving Confederate soldier.

The biggest changes I've seen in my life are the improvements. We did not have electric lights, although we had running water from the spring. We had a telephone as long as I can remember. My uncle Smith McBride generated some electricity down here at the mill. Some who lived close by got lights that they could turn on about an hour of a night. I have got a light bulb that belonged to Pete Mast and it still burns. My parents used it and then they got a radio and every time they turned the radio on the light would interfere so they had to quit using the bulb. That is why it is saved. They had the first radio in the community. Herman and I got a battery radio in the '30s and his mother and others came to listen to it. I remember well when we got our first TV. It was in the '50s. The World Series was going to be in Cleveland, and Herman and Dad were going up to visit relatives and go to the ball game. Herman was working on John Bingham's house in Boone. He came home one night and said, "What's the use of me a-spending all that money to go to Cleveland to the ball game. Let's get a TV so we all can enjoy it." That is why we got our first TV. We bought it from the old Ray Farthing store in Vilas. It was the first in the community and it was a black and white! The boys were in the service at the time.

Thankfully, the REA brought electricity to our hollar, but I don't remember when.

There are many things I am thankful for. As I grow older, I look back at many things. I certainly had a good upbringing, and an awful good mother and daddy. We didn't have any boys in the family; my sister and I did everything with Daddy and Momma. I have so many fond memories. I am thankful for a long marriage and good sons. I always had good neighbors. My church has been so important to me. I am thankful to have the church in my life. I am thankful to have lived to see seven grandchildren and five great-grandchildren. I want to pass my heritage on to my children and their children.

Girlie Palmer ... 100 Years Young!

Girlie Palmer

In the early spring of 2001 Nannie Greene visited with Girlie Palmer a few days before Girlie's 100th birthday party. The Greene family and the Palmer family have been friends for many years and have shared many memories. Nannie asked Girlie to tell her about her long life and some of her outstanding memories. From time to time, Nannie would prod her with questions, but basically this is the story as told by Girlie. Few people have such a wonderful opportunity to hear tales of the past.

In 2005 Girlie celebrated her 104th birthday. Her daughter now lives with her, but Girlie still likes to cook her own breakfast. She is an amazing lady.

Now why would anyone want to hear about my life? I am 100 years old and I guess I have seen lots of things come and go. But you know in some ways it doesn't seem so long ago that I was a young'un on Timbered Ridge. Yes, I remember the first automobile I ever rode in, and I remember how if an airplane went over we would go outside and look for it. I remember when people thought a moving picture show was a terrible sin. I wouldn't go back to them "good old days" for nothing. To tell the truth, I don't think they were so good. I love having electric lights, and an electric stove to cook on, a television, and a washing machine. I still hang my clothes outside to dry if I can. I hang them upstairs if the weather is bad. My telephone is my lifeline to the world. I have a sister 98 in Ohio, a brother 88, and one 84. I talk to them every week.

But you asked me about back yonder. I'll start with a secret, not many people know this: my real name is Sarah Jane. When I was born, at Forest Grove, my folks already had four boys: Spencer, Arthur, Stacy and Harvey.

Well, Harvey was just two years old and couldn't talk real plain. He went around telling everybody he saw, "We got us a girlie." The nickname stuck. Then a little later Harvey died and after that nobody ever thought of calling me anything except Harvey's name for me.

Sarah (Girlie) Palmer, at the age of 104, still likes to cook her own breakfast and have something on hand for guests to eat when they come by for a visit. She didn't ask to live this long, she says, but Girlie attributes her longevity to clean living, hard work, and keeping her nose out of other people's business (photograph by Bob Caldwell).

In 1903 my sister Mary was born and after that came Mamie and then Dock. When Dock was about a year old we moved to Timbered Ridge. Mamie was four and I remember how she would stand by the window, cry, and beg, "I want to go home!" At Timbered Ridge my parents had two more boys, Dave and Lewis. But, we were never ten children at one time. Stacy and Harvey were dead before the last ones came along. Stacy was just a teenager when he decided he was old enough to make it on his own in the world and one night he slipped off and went to Virginia to work in a coal mine. There was a mine accident and Stacy was killed. He was only 17. Ten children born to one woman was not so unusual back then, but it sure wore a woman out. My mama had heart trouble and was down for a long time. She died at age 48 when I was twenty. It wasn't unusual for little children to die either, as Harvey did. We did not have much to doctor with. These new medicines sure beat castor oil, quinine, and carbolic acid. Of course, some of the herbs worked pretty good too!

With a family as big as ours can you imagine how many shoes it took, even with going barefoot in the summer? We all got one new pair of shoes a year. Noah Isaacs was a shoemaker who went from house to house making shoes. We would be so excited when he came to our house. He would measure each foot, cut the leather to fit the measurement and then sew the shoes to fit. He had a room upstairs where he worked until all the shoes were ready. The shoes were kind of stiff, but they lasted well. One time I

In 1913 Girlie Dishman, the oldest girl, often was the babysitter for her two sisters, Mary and Mamie (at left), and Dock, her baby brother. Later two other brothers were added to the family (photograph furnished by Sarah Palmer).

thought I would like to know what store-bought shoes really felt like. So I got Lula Campbell to swap shoes with me at school. I thought I had made a good trade until I got home and my dad saw the exchange. I was ordered to come home with my own shoes the very next day. I imagine Lula got the same orders. Anyhow, we wore our own shoes home the next day.

My parents were Press and Etta Hodge Dishman. They grew up in the same general area. In those days, family members did not stray far from their birth home. Children lived at home until they married and then they lived pretty close to one set of parents or the other. If the parents owned land, it was willed to the children and they continued in the same neighborhood. My two youngest brothers still live not far from their birth home.

People used to move a lot. I guess they still do and for the same reason: to be near their work. Then if you farmed, you grew your own food and that took up all of your time. If you did not farm, you had to live within walking distance of your job. That's why people moved a lot. If you got a better job, you probably had to move, even if it was just a mile.

When my family moved from Forest Grove to Timbered Ridge, we were about ten miles from our grandparents. Back then, that was a long ways. Nowadays when people move they use a large truck. We just piled our things on a horse drawn wagon. Actually, it took several wagonloads to get all our stuff moved. It was not unusual to see a pair of oxen pulling a wagon with beds and dressers and other household plunder. The family's cow would be walking behind. The chickens and pigs would also be on the wagon.

As I said before, Mama was poorly for a long time. My brother Spencer had to help with the cooking and he sure hated that. One day when I was about ten or eleven Spencer came in and said, "This big girl should be doing the cooking around here." So, that night I made cornbread for the first time. My daddy bragged on it so much that it didn't take much encouragement for me to try some more. So, you see, I began cooking for the family at an early age. I still cook most of my own meals. I am happy to not have to cook my cornbread in the fireplace coals or on a wood stove! Lots of days my son comes and eats with me. I still like to make cakes, and I like to have a cake on hand to serve when someone visits me.

I usually think of my young years as being at Timbered Ridge, but I started school at Forest Grove when I was five years old. After we moved, I went to school at Timbered Ridge. I think I was nine years old. I went as high as the grades went, which was seventh grade. It was a two-room school. The school was also used as a church until the community could afford to build the Timbered Ridge Church. I joined the church when I was a young girl. The center of our life was in the church. There was Bible study, preaching services, hymn singings, revival meetings, church dinners, box suppers, weddings and funerals. Most of the families around attended church on Sunday. It wasn't unusual for company to go home with you for dinner after church. A big meal was usually cooked and left on the wood stove before the family went to church. You might have other company in the afternoon. Everybody stayed dressed up all day just in case company should come in the afternoon. We were pretty scattered out and it was too far to walk so people often rode a horse, or wagon or a buggy to make their visits.

There were some mighty good neighbors and friends who lived at Timbered Ridge. Mr. Bob Swift and his wife Bessie had seven children. I loved to visit them or have them visit us. Bessie was one of the finest ladies I have ever known. We children would swing on grapevines, climb trees, run and jump or just make up games. We would pick cherries or berries with the Swifts. Those were good times!

There were two boys that went to school at Timbered Ridge that would play a big part in my life in years to come. They were Partee Palmer and

Partee Palmer (left) and Dayton Greene loved horses and rode and worked with them most of their lives. They became best friends in their teens and rode their horses to visit their lady friends in the 1920s. Later Partee married Girlie Dishman and Dayton married Lula Campbell, her best friend. The four remained friends their entire lives (photograph furnished by Sarah Palmer).

Dayton Greene. They were best buddies and shared a lot of interests and remained best friends until Partee died. Partee learned to play the guitar and Dayton the banjo, and as long as they lived they got a lot of pleasure from playing music together.

I don't remember exactly when Partee and I got to noticing each other. But, I do remember Partee and my dad didn't care much for each other. One day Partee asked my mother if she cared if we got married. (I guess he figured he wouldn't get far with Dad.) She told him if he took me away she wouldn't have any help to raise her children. So we waited. When I was twenty Mama died. My sister, Mary, was already married and living in Saltville, Virginia. When their first baby was born, I went to stay with them and help care for the new baby. When it was time for me to go home Mary and her husband, Roby Guy, took me to Bristol to meet Partee. His cousin, Vance Palmer, had given Partee a ride to Bristol. Somewhere in there we decided to get married before we went back home. We rode the train from Bristol to Butler, Tennessee, where a friend picked us up and brought us home. We lived with Partee's parents, Jeff and Alice Palmer, for the first few months of our married life. Then we moved out on our own in the Cable house in Leander (now lower Bethel community). It was a big house and we had very little furniture so we used only two rooms at first. We lived there until Lois, our first child, was born in 1923. In those days, there was no such thing as a house number or even a sign that named a road. We identified houses by who built them or who had lived there a long time.

Later we moved into the Adam Greene house and Jay was born there. Dr. Jack Love assisted with that birth. Although I had only two children, I have six grandchildren, nine great-grandchildren and twelve great-great grandchildren; most of them live in Western Watauga County.

This was a happy time for us. We were young, had good health and were just as poor as everybody else was. Almost every weekend several families would get together and make music. The same people didn't play every time but there was always someone willing to take a turn. Some would play a guitar, another a fiddle, or a banjo. Then there were the unusual such as the washboard, spoons, Jew's harp or French harp. Those who could hum through a comb became a part of the band. Usually furniture and rugs would be moved out of the way to make room for guests, or the band, and for dancing. Sometimes there was someone who would do an old soft shoe, a flatfoot, or buck dance. Now and then, someone would know how to do the Charleston, and sometimes a couple might do the two-step. But square dancing was always the most popular.

Music was always an important part of our family's life. For a while, Partee was a member of a string band. He played a guitar, Dayton Greene played a banjo and Carl Farthing played a mandolin and Carter Farthing played a fiddle. They must have been pretty good because they tried out for a spot on the radio in Bristol, Tennessee, sponsored by Purina Feed Company, and they got the job. Because of problems they encountered, they were unable to cash in on the opportunity. One of the Farthing boys was about to be turned out of the church because they had to be in Bristol to play on Sunday and he owned the only car in the group. With heavy hearts, they turned down the job. Who knows? They could have become famous.

We moved from the Beaver Dam area to George's Gap. Again, we were close neighbors to Dayton and Lula Greene. By now, the children of the two families were beginning to feel like one family. The men helped each other with farm chores such as plowing, hoeing, putting up hay, shucking corn, making molasses or whatever was needed. We women helped each other with canning, making soap, making cheese, baking, hooking rugs or quilting. Doing things together made the work more enjoyable.

Later we moved to Phillips Branch, where our neighbors were Ed and Chloe Stokes, Claire Simpson, and Dwight and Nannie Edmisten. Wherever I have lived, I have had good neighbors and I have tried to always be a good neighbor.

My husband, Partee, was always good with horses and mules. No matter how peculiar a man was about his best team he would always trust it to Partee. Some said he could talk to the horse and it understood. In the 1920s and '30s there was a lot of logging going on and it was done with horses. This was hard work but Partee did not mind because he was working with the best teams of horses. But, when the logging played out he had to seek other work. That's when we moved into Boone. Appalachian State Teachers College owned a big farm in the area of the swim complex (that is how State Farm Road got its name). The farm produced fresh vegetables and had a dairy that provided milk for the college. Well, Partee got a job working at the dairy. Part of his job was to haul milk in a cart to the college. The cart was pulled by jennies. We lived there until 1945, when we moved to Perkinsville. After we moved to Boone, Partee bought his first car, a Model-T Ford. When he died in 1960 he owned a Chevrolet, but I don't think he was ever as happy driving a car as he was driving a horse!

After Partee's death, I went to work outside the home for the first time in my life. I worked at IRC for a while and later at the laundry at Appalachian. I retired in 1974.

Any place I have lived the church has been a big part of my life. I joined the church at Timbered Ridge when I was just a teenager. When we were living at Phillips Branch there was not a church close by until Dwight and Nannie Edmisten helped get one organized. I belonged there. In the late 1940s the Perkinsville Baptist Church was organized, and I am the only living charter member. The Good Lord has seen fit to bless me with a long life and I am thankful.

Most of my life has been spent right around here. But I want you to know I have been to New York City, Connecticut and Massachusetts. I saw the Statue of Liberty and Plymouth Rock and lots of other things. But, after three weeks I got so homesick that I caught a bus home. It took two days to get back to Boone, but it was worth the ride to get home.

On March 11, 2001, exactly 100 years from the day I was born, over 200 people came to my birthday party. I reckon they just wanted to see what a person who has lived 100 years looks like! I think I talked to everyone there. Some I knew, some I did not know. Many asked me what reason I could give for living such a long life. I told them, "It was hard work, clean living, and keeping my nose out of other people's business. I never asked for this long life."

School Days Circa 1930

Helen Banner Williams

This is from an interview conducted by Nannie Greene with Helen Banner Williams, September 2000, at her home in the Mabel community. Mrs. Williams was born in 1918, the seventh child of Alice and Bill Banner.

I have a lot of good memories of going to Cove Creek High School even though it was during the Depression. My favorite subjects were math and music. Mr. George Farthing was my math teacher and he was really good. He also liked to play the banjo and on Sunday nights I would play the piano and he would play the banjo at Henson's Chapel Methodist Church. He always wanted to play *When They Ring Those Golden Bells*, every Sunday night. Boys, he could make that banjo talk. I loved music and I had a wonderful teacher, Mrs. Maude Spainhour. She came to the schoolhouse and had a little room just off the stage of the auditorium where she had her lessons. I don't remember how much she charged. Because she only taught the classics, I learned Bach, Handel, and many of the great composers.

At the end of our junior year, that was 1935, we went on our senior trip to Washington, D.C. Our teacher was Miss Grace Blalock, who later married Dave Mast. She went with us. The trip cost ten dollars. That paid for our transportation, our hotel, and I don't know what all. I know we had to buy our own lunch. While we were there, we went to a movie. I can still

Helen Banner Williams was the fourth girl in a family of 17 children. She was a talented musician and was awarded a music scholarship for college that she didn't use. This photo shows Helen, her parents, and 13 of her siblings. Billy was not yet born. First row (from the left): Mack, Eva Nell, Luther Martin, and Charlotte; second row: Tony and Josephine; third row: Mother Alice holding baby Johnny, Helen, Blanche, Ruth, and Susie; and in the fourth row: Daddy Bill, Jim, Joe, and Bob (photograph furnished by Charlotte Banner Martin).

remember it. It was *Naughty Marrietta* with Nelson Eddy and Jeanette McDonald. We had to pay for that and I sat in the fourth balcony because it was cheaper. We were so far from the screen it looked like the actors were in Egypt! Funny how I can remember that when I can't remember what happened yesterday.

We went to all of the government buildings and the famous monuments like the Lincoln Memorial and the Washington Monument and the Smithsonian Building. While we were watching the Senate, we saw Huey P. Long give a speech. That was not long before he was assassinated.

Just think about all that for ten dollars! The way I got the ten dollars was my cousin Mary Lizzy told Grandpa Banner I couldn't go to Washington because I didn't have ten dollars and he dished it out. My daddy was sick and couldn't work but Grandpa had a little pension from his service in the Civil War. I had a little money left when it was time to come home (my spending money) and I bought a little gift for each of the little young'uns at home. Probably nothing was worth more than a dime. I remember I bought Eva Nell a little ring with a set in it.

Another thing I remember is we didn't ever stop school because of bad weather. They would put chains on them buses and they would go right on. I do remember sometimes if there was a funeral at Henson's Chapel or Cove Creek Baptist Church they would let school out at dinner and if the students wanted to go they could. They were not required to go.

The only time I remember ever getting into trouble at school was playing the piano for people to dance. Nobody was supposed to dance at school, or anywhere else, I guess. Anyhow, we were upstairs in the auditorium, I was just playing away, and some girls were just dancing. Mrs. Grace Bingham Campbell was on hall duty and she asked the girls to quit dancing. They didn't quit right then. She was getting pretty upset and finally told me if I'd stop playing they would stop dancing. I let on like I couldn't hear her. I don't remember how we were punished but we had to go to the office.

Commencement was a big community thing back then. Everybody went. There would be a big dinner on the grounds. The commencement I remembered best was in 1936. I graduated valedictorian and I played the piano for graduation. Later that year Ralph Williams and I got married. I was offered a scholarship to Meredith College in classical music but I chose Ralph instead.

Through the years, I have enjoyed my music and have played in church at various times and sometimes at school functions if they needed me.

The Awesome Aldridges of Foscoe

Catherine Stokes Sheppard

Tucked in the shadow of Grandfather Mountain is the community of Foscoe, about halfway between Boone and Banner Elk, on Highway 105. Today the passerby sees neat homes, shops for the fisherman and other tourist attractions. But past generations knew this area as a logging and sawmill community, complete with a train stop. To get a firsthand view of Foscoe's past one has only to have a visit with the Aldridge sisters.

To separate the Aldridges from Foscoe is like separating peanut butter from jelly. The two just naturally go together. One of the early settlers in the Foscoe area was a famed bear hunter named James Aldridge. From him have descended many people bearing that name. One was a grandson named Roy James Aldridge, who married Gladys Taylor from Tennessee.

They had fourteen children, seven boys and seven girls. Most of these children grew up and remained in the community of their forefathers.

I had the opportunity to visit with three of the sisters one afternoon, and I must say it was a delightful encounter. The three I talked to were Carmalee Ellis, Verlene Roark, and Bernice Byrd. Their sister Blanche Byrd could not join us but she does still live near the others. These ladies did not look to be the ages they claimed, yet I soon realized they had worked hard all their lives. They had such a cheerful demeanor and positive outlook it was not hard to see what kept them youthful. They especially enjoyed telling me about their days of galacking (gathering galax leaves and various roots and herbs). This is their account:

> Our dad was a sawmill worker and a hard worker, but there was 14 of us kids and we all had to pitch in. We girls used to get up before daylight, fix us a lunch of pork and beans, fried fatback, and taters and head out for the Bench Field, First or Second Ridge, or even Grandfather Mountain. Back then, there was plenty of galax and it was legal to gather all you wanted. We would cut it off and not disturb the roots. We carried two sacks on our shoulders. When we sat down to rest or eat our lunch we would tie the galax stems into bunches of 25. We sold them by the thousand to Richard Sluder. The galax was used to make the base in funeral wreaths. We would put our sacks on a sled, hitch up the horse and haul the galax to Mr. Sluder. If we made five dollars a day, we thought we had done really well.
>
> We picked and gathered anything we could sell. There was just no money to be had! We gathered May apple roots, blackberry briar roots, we skinned wild cherry bark and bear bush bark. We would sell these to Wilcox Drug; they would send a truck about once a week. We would also gather sacks full of moss off logs in the woods. In the summer we would take a lantern before day, go out, and pick wild huckleberries and blackberries. We would catch the Tweetsie train and take the berries to the hotel at Linville and walk back home! Oh, those were good days! Today you can hardly find a big bed of galax and if it is on government land, it is illegal to gather it.

Other good Tweetsie memories the Aldridge sisters shared were catching the train, riding to Johnson City, and getting another train to Bristol, Virginia, to visit their Taylor grandparents. Carmalee recalled that she and her husband took their new baby and a baby pig (in a sack) and rode the train from Foscoe to Montezuma to visit her husband's parents. Today she laughed at what a sight they must have been. The train tracks washed out in the '40 flood and were not put back into service. Lots of good memories is all that is left of the train today.

Looking back, the sisters remarked that in all their galacking treks they never remember being frightened. They never came upon a bear, a snake, or a stranger that was cause for fear. Something tells me that if they had, they would have out-witted either. (Even now it is not unusual for a bear to wander down from Grandfather Mountain and disturb the peace of this quiet community.)

Lest you think the Aldridge sisters are living in the past, let me hasten to assure you they are not! Nor do they limit themselves to Foscoe. They have standing appointments with hairdressers in Boone and every Saturday morning they make a regular visit to Boone Drug Store. They even have reserved seats in that institution, and if some uninformed customer happens to occupy their seat when they arrive, the management will firmly but politely ask the intruder to find another seat. These ladies told me they have made several trips to California and when I talked to them they were preparing for their annual trip to Myrtle Beach.

Galax is an evergreen plant with shiny leaves and small white flowers, and is sometimes used in wreaths. It grows in the higher elevations of Watauga County. Children in the Aldridge family gathered galax to sell and to supplement the family income. Each person had to do his part to support a family of 14 children during the Depression years (photograph by Catherine Stokes Sheppard).

When I asked them to comment on the greatest changes they had seen in their community they all agreed it was the influx of outsiders. They commented that some of the outsiders were real assets to Foscoe. They join in the community activities and become a part of it. Unfortunately, others set about to mold Foscoe into the place they have left. When I inquired about their hopes for the future of their community they in unison declared, "Stop tearing down our mountains to build vacation houses and stop ruining the water." They want their children and grandchildren to be able to occupy the land of their forebears. Is this too much to ask? It is a wonderful heritage for people to be able to trace their ancestry several generations in the same location. The Aldridges take great pride in theirs. Awesome!

Howard Cole Remembers

Howard Cole

This story was submitted by Howard Cole (1926–2005) in 1999. At that time, he was living in Avondale, Pennsylvania.

When I was growing up home life was very simple. No one had money and everyone "lived at home," meaning we used what we had or did without. When I was very small, I recall going with my mother to pick up chestnuts. (I also remember sitting down on the burrs and how painful the removal was.) Since we did not work on Sunday, we boys often would pick up chestnuts on Sunday and take them to the store on Monday. These native chestnut trees died out in the '20s and '30s from a disease called Chestnut blight.

One thing we were taught at home was respect. We called all older people uncle or aunt even if they were not related to us. I recall saying Uncle Newt Banner, Uncle John McBride, and Aunt Nancy Eggers. Others we called Mister or Misses but not by the first name alone. Another thing we learned at home was not to use vulgar language. I quit one job early because one of the men I had to ride with used such foul language.

We did whatever we could to earn an honest dollar when I was young. My father, William Cole, kept bloodhounds for the Watauga County Sheriff's Department. These were used to track criminals. In order to keep the dogs in good shape Papa would have me walk the dogs up and down the hills and return home from a different direction.

Papa also kept honeybees. He usually had an average of 10 hives until a disease killed them. He was rarely stung and had no fear of bees. It was not unusual for him to spend a Sunday afternoon napping on the ground around the beehives. Most years he would harvest about 100 gallons of strained honey. It takes 10 pounds of honey to make one pound of honeycomb. He made his own extractor to take the honey from the comb but he never cut the comb. Papa always robbed the bees early enough for them to refill their combs with enough honey to feed themselves until the next spring.

Another job I remember well was picking beans for a neighbor. My pay was seven cents an hour and dinner. (I still call the noon meal dinner!) Back then, lunch was always a part of the pay. In the '40s the custom changed; you either carried your lunch or went home to eat. When I was in high school, World War II was in high gear. A factory was built in Morganton, N.C., and I got a job as a carpenter for 45 cents an hour. That was really big money for me. The catch was I had to leave home before day, ride on the back of a flatbed truck and get home after dark. A teenage boy did not get into much trouble with hours like that.

As I said earlier, everyone lived at home. We grew our own corn, shelled it and took it to the mill to be ground into meal. The man at the mill would take out some meal as his pay. Sometimes there would be red ears mixed with the white. Once my brothers and I shelled all red ears and went to the mill. The bread Mama made from this meal was so bad we could not eat it. If a small amount of red got mixed it was okay. Our mama may have invented tube socks because when the toe of a sock wore through she would sew across the end. Then, we'd just have shorter socks.

My dad smoked Stud tobacco. Two hen eggs would buy a five-cent bag of Stud. Once I was sent to find two eggs but the hens did not cooperate and I found only one egg. My dad did not believe in going in debt for anything he did not have to have. Papa tried to cut up some plug tobacco but that just did not do the same. I suppose we had to wait for one more egg, though I don't recall.

Back then, recreation was limited by both time and money. On Sunday afternoon in warm weather, the men might gather on the porch at Sherwood's store and swap tall tales. Sometimes it got to be a contest to see who could tell the biggest one. Papa thought his were the tallest. He also liked to play tricks. He had a small, round steel tape that he carried in his watch pocket. It gave the impression of a watch. Once a stranger asked him the time of day and he pulled out the tape, glanced at it and gave the man an answer. We boys went swimming in the Pogey Hole, fishing in the creek, and did a little hunting for fun (and for hides if we were lucky).

My brother Carlton complained that his eyes were bad and he thought he needed glasses. My parents did not believe him and couldn't afford glasses anyhow during the Depression. Not long afterward, we were hunting with our little dog, who scared up a polecat. Carlton announced that he would catch the polecat (skunk) but the skunk got him first in the face and eyes. We were near a branch and he washed his face and eyes. He never complained again about his vision. He is in his '70s now and only uses glasses to read. Maybe skunk spray was good for his eyes.

Most doctoring was done at home when I was growing up. The medicines I remember were castor oil, Black Draught, Calatabs, 4-Way cold tablets and tallow rags. I guess we were just tougher back then before the days of "wonder drugs."

When I was about 12 years old, Grandpa Reeves Cole died. Family and friends took care of preparing the body for the burial. While Papa went to Boone and bought a casket, men in the neighborhood dug the grave and the ladies brought in food. I remember how the men prepared the body.

After giving him a bath, they put on a pair of long underwear, then a shirt, tie and suit. They placed a bag of salt on his abdomen under the suit and changed it often. Papa said this was to keep down any odor. People were usually buried three days after death.

DeWitt Brown's Garage

Catherine Stokes Sheppard

The following is based on recorded conversations with Paul Brown in 2003.

Sometimes a man's work is so intertwined with his personal life that it is difficult to think of one without the other. So it is with the memory of DeWitt Brown and his garage.

When Highway 421 was paved from Boone to Mountain City and cars became fairly common, it was only logical that repair places and gasoline sales would be needed. DeWitt Brown recognized this need and acted accordingly. In the early '20s he built a brick building that ever after was referred to simply as "The Garage." Actually, for many years it was the only such business in Western Watauga.

Paul Brown said that his father learned auto mechanics simply from trial and error. He had no formal training and cars did not come with manuals. If the automobile did not run right DeWitt would take one part off and put it back on until he found the part causing the malfunction. Pretty soon he could tell right away what was causing the problem. No doubt, he was born with a mechanical talent that made this learning easy for him. Early on he became a very respected mechanic. He worked from early in the morning until late at night. Before many years had passed DeWitt had to hire other mechanics. Paul told me that for years, the garage had no cash register, only a cigar box, but his father always knew how much money was in it. His daughter Billie did the bookkeeping before she went to college and afterward when she was at home. The two sons learned early to pump gasoline and to wash windshields.

"The Garage" was more than a place to buy gas and get a truck repaired. Since the clientele there often came from outside communities, there was usually news to learn. Many stopped to buy gas whether they needed it or not. There were always jokes to hear and often practical jokes were being played on someone. These jokes were not instigated by DeWitt; it was just that his place was a sort of social hub. He was a very quiet man.

DeWitt Brown's Garage, built in the 1920s, was the only garage in Western Watauga County for several years. DeWitt is standing by the car on the right. The others are unknown. A local organization, Cove Creek Preservation and Development, is interested in restoring this community landmark to museum status (photograph from a collection of CC Grange).

Most who remember DeWitt from the garage may have overlooked that he was first a farmer and always a farmer at heart. His pride and joy was in owning white-faced cattle. His son Paul remembers that his dad could not bear for anybody's hands to be idle and there was usually a farm job waiting for him after school. As automobiles became more complex, DeWitt chose to leave the garage and move to his orchard at Zionville. Here he could devote his time to full-time farming.

When World War II ended and Paul came home from the Navy, he knew he did not want to farm or to go back to school. Like his father, he was very mechanically inclined. Paul had seen bulldozers operate and was fascinated by them. He appealed to his father to buy a bulldozer and thus Brown Brothers Construction Company was born.

DeWitt Brown was a quiet family man. His children were Billie Brown Southerland, Paul Brown, Josephine Brown Bingham, and D.T. Brown Jr. His wife was Bessie Moody Brown, who was also a hard worker. Mrs. Brown taught school and managed the house and some of the farming. Both Mr. and Mrs. Brown were generous, good-hearted people who extended a helping hand where needed. Paul told one story that pretty much reflects their family bonds. One Christmas all four kids got roller skates for Christmas and for days, the basement became a roller rink. The parents did not mind the noise as long as the kids were safe and happy. They also encouraged their children in their dreams. The daughters chose to go to college, while the sons chose to work. Mr. and Mrs. Brown gave each the opportunity.

The Wanda Inn

Catherine Stokes Sheppard

In the 1940s teenagers in the rural communities did not have places to hang out. Our fathers had the country store. Our cousins in the towns or cities had the local drug stores. About the only place teens could hang out was at school events, unless one lived at Cove Creek. There was the wonderful institution called the Wanda Inn.

The Wanda Inn was built in the early '40s by Dana Farthing. This was our mini-mall. The complex consisted of an auto repair shop attached to a grocery store, which was attached to a restaurant. Upstairs was one or

The Wanda Inn was named after the owner's daughter, Wanda Farthing. Look closely and you can see her playing near the gas tank. This inn was the only such establishment in the area. It had rooms for rent, a restaurant, a garage, and gas (photograph furnished by Willis Farthing).

more apartments, as well as rooms for rent. One of these housed the Sugar Grove telephone switchboard for a short time. The rooms were very nice and, especially, I recall the beautiful hardwood floors. The part that captured my memory was the restaurant. It had booths, a counter with stools, and a big jukebox.

There were several families who operated the business over a period of years but the family that I remember was Mr. and Mrs. Roy Brown and their daughters Lavola and Lennis. Mr. Brown ran the repair shop and his wife and daughters took care of the grocery store and restaurant. The food was clean, tasty and served with a smile. It soon became the hangout for the after school and the after ballgame crowd. Dancing was not allowed (there or anywhere else in the county) but for a nickel we could hear the Big Bands. It even had the approval of our parents.

Today all that remains of the Wanda Inn is a lot of crumbled concrete blocks and junked cars. Well, not all that remains; many good memories remain of wholesome fun and swing music!

Hattie's Hill

Genevieve Sherwood Henson

We visited with Genevieve Sherwood Henson and taped her story in October 2000.

As one drives across the Watauga River going towards Bethel one sees on the left an interesting-looking country lane with a road marker that says Hattie Hill. The story behind the sign is very interesting. Who is or was Hattie? Genevieve Sherwood Henson explains here.

Hattie Mae Farthing was the third child of John (Jack) Young and Polly Farthing. Jack was a brother to my mother's father. But, the strange story begins before that.

Polly Farthing was in love with Jack's brother but he was killed in the Civil War. Although she was a first cousin to the brothers, she did marry Jack when he came home from the war. They built a beautiful house at Timbered Ridge. The house had seven fireplaces and a basement under part of the house. A basement was a rare thing in those days. The house had beautiful furnishing. The family lived well; they had two large barns, and beautiful horses. Their first child was a son named Robert Lee, the first daughter was Victoria, and the third child was Hattie Mae. Robert Lee was slow-witted. Victoria was a pretty girl who defied her parents, married a Greene, and moved to Athens, Tennessee. Hattie grew up to be a beautiful and popular girl, much prettier than Victoria. Even before Victoria married, Uncle Jack and Aunt Polly decided Hattie should not have boyfriends. If Hattie went to church, Victoria was sent to spy on her to see if she talked to boys. After Victoria left they would even have a hired man spy on Hattie.

When Hattie was about seventeen, a young man called on her one Sunday afternoon. They walked out on a hillside a few hundred yards from the house. Aunt Polly made Uncle Jack go out and run the young man off. That night the young man put all of his belongings into a pillowcase, slipped out the window and left home to go out West. It was many years later before he returned. (Hattie told me this story when she was about 70 years old and as she talked tears rolled down her cheek.) She loved this man till the day she died. She said that every time he came back to this area he always came to see her, wife or no wife. After the parents died another man called on Hattie and asked her to marry him but she refused. She told him, "I am not the woman I used to be." Of course, she knew she must look after Robert "Bob" Lee.

After Uncle Jack and Aunt Polly died, Hattie and Bob remained in the homeplace. Sadly, neither of them had been trained to take any responsibility. They did not know how to do anything. They did not cook and eat; they did not wash, clean or anything like other people. I never saw Hattie sit down and eat a meal. She would eat a bite here and a bite there. Bob would often go to my mother's house on the pretense of cutting wood for her. She would fix him a plate, and could he eat! Once I saw him eat 13 large sugar cookies. Neighbors said Bob would have been a strong man if he had had anything to eat, that is if he did not eat himself to death. Bob could work if someone would show him what to do. He could do simple sums and he could remember dates that certain events had happened right down to the month, day and hour.

Sometimes they would hire someone to come in and cook for them. They never had electricity in their house, so there was no way to keep food from spoiling. That did not seem to matter to them; they just kept eating the food till it was gone, spoiled or not. I have seen Hattie scrape mold off canned sausage and eat it. It didn't seem to hurt them. They would buy cheese and eat it, mold and all.

Their only heat was from a fireplace and there was never more than a handful of fire then. I do not know why they did not freeze to death. The house was always cold. I never knew them to wash anything, but they must have.

They had plenty of money. Their parents bought government bonds and they got income from that. They had good farmland but they did not know how to tend it or how to rent it out. They had a battery-operated radio, one of the first in our neighborhood. As long as Hattie could see to read, they had newspapers. Bob could not read and Hattie's vision became so bad she couldn't either. People tried to take her to be fitted for glasses but she had motion sickness so bad she could not ride in a car. Hattie was very intelligent; she could remember and recite beautiful poetry.

Hattie or Bob hardly ever left home. He liked to go to funerals. On rare occasions, she would go to my mother's house or to the store. I remember sometimes she would order things from Sears. Once in a while she would get a notion to fix up a room. I remember once she ordered new chairs and fixed a beautiful room. They got a chandelier they hung a lamp in, a pretty thing. They had fine furniture. A time or two Hattie would order cloth to make me and my sister Catherine a dress. Mama was kind to her and other people tried to be. You just could not help them.

The end of their life was just as strange as any of their life. Bob lived to be 89 and Hattie was 87. Although he died at home, no one seemed to know how long he had been dead when help was called for. They died in the lifestyle of paupers. Yet in their attic were valuable bonds and gold coins. Today they lie side by side, along with their parents on Hattie's Hill.

Making Rugs

Peggy Hagaman

This piece is based on notes and recollections submitted by Peggy Hagaman in 2002. She lives in Sugar Grove.

During the 1940s and early '50s the people of Western Watauga still felt the pangs from the Depression and later, the aftermath of World War II. My mother, Myrtle Reece Gentry, and the mothers of most of my friends did not work outside the home. We all had to be thrifty and make the most of what we had.

My mother turned to an old mountain craft: making hooked rugs. She learned the craft from her mother, Nancy Jane Guy of the Whaley community. My grandmother, mother, and some of my aunts would make rugs and take them to Blowing Rock and Bristol to sell. In Blowing Rock, they took the rugs to the Dangerfield House, which is now Westglow Spa. After she was married and had children, Mother began to trade the rugs for clothing. I'm not sure how she got the names of women she exchanged with, but my sisters and I did have very nice clothes.

The method of construction was to dye burlap sacks, ravel them out, and wind the strands of burlap into a ball, which was used to hook the rug.

They would use two or three strands of burlap at one time. Another burlap bag was used for the background. The design was drawn freehand onto the bag, which had been attached to a wooden frame. The design was drawn with black dye and a small brush. Using a metal hook with a wooden handle, Mother would pull a loop of the burlap thread through the burlap bag backing so that only about one half inch of the loop showed. She would finish with one color and then go to another color.

In later years, Mother used nylon strips, which came from the Bemberg plant in Elizabethton, Tennessee. She would dye the nylon and use it as she had the burlap. My aunt worked in that plant and would bring discarded nylon to my mother. These rugs were quite beautiful, and if one is located in an antique shop today it is very expensive. As far as I know, my mother never kept any of the rugs. I certainly would love to have one of them today.

My Memories of Oak Grove

Edna Ward Ellis

Edna Ward Ellis submitted the following in 2001 in response to our requests for reminiscences.

My happiest childhood and teenage memories revolve around the community of Oak Grove Baptist Church.

The Ward family, Lionel, Birdie, Edna, twins Jack and John, and Uncle Daniel (called Dan'l) moved from Laurel Creek to the Oak Grove Community near Boone in the summer of 1927. A few years later Grandpa Jackson Ward came to live with us.

The house Papa bought, not far from the church, was a two-story frame structure with a porch across the front and the sides. We had no electricity or indoor plumbing, and the house was heated by a fireplace and a wood-burning stove in the kitchen.

At that time, the Oak Grove Church was located on the corner where Hodges Gap Road turned off the Oak Grove Road. It was a white-frame building with double front doors. We sat on slatted wood benches, and the Sunday school "rooms" were made by closing green burlap curtains on wires strung across the walls. The choir was on the right side of the pulpit with barber Bill Hodges as the leader. Ralph and Laura Green organized the first B.Y.P.U. for the young people. During the winter, the children would huddle around the big iron stove, which was the only source of heat.

I started to Oak Grove School in the second grade, having gone to Windy Gap School before we moved. The school was a two-room, white frame building between our house and Mr. Cleve Gross's house. Richard Hodges was my first teacher there. My brothers, John and Jack, started sometime later. Mrs. Ethel Gross was their one of their teachers.

A new two-room red brick schoolhouse was constructed about 1928–30. It was located on the hill above the church. We were a proud group of children when we moved to our new school. Mrs. Annie Walker (we called her Misannie) taught the first three grades, and Mr. Cleve taught the fourth through seventh grades.

At that time, no one had even thought about separation of church and school, so when it was time for revivals we would practice our songs over and over again. Mr. Cleve would march us to the 11 o'clock service with stern instructions to behave and sing loud. We would sing "Throw Out the Lifeline" and "What a Friend We Have in Jesus" at the top of our voices. Preacher Watts was pleased to have the pupils in attendance and he always praised our singing and our behavior. The school closed in the late 1930s and the children transferred to Boone. In 1932, there were 71 students and 2 teachers. The years passed and we grew up, finished high school, and many went on to college or moved away. Oak Grove School was not a bad beginning!

The whole community was excited when the new church building was under construction. Mr. Jim Gross gave the property across the road from the old church. On Sunday afternoons, the children and young people would go and play or "court" around the piles of brick and lumber. Finally, the beautiful red brick church was ready for the first service, March 7, 1937. I remember how thrilled Mama and I were when we heard the church bell ring for the first time.

I graduated from Appalachian High School in 1939 and attended Appalachian State Teacher's College for one year. By then it was wartime and I went to Norfolk, Virginia, to work. There I met and later married a naval officer from Georgia. When he was sent to the Pacific to serve on an aircraft carrier, the U.S.S. *Franklin*, I came back to Boone to live with Papa. (Our first child was born in 1944 in the old Watauga Hospital.) My brothers were also away in the Air Force; John was a nose gunner on a B-24 in Italy, and Jack was stationed in India. Papa had been in World War I and was then the Veterans Service Officer. His job was to work with veterans and help them find jobs after WW II. He also helped them get to the veterans hospital either in Johnson City, Tennessee, or in Asheville, N.C. I remember how proud Papa was of all the young men who were serving their country.

Because I was a Navy wife, I lived in quite a few different places both

Edna Ward Ellis remembers when the new Oak Grove Baptist Church was built. It was just across the road from the old one on Hodges Gap Road. In 1968 this picture was made at the groundbreaking ceremony. From left to right are Fred Baumgardner, John Ward, Andy Kirby, Joseph McNeil, Vance Calloway, Ben Fox, Vance Culler, Lewis Hodges, Ralph Beshears, Ronda Hodges, Lee Eller, and in front, Pastor Fritz Hemphill (photograph furnished by Kathleen Ward).

in the USA and abroad. But, I always came back "home" as often as possible. It was always a joy to visit the church and community where I grew up. After my husband, Capt. William Ellis, retired from the Navy, we moved to Athens, Georgia, where we have lived since. In 1989, we began restoring the old Ward homeplace. Now my children and grandchildren can share my enthusiasm for their roots. My husband died in 1991, my brother Jack died in 1994 and his twin brother John died in 2002. I still spend as much summer time as I can with my brother John's widow, Kathleen Ward.

I thank the Good Lord that I was privileged to have grown up under the guiding light of the Oak Grove Baptist Church in the majestic mountains of Western North Carolina. On Sunday mornings when we are at the "Old Homeplace" I am sure I can hear the church bell ringing off in the distance, even though I am told the bell has not been used for many years. Oh, the magic of memories!

The Conniption Fit

W.T. Payne

W.T. Payne lives in Asheville, N.C. He submitted this story in 2003.

This situation occurred long before my time at the Cove Creek Baptist Church. This was back in the days when a visiting preacher would stay with one of the lay members during a revival. At one particular revival, the visiting preacher was staying in the home of one of the church deacons.

According to the story I heard, the revival was going very well, in fact, so well that it had to be extended for another week. The preacher was outstanding! The entire event had been a big success—until he left. It seems that when he left Cove Creek the deacon's wife left with him. When the word got around the community of what had taken place, I heard that many of the women in the church had a conniption fit. However, I never did hear if the deacon got his wife back.

Strawberry Picking

Mary Alice Palmer Hanna

Mary Alice Palmer Hanna lives in Johnson City, Tennessee. She submitted the following in 2004.

When I was a little girl, we lived one mile from the North Carolina–Tennessee state line. My parents were Richard and Della Palmer. Our father was a carpenter and often worked away from home, but our mother was always at home with us kids. My three sisters were Georgia, Myrtle, and Chloe. Our one brother was Ronald and he owned a donkey.

Ronald kept the donkey pretty busy. He used it drag poles and small limbs from the woods to burn under the black wash pot outside. On days that he did not need to work the donkey, he could use it for fun things.

One morning Mother announced that we would all go pick wild strawberries. (If you are not acquainted with wild strawberries you need to know that they are about a third the size of cultivated berries.) So here we go, Mother, all four girls, Ronald, and the donkey. We all worked hard picking strawberries and finally got all our buckets full. Ronald decided to tie the buckets across the back of the donkey to be carried home. We all went up the hill happy to have an animal doing our work for us. Our happiness lasted until we started washing the berries. The berries were well mixed with donkey hair. The berries could not be used. It is funny that we never noticed that the donkey was shedding his winter coat! I don't think I've ever seen my mother so mad. We had all worked so hard to fill our buckets.

The moral of this story is when you go strawberry picking, don't ever take a shedding donkey with you!

RACE RELATIONS AT COVE CREEK

Catherine Stokes Sheppard

Facts presented here are from The First 200 Years of Cove Creek Baptist Church 1799–1999.

From the time of the first settlements in Western Watauga, almost everybody farmed, but always the farms were very small. Consequently, there was never a great need for slaves. That fact and the climate of the area resulted in a small population of Negroes as compared to other parts of the rural South.

Of the black people who came here some were slaves but others were freedmen.

The First 200 Years of Cove Creek Baptist Church (published 1999) tells far more than church history. It reveals much about the culture of Western Watauga County. The church was established in 1799 and the history states that "racism was no problem in the early church." It goes on to say that two Negro women belonging to Samuel Hix and Noah Mast, respectively, were taken into membership in the church. While these were the first Negroes to be received into the church, several other black people were members in early years. In 1884, the black people wanted their own church and were assisted in the establishment of one by the Cove Creek Baptist Church. However, some black people chose to remain where they were. George Whittington, Mary Whittington, Jesse Mitchell, Rachel Mitchell, James Mathis, E.P. Whittington, Lucinda Whittington, Jose Mathis, Glenda Mathis, Ambrosette Mathis, and Drucilla Mathis withdrew from Cove Creek to become charter members of the Little Zion Church, which later merged with the Mennonite Baptist (Brethren) Church in Boone. It was also noted that several black people were buried in the Cove Creek Cemetery.

As recent as 1970, John Henry Whittington preached at Cove Creek Baptist. The Rev. Whittington was born and reared in the Cove Creek community. His forefathers were among those who left Cove Creek to establish Little Zion. After he graduated from college and seminary, he became a Presbyterian minister.

From these notes, it appears that the distance between blacks and whites is not nearly as great in Western Watauga as it is in other parts of our state, past or present.

Race Relations at Bethel

Genevieve Sherwood Henson

As told to Jo Harris and Nannie Greene in 1999.

Growing up in Bethel I never knew there was such a thing as racial discrimination. Since I was white, opportunities were not limited to me and therefore I did not realize there was a different way of life for my black neighbors. Of course, they went to a different school. There was a small school over on Stone Mountain for colored children and the teacher was named Frances McQueen. (I believe there is a road over there now named for Mrs. McQueen.) Later the children rode a bus to Boone to their school. That bus was not allowed to pick up white children, but in very bad weather, the driver would bend the rule and allow white children to ride if they had to walk a long distance. The bus would drop them off in an easier walking distance to their school.

Baptist was the only denomination in the Bethel community and anyone who lived there came to the Baptist Church. I remember quite well when colored people came also, especially when we had revivals. Uncle Calvin Farthing was the minister and he would call on a black man to lead in prayer.

There were never many black people at one time living in Bethel but there were some mighty fine black people. I remember Aunt Laura and Aunt Jane Thompson and the Tom Banner family. (There was a white man and a black man named Tom Banner.) The Moores were a fine family. If there was a need, we helped them and they helped us. Clarence Moore's children still live in Boone.

Recollections of the 1940 Flood

Baxter G. Farthing

Baxter G. Farthing lives in Manassas, Virginia. He submitted this story in 2000.

When the big flood occurred, August 1940, our family was living at our farm in Laurel Creek Township. Our house was located on the hill overlooking the large bridge, which crossed the Watauga River. The bridge was a large self-supporting type structure with the huge steel framework overhead. There was a concrete pier on the bank on each side of the river for support; however, there were no piers in the river itself. This type of structure was typical of many of the earlier bridges. This type of construction gave the bridge somewhat of a flexible or springy aspect. On Tuesday, August 13th, 1940, the river started rising and by noon the water was halfway up to the bridge floor. That afternoon as the water level continued to rise, much debris was being washed down the river. Cove Creek entered the river a few hundred feet north of the bridge so the debris was coming down from Cove Creek as well as Watauga River valley. By mid afternoon, there were multitudes of haystacks being washed down the river. As the water level got closer to the bridge floor, these haystacks would hit the bridge with enough force to cause it to shake back and forth. Sometimes a clump of three or four haystacks would hit the bridge at one time, which would cause the bridge to spring violently back and forth from the force. I distinctly remember some of the haystacks had large rats scurrying about before they would hit the bridge. I imagine they thought they were taking one heck of a ride! Large trees were also hitting the bridge as they floated down the river.

The largest flood on record before 1940 was said to have occurred in 1916, and there was a large mark left on a tree across the river, which was always said to mark the height of the 1916 flood. My brother, Wheeler, who was a member of the faculty at Cove Creek High School, knew where the mark was located. Just before the water started sloshing across the bridge floor, he ran across the bridge to see if the high water mark from 1916 was still visible. He came back and reported the water level had already risen above the 1916 flood mark. This meant that we were having a record-breaking flood.

About dusk that evening, my dad, Ben Farthing, went out in the yard to get another look at the river. He had expressed concern all evening that the bridge might be washed out. He came back into the house and these were his exact words, "Well, the bridge is safe now. The water level has gone down a few inches, and there is no more trash coming down the river." At that split second, we hear a loud CRASH. All of us ran outside to see what happened. A house had washed in against the bridge.... It was the house of Ms. Polly Ward which had been located about one-half mile from the bridge on the opposite side of Cove Creek. It had floated around in the bottom land that afternoon. Finally, late that evening it got caught in the main current of Cove Creek and was then resting against the bridge. The house started pushing slowly against the bridge, and would move it a few inches, then it would stop pushing for several seconds after which it would start pushing again a few inches. This caused a "blood curdling" screeching sound, which I will never forget. After it slowly pushed the bridge a few inches at a time, the bridge finally toppled off the piers and went under the water.

Early the next morning after the water had receded we discovered the bridge had landed just below the huge rock, which is located in the middle of the river about 400 feet downstream. Needless to say, it was warped and twisted in all kinds of shapes.

During the weeks that followed, the state removed all of the bridge debris and built a new bridge, which was completed about December 1940.

During my lifetime, I have seen few incidents as dramatic as when the house pushed the bridge off the piers into the Watauga River that Tuesday evening during the great flood of August 13, 1940.

Baxter G. Farthing lived right at the bridge on Watauga River in 1940. He remembers vividly when a house in the water pushed that bridge off its piers on August 13, 1940, and the terrible screeching sound it made. This photo shows piers like the ones on that bridge. What a force it took to cause such damage! (photograph furnished by Leo Mast).

The Day Cove Creek Gym Burned

Hensel Stokes

Hensel Stokes (1917–2004) graduated from Cove Creek High School in 1934. The following is from a taped interview conducted by Catherine Stokes Sheppard in 2003.

The Cove Creek gym burned in 1939. It was on a Saturday, not long before dark in late May after school was out for the year. A lot of tales were told about how it caught on fire, but I believe what I heard and saw.

My brother Roger and I had lived with our Grandma since we were

Hensel Stokes and his brother, Roger, witnessed the burning of this beautiful and spacious gym in May 1939. They heard each bus explode as the fire reached it and saw the flames light up the sky. They feared those flames would cross the road to the gas tanks at the garage and cause even more havoc. It happened during a summer storm with lightning playing all around (photograph from CC Grange Collection).

just little fellers. Her house was the first house past the old Cove Creek gym, same side of the road, just on up the road in the direction of Tennessee. Our rooms were upstairs where we could see the gym good from the window in Roger's room. The awfulest thunder and lightning storm you ever saw came up. It wasn't raining at first, but the thunder and lightning was just a cracking. I was upstairs laying on my bed and Roger was in his room on the bed. In a little bit they came a crack of lightning and I heard something POP. It was a big pop. I run across the hall to Roger's room and looked out the window and Boys! The smoke was roaring out of the gym. In no time there was a blaze in there I bet 75 feet high. Across the road from it was DeWitt Brown's garage with them gasoline pumps out front. I think to myself, "They will blow up!" It was a good thing that it was Saturday night and nobody was at the garage. People didn't have any way to fight such a fire so they just had to watch it burn.

There was more than just the gym a burning too! Since school was out, all the buses were stored in the gym for the summer. I believe there was 15 buses in there. As the fire reached each bus, its horn would begin to blow. That was a mournful sound, believe me. Then when the fire reached the gas tank there would be another explosion. They were old buses, but they would run.

After the fire died down we boys went over there and was looking around. I remember Sam Horton came up and said, "I am glad we had all the old buses in there. The insurance will pay for all of them." So then, we did get all new buses. The old buses were valued at $1000 each.

My First Job at the Carolina Pharmacy

Reba Cook Farthing

Reba Cook Farthing lives in Manassas, Virginia. She submitted this story in 2000.

In 1945, I started my first job at the Carolina Pharmacy. An older sister, Ora Lee Cook, was working there and she was instrumental in helping me to get the job. She provided the transportation to and from work. My duties were to serve customers sandwiches, drinks and ice cream, including sodas, sundaes and cones.

Some of the waitresses with whom I worked were Lennis and Lavola Brown, Mary Jo Ragan, Marlene Shull, Nina Taylor, and of course, my sister, who was most helpful.

Our salary at that time was about $16.75 per week, excluding our meals. We were pleased with that salary range, as it was considered to be a fair wage during that period.

I recall having my 15th birthday while working there. Dr. Mock was shocked to learn that I was only 15, and he remarked that if he had been checked by the employment officials, he could have been in real trouble for employing a person under age. I worked there for four months while I was in school at Cove Creek High School, and for about a year after graduating. Working there was a good learning experience. It gave me confidence in myself to face future employment possibilities.

Many good friends were made through working at the Carolina Pharmacy!

Boating on the Creek

Hensel Stokes

Hensel Stokes (1917–2004) lived in Cove Creek many years. His story was recorded by Catherine Stokes Sheppard in 2003.

One day my Uncle Don was in Newton and saw an old boat for sale. He said, "Let's get that boat and fix it up and put it on the creek." I said, "That's good!" Well, we got it turned bottom side up, dried it out so we could load it, put it on the back end of his old Dodge pick-up and brought it home. We worked on it a little and put it in the creek. Now you gotta understand that creek had always been there but nobody used a boat anymore. Well, everybody that came along wanted to ride the boat.

The first thing that came to my mind was to wet 'em. I'd take 'em out to where the water was waist deep (I didn't want to get nobody drowned) and I'd turn 'em over. Oh, you never heard such squalling and carrying on, and hollering in your life. Now that is what the boat business was! We'd take any of 'em. I had a bunch of teachers in there one time. I didn't want to wet them. They trusted me enough to get in that boat and I was going to get them out safe. I got them to the bank safe. They made a pass for the bank and got to it too. That was the only boat I ever knowed of on Cove Creek.

I was running the mill back then and I kept the boat tied to a post in the milldam. Anybody that come along and wanted a ride I'd let 'em use it. Ed Isaacs and Don Isaacs used to live up Isaacs Branch and when they'd bring corn to the mill, while I was grinding they'd go boat riding. I'll guarantee every time they'd go they would come back soaking wet.

I didn't use a paddle, I used a pole and we just went in the milldam. I remember one time I took Hattie Perry for a boat ride. Now if you remember, Hattie Perry was a very heavy girl. It was a Sunday afternoon and Hattie came by and I said, "Hattie, do you want to go for a boat ride?" She said, "No, you'll just get me wet, but if Edward will go I will." Edward was a younger brother of mine and Hattie was sort of sweet on Edward. He agreed to go. Well, we took Hattie for a boat ride. We went up behind the schoolhouse where the water is about waist high. I decided we'd better not go any deeper. Of course, we turned the boat over and Hattie went plumb to the bottom! We got her up. Edward had one arm, I had the other, and we aimed to get her out of there. I said, "Just a minute here, this thing was a joke but it ain't so jokefied now! We got to get her out of here." Edward said, "All we got to do is lead her over to the bank." I said, "No you won't either. Hell, she'll mire up in the sand. We can't leave her out here; we have got to get her out of the milldam." Then I had an idea. We turned the boat bottom upwards and we got Hattie across it and floated it to a sand bar. That's how we got Hattie out of the mill pond. Ed allowed as to how this wasn't much of a joke after all. We had expected Hattie to be mad but she took it good and laughed. Of course she was wet from head to toe, so my wife took her in the house and Hattie took off her clothes and my wife put them in the sun to dry. We lived then in the little house beside the mill. We had a

Hensel Stokes was the "miller" at this gristmill. He would grind the corn into meal when people brought it to the mill. He and his wife Pearl lived in the white house beside the mill. It was on the creek just above the milldam where he gave people a ride in his boat. He and his brother, Edward, liked to see most of them get wet during the ride, too (photograph from Cove Creek Grange collection).

lot of fun with that boat. We played a lot of pranks in those days. We had something going all the time around that mill.

The Run-Away Car

Baxter G. Farthing

The following was submitted by Baxter G. Farthing in 2000.

In the late 1930s, the North Carolina State Highway Department straightened and rebuilt Highway 421 through the Brushy Fork area and up the mountain to Boone.

Soon after the road was straightened, paved, and opened to the public I went to Boone with my dad. This was the first time we had been to Boone since the new road opened. Our car was a 1935 Chevrolet two-door sedan with mechanical brakes. We came out of Boone on the way home to Sugar Grove and when we got to the top of Boone Mountain, my dad put the car in neutral to let it coast down the new highway towards Brushy Fork. Naturally, the car started picking up speed, and as it did so, he started tapping the foot brake with his foot but the car would not slow down. I had remembered my older sister, Frances, complaining about the brakes not being very good. Since the foot brake would not slow it down my dad pushed in the clutch and got a hold of the gear shift, which was mounted on the floor, and tried to put it back in high gear. However, it would not go into high gear but stayed in neutral. My dad was chewing tobacco and he spit tobacco juice out the window, but the window was up and it splattered all over the inside of the window. Then he rolled the window down and continued to spit out the window several times, as he kept pressing the foot brake and also trying to get it back into gear.

After we got home, we noticed tobacco juice had flowed along the outside of the car towards the back in very graceful, artistic curves. Also, we found that considerable tobacco juice had actually been blown into the back seat by the wind. This is an indication of how fast the car was traveling down the mountain.

After trying several times to slow it down by pressing the foot brake and after being unable to get it back into gear, he just held onto the steering wheel. I do remember he never did reach for the emergency brake, which was also mounted on the floor in that model Chevrolet. Fortunately, there was virtually no traffic on the road at that time, and as we passed the Dock Mast store area the car was traveling at a very good clip. As the road began to level out through the Brushy Fork area, he continued trying to get it into high gear. Finally he got it into gear along about where the Adam's Building Supply is located today. With that, my dad made the most emphatic sounding statement that I have ever heard, "Boys, I'll never do that again!" That's the last time I ever saw him coast.

A Boy and His Pony

Bill Stokes

Bill Stokes (1927–1999) submitted this story in 1999. He lived in Chilhowie, Virginia.

The year was 1939 when I turned 13 and left home to live with my grandmother, my aunt and uncle. They lived near the Cove Creek School. Even if Cove Creek was only a few miles from Phillips Hollar it was a world away to me. My uncle bought me pony and a green pony wagon. I was probably the proudest boy in Watauga County.

A boy has various uses for his pony. Bill Stokes (standing on the pony wagon) wanted to earn some spending money so he hauled his neighbor's extra milk to the Coble Dairy. Five-year-old Daren Campbell (seated in the wagon) was always happy to keep him company (photograph furnished by Jerry Adams).

I used this wagon to haul anything that needed hauling. The Coble Dairy had built a milk receiving plant near the Sugar Grove Post Office. My grandmother had a little milk to sell so I had a job! All I needed now was more milk to haul so I got out to see if I could find other people who had extra milk. I had plenty of room in the wagon to transport four big old milk cans and my pal and neighbor Daren Campbell, who was 5 years old. He became my helper as well as my companion. I think we finally got three customers. One of them was Tom Moody, a teacher at the elementary school and the owner of the store across from the school. Tom had a two-gallon bucket that he sent out daily with one gallon of milk. The plant workers really hated to see that bucket come through because it would not go through the washer and they had to wash it by hand. It finally wound up with a nail hole in the bottom (maybe on purpose) and couldn't be used any more.

Each customer paid me five cents a trip, but the job only lasted through the summer. Money could not buy the feeling of wealth and maturity I enjoyed with that job. I was grown and rich!

That pony was good for riding as well as for pulling a wagon. A few years after my milk job, my brother Ralph and I were riding our ponies and decided to check out the WPA job that was building a stone schoolhouse not far from Grandma's house. Since it was Sunday, there were no workers present. We rode around the building and commented on the progress. As we rode behind the building, we saw a ramp going to the top of the structure. I am sure the ramp was designed to push wheelbarrows full of rocks, cement, and other materials to a higher level. As it grew, the building became more and more beautiful and the community was so very proud of it. Often farmers would bring a load of stone to the building site. It was a big job! Well, Ralph and I looked at that ramp and began to calculate in our minds if it would hold up two ponies and two boys. We decided to test it.

Up we went! What an adventure. My pony seemed pretty nervous about the whole thing, and consequently left her calling card on the roof. I have always wondered what the workmen thought when they arrived on Monday morning and found her message.

I have many wonderful memories of that first pony. Not only I but many friends enjoyed jaunts on the wagon and on the pony.

Duck Eggs

Catherine Stokes Sheppard

Western Watauga County was a wonderful place to grow up in the early '40s. I have so many fond memories from there. My cousin Bill Stokes was two years older than I and he was the best buddy a girl could have had. We both went to our grandmother's home when we could. In the summertime, we spent many happy days riding horses or, more likely, ponies. Our grandmother, Lou Stokes, was a no nonsense person and always had chores for us to do. Therefore, we stayed out of sight if at all possible. But, one day she had a chore that was made to order for us. We were to hitch a pony to a pony wagon and go to Mrs. Sheffield's and get duck eggs to set. This journey was a distance of two or three miles and on an unpaved road. I do not recall what we used to pay for the eggs, but I am sure it was barter. I clearly remember the basket that she padded with a flour sack to give the eggs a cushioned ride home.

Feeling very important to be sent on such an errand, we sallied forth. The day was so clear and gloriously warm (as only Watauga days can be)! I do not remember much about the trip going, the fun was the trip home. The pony was lively and so were we, so we decided to see just how fast the pony could run on the gravel road. About the time we got back to the Cove Creek Baptist Church and the paved road, the truth hit us that maybe racing the pony had not been too smart. Too late now! A few minutes later, we were back at Grandmother's with a basket of broken eggs. We both feared the death penalty. Maw (we were never allowed to call her anything else, not even Ma) had never been accused of mincing her words and that day was no different. I distinctly recall her expletives being such words as "foolish," "no sense," and "crazy." Today when my grandchildren do something totally stupid, I have to remember this event. We certainly did not help the duck population any, but we built a great memory.

Catherine Stokes Sheppard recalls many happy days spent riding ponies and playing in Cove Creek during her childhood.

Ned Walks

Ned Trivette

As told by Ned Trivette of the Timbered Ridge community to Catherine Stokes Sheppard, October 1999.

Sometimes when I see a young man get a fast new car for his 16th birthday, I chuckle to myself and remember how I traveled at that age. Specifically I remember in the 1950s going to a basketball game in Boone when I was in high school at Bethel.

After school, I caught a ride into Boone, giving little thought as to how I would get home. After all this was a big game and surely someone from my general area would also be there, and I would just catch a ride. Near the end of the game, I realized I had better start surveying the bleachers to see if I could find someone from Timbered Ridge.

Suddenly I realized I was among strangers! I did not know one person in my vicinity except the Banner brothers who lived at the base of George's Gap. They were glad to give me a ride as far as their house and I just knew that if I started walking, soon somebody would come along and give me a ride. So, it was a right and a left.

To my utter astonishment not one, repeat, not one motor vehicle came along. Anyone who is familiar with the terrain from the base of George's

Ned Trivette still lives in this beautiful home on Timbered Ridge built in the 1890s. When he was 16 he went to a basketball game in Boone without making plans for a ride back home afterwards. Ned caught a ride with two Banner boys to their home on George's Gap Road. That was about halfway home. From there he walked the nine and one half miles to get home. It was a very cold night and it took him about 5 hours (photograph by Catherine Stokes Sheppard).

Gap to Timbered Ridge knows that it is not a stroll in the park. There are a lot of ups and downs. Making matters worse, I think it was the coldest night I ever felt. It is about nine and one-half miles from the Banner home to mine. But I made it in five hours. That was a long night and my Mother was worried about her son.

Itch Cure

Odenia Miller Rowe

Odenia Miller Rowe lives in San Diego, California. She submitted her story in 1999.

When reminiscing about my early years on Cove Creek, I recall how blessed we were with the lovely mountain setting and the neighbors' generosity in sharing recipes, home cures, and folklore, which enabled us to survive with few doctor visits.

Regarding such cures, I laughingly recall an instance in which my sister, Ruth, and I had caught the itch (scabies) from friends whom we had kept overnight and with whom we'd shared a bed and towels. Refusing to use the tried and true sulfur and lard remedy, which smelled to high heaven and made the greased person an instant social outcast, we decided to try a new remedy our mama, Mary Miller, had heard of. It consisted of discarded auto engine oil, which we acquired from DeWitt Brown's garage next door.

Mama had us wash up and she applied the thick oil from neck to ankles, over which she had us put on a pair of Dad's drop-seat knit union suits (long johns). Then she tied that at the wrists and ankles. Since we were "treated" on the weekend, we were housebound for two days and washed down with lye soap and hot water in a galvanized washtub. We scrubbed until we were nearly raw and even though it cured the itch, I have often laughed at the experience and believe that the removal of our skin by rubbing with lye soap was probably the true cure.

The County Home

Nannie Greene

Before the days of Social Security and retirement benefits, it was not unusual for elderly people, particularly women who had never married, to find themselves with no funds for sustenance. Sometimes these unfortunate people would find a home with some relative. If there was no one to take them in, it could be necessary to go the county home.

The first Watauga County Home was located in the Brushy Fork Township where a church is located now on the 105 Bypass. A second location was near the intersection of US 421 and the 105 Bypass where a new brick building was erected. The county paid a set amount for each resident living in the home. It was not only a home for the elderly, but also for the mentally retarded and crippled who had no one to care for them. Some folk remember Little Jim Greer who lived there. He took care of a polio victim, Jimmy Andrews. One person recalls that every time she went in to visit a resident, Little Jim would shake his small change purse at her. Perhaps he never had much money in his purse to shake.

One lady remarked that while she never saw the inside of a county home, her mental image was vivid! She could just see the institution as something right out of Charles Dickens. No doubt, the fare was meager, and poorly paid attendants may not always have been kind. We do know that the anecdotes about the county home caused one to shiver. These homes were also called the "poor house."

Today one might hear a younger person refer to the "poor house" and we know quite well that the youth has absolutely no idea what a poor house is. The name worked into our language as a representative of poverty.

The county home has been replaced by nursing homes and assisted living homes. We can all rejoice that the county home has disappeared, necessary as it was in its day.

Earline Huffman Came as a Tourist

Earline Huffman

Earline Huffman lives in Summerfield, N.C. She submitted her story in 2000.

Even before I was born my dad, Earl Sigmon, and my grandfather, George Setzer, would go to the mountains around Blowing Rock, Boone, Valle Crucis, and Sugar Grove to buy white-faced steers and drive them down the mountain. Dad always took cash to buy the cattle because no one would accept anything else.

Dad loved the mountains and the people who lived there and prided himself on being their friend. As a result, my brother, my mom and I would spend our vacations there. We were never treated as a boarder, but always as members of the family.

Even before I began school, about 1930, we would stay with a family across the road from the Mast Store in Valle Crucis. I cannot remember their name but I do remember the creamed corn and biscuits we had for breakfast — still my favorite foods.

Later we started staying with the John Bingham family in Sugar Grove. John Bingham was a retired judge. I would often walk with him and listen to him talk. And did he love to talk! One of his favorite sayings was that he wanted his flowers while he lived, not after he was gone. He always laughed and said he had one old family of children and a new family. Those two families, but with the same wife, included: Finley, Joe, Ophie, Don, Roxanna and Bob White. An older daughter was a teacher and taught in a school she said was built over a creek and where the children were sewed into their long underwear in the fall and taken out in the spring.

Judge Bingham set a good table and his special luxury was orange blossom honey, which he had sent up from Florida. Another treat for me was cake with lemon sauce and I always requested it when asked.

Clyde Mast General Store was usually buzzing with activity in the 1930s. People came there to buy, trade, talk or play croquet. Because there were few cars in the Sugar Grove area, most people walked or rode a horse to get there. One day during her summer vacation Earline Huffman waded the creek to get there because some boys would not let her use the bridge. She had to get to the store to buy her daily supply of candy (photograph furnished by Mildred Mast Farthing).

The Bingham house was a large, white two-storied house with a wide, covered porch on three sides where we could play when it rained. A yard full of flowers surrounded the house. Don's son and I were special friends and I remember that we spent hours trying to catch many butterflies, without hurting them of course. We became quite proficient at it.

When my dad brought us up he would always empty his pockets of change and this was my candy money. Another Mast store was across the creek and I crossed the footbridge every day to go there for candy. One day my brother, George, and Bob White decided to tease me and they would not let me cross the bridge. Scared silly, I waded across the creek holding the bottom of the bridge, but I got my candy.

Although Roxanna was several years older than I, she took me under her wing. We walked and visited all around the area. I especially remember Jim Mast, who lived around the curve from the Clyde Mast Store and whose front door was always open. Further down the road, we visited a family who had a small, cold stream that ran through the basement, where they kept butter, milk and such. We scouted the hills for small nuts called chinquapins. These grew in burrs like chestnuts, were smaller and much better. I was especially delighted with their family graveyard, which was on the top of the mountain so the dead would be nearer to heaven.

Not far from the Bingham house was a small cheese factory. It was fascinating to watch the cheese being made. I still love mountain cheese.

Around 1940, my dad bought a small house where the old Blowing Rock Road crossed the New River, on what is now called Austin Road, so we no longer stayed in Sugar Grove. There we soon made new friends with the Shores and the Austins. We met Edell Shore and her daughter Murlee Austin one day when they were fishing under the bridge. Edell's favorite thing was fishing in that river and she spent hours sitting on the riverbank.

Tom Shore and Edell were married when he was only nineteen. Six months after their wedding he woke up one morning to find that he could not straighten his body and for the rest of his life he walked and lived with his body from the waist up almost at a right angle to his lower body. He was in great pain from this awful arthritis but he continued to work every day and I never heard him complain even once.

I spent many happy times with these wonderful people. They would all gather around the piano to play and sing for hours. Many times, we cooked and ate together. I especially remember one evening Murlee and I made walnut ice cream. We cracked black walnuts and bragged about how good that ice cream would be. We turned and turned long after it should have frozen and finally decided to open and serve the soft ice cream. One bite told us the problem. The container had a small hole and our good ice cream was full of salt. We still laugh about that when Murlee and I get together.

The Shores and the Austins attended a small Baptist church several miles from Boone and I went with them to Sunday services, homecoming dinners and church outings. Again, I was accepted as if I belonged.

Never did I hear any of the friends I know complain except once. There was a preacher around Hickory who called himself "The Parson of the Hills." My friends were upset to hear him talk about the poor mountain folks. They were never poor. Indeed, they were far richer than many wealthy people were. I know they taught me all I know about patience and kindness.

George Sigmon Visited Too!

George Sigmon

George Sigmon lives in Maiden, N.C. His story was submitted in 2000.

In the 1930s, we went to the mountains more times than I can count. Blowing Rock and Boone were just places to pass by. To us Sugar Grove was the place to be. We stayed at John Bingham's. He was a retired judge of Watauga County. He liked his large front porch where he could talk to all who came by. If you were there at lunchtime, you were always invited to eat. The table was full of food. The center of the table would revolve so you just turned the center to what you wanted. I do not know why we started staying there unless Dad just passed by and was asked to come back, and we did lots of times. There were several large stores on Cove Creek; the largest was at Sugar Grove. The mountain folk would bring hams, chickens, eggs, bark, etc. to the store for which they would get due bills instead of money and then use those to buy whatever was needed. There was a small cheese factory where they would sell cheese and cream. Dad would always take a hoop of cheese home.

We stayed at John Bingham's a few days at a time, but one summer I spent a whole summer there. Joe Bingham was John's oldest son and he did a lot of farming. We cut wood up on the mountain and brought it down on a large sled. A wagon was no good on the mountain because it would run over the horse, but a sled would not. Finley was a very fine man. Ophie was a schoolteacher. Bob White and I were about the same age so we did more things together. We helped Joe on the farm, fished and hunted, and sometimes got into trouble. Mr. Bingham would twist tobacco, which he used for chewing. Bob got into it once and while we were on top of the silo, we used some. We got so sick that Finley had to get us down. Sometimes we would go to the cheese factory to buy cheese for Mrs. Bingham but at times all of the cheese never made it home.

I remember that Bob White finished school without ever missing a day.

Character Building Comes with a Price

Landon Stokes

Landon Stokes lives in Lexington, N.C. He submitted this story in 2001.

Most people can remember an event or two from their school days that stand out and come to mind occasionally. I can remember that when a reference was made to school, it was called either grade school or free school. In my home, it was referred to as grade school. There may have been a reason for that, rather than using the term "free" school. When school began in the late summer each year, there was more required than just telling the teacher your name, it seems there was a 50-cent library fee to be collected from each student.

The collection began after all the students' names were on roll and each one had been assigned a desk and chair. The prodding began in earnest about the fourth week of school and by the fifth week the screws were being tightened a bit more each day. All of us, being graduates of the first grade and now in second grade, surely can understand the teacher when she says, "Each of you that hasn't paid the 50-cent library fee by next Monday will stand at the front of the classroom, in front of the blackboard, and tell the class why you haven't paid your library fee." Those words seemed very gentle compared to the words I heard at home whenever I was told, "If you don't...." The Depression may have been over some places in the mid-thirties, but at our house it was still in full bloom and there was no money for such foolishness as library fees.

Anyway, the lineup began at school. Scrawny little lads, half-clad in bibbed-overalls with patches on both knees and worn-out Wolverine shoes, along with several little lassies clad in flour sack dresses, lined up in front of the class and began explaining why the fee had not been paid. When each one gave their familiar "I ain't got it" they were allowed to return to their desk and sit down. This was a daily routine until the fee was paid or the teacher just gave up.

As days and weeks went by the lineup grew smaller but the demand to pay up was not lessened in any way. However, there was a very tiny ray of hope that shone through for me, and maybe, just maybe, I could get out of the lineup, which by now was very small. It seems my older brother Ralph had heard of my plight and was anxious to help me. He had no means either, but as the saying goes, "Where there is a will, there is a way." The school janitor, a lame man named Don Swift, who rode a horse to school each day, had a need himself. The school rooms needed to be swept clean each day after school and Mr. Swift, as we students called him, could use some help. Ralph, who lived with our great-uncle Will Moody, within walking distance of the school, applied for the job. The wages, as I remember, were approximately three dollars a month. Anyway, we were way into the fall of the year when that tiny ray of light shone brightly for this little second grade boy who would no longer have to stand in front of the class each morning to say, "I ain't got it," because he had an understanding older brother.

I was too young to realize at the time that this pressure was put on us kids because the principal was putting pressure on the teacher. But, as humiliating as it was, now I like to think it did help me to build character. Something good should have come from such suffering.

The Big Game

Landon Stokes

Landon Stokes submitted this story in 2001.

When I was in the eighth grade at Cove Creek High School in the mountains of Watauga County, something happened to me that has much more meaning now than it did then. Our family lived near the school, and often after school was dismissed for the day, I would hang around and watch the basketball team practice. The coach of the men's team was a short, stocky fellow whose name was Sam Osborne. I don't know what his coaching secrets were, but he turned out some champion basketball teams. One of his teams (I believe the year was 1945) was champion of the WSJS Northwest North Carolina Basketball Tournament held annually in Winston-Salem.

The WPA had built our gym in the late thirties. It was an unfinished shell with no ceiling and partial inside walls maybe eight feet up from the floor. It did have a hardwood floor, sanded but unfinished, with some black painted lines outlining the playing court. Coach Osborne, whose trademark was rolling a piece of bubble gum into a small ball and then rolling it around on his lips with his index finger, learned my name because I was Len's brother. Len, the tallest and toughest of the Stokes boys, had by this time become a star on the high school basketball team, so Coach Osborne grew to like me.

When the gym was built, no consideration was given to dressing rooms for changing from street clothes to playing uniforms, so two small buildings, which were regularly used as bus houses (buildings used at bus stops to shelter schoolchildren while waiting for the school bus), were located at one end of the gym. One was for the visiting team, one was for the home team, and each was equipped with a small pot-bellied wood or coal stove.

The night that I remember so well was just after basketball season opened and cold weather had arrived. A big game was coming up and Coach Osborne wanted everything just right. We had hauled sawdust and put it on the gym floor where all of the different classes played with the sawdust on the floor. Talk about some spills! It was so slippery one could hardly stand up. Nevertheless, it must have accomplished something. On the afternoon before the game was to be played, we swept the floor clean of the sawdust. Maybe it served to clean the unfinished floor.

Then Coach's thoughts turned to the dressing rooms. "Could we build a fire in the stoves?" Coach spotted that little, skinny, bib-overalls-clad boy

When the big school gymnasium burned in 1939, Cove Creek volunteers rallied to help get another one built for their basketball teams. The new gym had only bare necessities, including pot-bellied stoves for heat. Even the dressing rooms were built on the outside of the building. Landon Stokes was in charge of building the fires to warm the dressing rooms for the big game, which he didn't get to see (photograph from the Cove Creek Grange collection).

named Landon. Coach Osborne knew I was familiar with wood or coal stoves, pipes, ashes and what it took to make use of them. "Landon could check it out." I was more than happy when Coach asked me to be in charge of providing heated dressing rooms for the teams.

My first task was to check each small building to see what would be required to bring them up to Coach's expectation. Having had previous experience in faulty flue pipes, especially ones that were flattened, I noted that two sections were needed to make it safe to build fires in the stoves.

The next step took much thought and consideration. There was a problem: since Coach had put me in charge (actually I was the only one, so I didn't have much of a personnel problem), somehow I needed to get two sections of 6-inch flue pipe. There was a country store about a mile away that I knew would have metal flue pipe, but there was another problem: that pipe would not be free, even for the school.

Knowing for weeks about the big upcoming game, I had saved and scrounged to have enough money to pay my way in and have enough extra for a Pepsi-Cola and a Moon Pie from Tom's Store. Tom Moody owned the store and was also the principal of the elementary school. The schools and the store were all grouped together, separated only by US Highway 421. I had 50 cents, more than enough to get into the gym, eat Moon Pie and drink Pepsi, so I was well prepared. Anyway, Tom did not stock flue pipe, so I would need to walk to Sherwood's Store a mile away to get pipe. After all, I was in charge, and I must not let Coach Osborne down now.

A bright idea hit me: I could use my money to buy the pipe, and Coach would reimburse me before game time. So, off to Sherwood's Store I went. I told the clerk what I needed, and he probably thought perhaps the ones at our house had become flat; but I quickly told him that I was in charge of having heated dressing rooms for the school basketball teams. He told me that the total price with tax would be 40 cents. I had enough to accomplish my mission. Down the road I went, whistling. I was a worthy person for Coach to put in charge.

Back at the dressing rooms all went well with the flue repairs. It was time to build fires to check out the flues. All went well there, also. I cleaned, swept and had everything ready for Coach Osborne to inspect, and most of all, to brag on what a fine job I had done, and to reimburse me for the cost of the two new pipes. I waited in anticipation as the dressing rooms became warm and cozy. I wondered, "Where is Coach?"

I had not been home since school was dismissed, so I had not yet eaten supper, but that was not unusual for the day of a big game. What was most important to me was having two warm, cozy dressing rooms. "Where is Coach? It's near dark and I haven't seen him, but don't panic, he'll be here soon."

Cars began to park alongside the highway, with some people going into Tom's Store to get refreshments for the game. Members of the girls' team began arriving. They had dressed in their uniforms at home and just wore a long winter coat over them. "I know I don't have anything to worry about, Coach will be here, and besides, his wife collects the admission fee for the games at the door."

Some of my school buddies had arrived and were doing all the things that we young boys would do before game time, but I couldn't join them; I was in charge of the warm, cozy dressing rooms. "Where is Coach Osborne?" I wondered. The gym was packed full of loyal fans and I began to hear the noise of feet running on the cleanly swept floor. It was the girls' teams warming up for the first game. "Don't worry, Landon, Coach will not forget you."

By now, all my school buddies had stopped their outside play and had entered the gym. "I'll take a peek inside the gym door to see if I can see Coach anywhere." Standing near the door was Coach's wife, with the cigar box holding the receipts for the night's game. I only had a dime, and it cost

15 cents to enter. I could tell Coach's wife my plight but that would hurt my pride, letting her know I didn't have 15 cents. No way was I going to do that.

By this time, I heard Dale Adams blow the whistle, signaling that it was time for the game to start. "So what? I don't care all that much about the girls' game, anyway." Dale was a local citizen who knew the rules of the game, so he would be the referee for both games, and he was always fair to both teams. "Where is Coach? Maybe he is across the road at Tom's Store getting stocked up on bubble gum, because he'll roll lots of little gum balls this night."

It was dark now, and feet were pounding up and down the gym floor. People were yelling, the whistle was blowing. "I'll check Tom's to see if he's there." So I entered Tom's Store, and around his large, pot-bellied stove stood Tom and his wife, Eude, Hensel Stokes, DeWitt Brown, and maybe one or two others. All eyes were upon me as I came in, because after all, every other boy and girl my age in that community was inside the gym watching the ball game. "Why aren't you at the ball game?" Someone asked. "Oh, I don't care much about the girls' game," I replied. "I'm waiting for the boys' game, and besides, I'm in charge of providing warm dressing rooms for the boys' teams." Needless to say, Coach was not there.

Back across the road I went, thinking, "It's only the girls' game now; I'm not missing a lot. The roaring inside the gym had ceased, and so had the sound of pounding feet. It must be half-time."

The boys' teams would be approaching any minute now to dress for their game following completion of the girls' game. They began arriving and talking about the warmth of the dressing room. "What a change," someone commented, which made me feel so good I forgot for a moment that I still had no means to enter the gym for the boys' game. There was so much noise and jabbering while they were getting dressed that I became one of the groups. After all, Len was in the group. Someone yelled, "Boy! Did you see what pretty legs that number 5 girl had?" Someone else answered, "No! I was watching that number 11. Isn't she a beauty?" Well, one by one, they got dressed and returned to the gym to watch the pretty legs and faces, which is a wonderful part of growing up. Pretty soon it was down to one person left in the dressing room — Landon.

By now the thought had begun to creep in that the coach was not looking for me, I needed to be looking for him. But he was inside, and I was on the outside. I should have found him early in the evening, instead of staying in the dressing rooms to receive all those pats on the back for my job well done. He had been there all the time, but I wouldn't dare leave those dressing rooms, for fear of missing a pat on the back.

The girls' game ended and the boys all put their eyeballs back into their sockets. They were racing around the gym floor, getting warmed up for their battle with the opposing team.

The whistle blew, and the teams took their positions. The ball was tossed into the air and the game began. The coach's wife was still just inside the gym door with her cigar box of receipts, waiting for any latecomers. "Now, all I need to do is tell her, and she will see me through. But, wait, she won't know anything about me, the flue pipes, and the dressing rooms. She'll think I'm just another student trying to trick her. It's obvious now, no one but the coach can get me in. But, it's too late. He's on the inside, I'm on the outside."

I couldn't go home because Mama would ask why I wasn't at the game, and if I told her, then Dad would whip me for spending my money for the flue pipes, all the while laughing and telling me what an idiot I was, and what a good lesson I had learned. There was nothing to do but stay around until the game was over. At least I could keep warm. The dressing rooms were not locked, no need for that back then. There were no valuables and very few thieves.

Well, the game was over, some team had won and I guess I was the real loser. It took me about fifty years to figure out the moral of this story. "Pride goeth before a fall."

Part 2: Law and Order … and Sometimes Justice

From Sunday afternoon visiting on the front porches of Western Watauga County to the cell phone chats, one of the most frequent topics of conversation has to do with law and order. Ordinary happenings just cannot measure up to the suspense and entertainment provided by crime. Stories get told and re-told, added to and altered by various participants. Sometimes convicted felons become folk heroes, and just to spice up the talk, sometimes humor is woven into the fabric of the plot. Often legal justice is not the main ingredient in these social discourses.

Although we have heard stories of how young men from the Tennessee–North Carolina border communities would get alcohol happy, ride their horses into the neighboring communities, yell and holler and frighten some people, they did no real damage. We were never able to get firsthand accounts of these handed down tales. Likewise, other stories tell of how young men in the Timbered Ridge area would not allow guys from outside to go courting on their turf. They would hide in ambush for young men who had shown interest in their girls. Mostly, they roughed up the intruder and frightened him off.

Unfortunately, there were some crimes committed that brought great sadness to entire communities. Family reputations were damaged for years to come. However, by and large the people of Western Watauga County are law-abiding people but now and then it becomes convenient (if not necessary) to circumvent the law in order to provide justice. Some of the following stories are examples of seeking justice outside the law, some of which resulted in a great deal of humor.

From the Bible to Hollywood, as well as every day life, we still find entertainment in sex and violence!

A Post Office Burglary

Jean Ward

Very few burglaries occur in Sugar Grove, N.C., these days, but in 1969 it was even more of a rarity. Nannie Greene interviewed Jean Herman Ward (Mrs. Cannon Ward) in the summer of 2004 and was surprised to hear about this robbery.

Cannon Ward was the postmaster at Sugar Grove Post Office for several years. One morning he got a telephone call just after 6 A.M. from the man who delivered newspapers in the area. He wanted Cannon to know that the main door to the post office building was open. Mr. Ward immediately rushed right over to the post office.

When he arrived at the site, he was appalled at what he found. Not only had the main door been forced open, so had the door to the room where the safe was located. The safe had also been damaged. Cannon immediately called the sheriff and then began to inventory the missing items.

Sheriff Ward Carroll arrived in about 30 minutes. He noted that the burglar had used a crowbar or some large object to open the doors. He determined the burglar must be a professional because he knew exactly where to put the charges of dynamite or the TNT he used to blow open the safe door. After talking to people in the surrounding neighborhood, the sheriff could find no one who had heard a loud noise during the weekend.

The burglar had made a big haul! Social Security checks which were to go out on Monday were gone, all $11,000 worth of them. Also missing were about 50 money orders, $4,000 in stamps, but only $11.48 in cash. That was a big heist!

All the Social Security checks were issued again so no one lost money. They just didn't get it on time. But one of those checks led to the burglar. Someone in South Carolina called the Watauga sheriff's office to see why one of those checks would be in their city. The man who cashed that check was already in jail in South Carolina for another crime. No one is sure whether or not he or anyone was ever prosecuted for this crime. After all, that was in 1969!

A Burning Cross

Catherine Stokes Sheppard

In the late '30s and early '40s lifestyles were quite different from those of the 21st century. I have a clear recollection of looking up on a hill not far from our house and seeing a large, flaming cross. It was a clear summer evening and there was nothing to obstruct the view. There were men milling around the cross but I saw no robes or hoods. The men were, however, too far away to be recognized.

At the foot of the hill where the cross burned, there were a man and a woman living together who were not married. This situation had inspired a great deal of discussion in the neighborhood. In our house, at least in my presence, there had been lots of whispering. The woman's husband had committed suicide just prior to the new living arrangement. Shortly after the burning cross incident, the man hurriedly moved out for parts unknown. I realize now that this was the neighbors' way of telling the couple that they were not happy with the pair's living arrangement. Perhaps today we would label this event as a nonviolent demonstration.

An Angry Husband and a Dead Lover

Catherine Stokes Sheppard

The following is compiled from an interview published in the Watauga Democrat *on February 22, 1999. Dr. Lynn Getz, of the Appalachian State University History Department, conducted the interview with Kermon Hagaman. Dr. Getz is past president of the Watauga Historical Society.*

In about 1875, Elisha Trivette was having an affair with Evelyn, the wife of Ephraim Harmon, although they were first cousins. Ephraim learned of the situation and warned Elisha to stay away from his wife. Apparently, Elisha did not heed the warning. Ephraim suspected the meetings were still taking place so he called on Elisha and asked to borrow a gun. His pretense was that he was going up on the Beech the next day to salt his cattle. Early the next morning Ephraim left, but instead of going to Beech Mountain he concealed himself where he could watch his house and the surrounding area. A little later, he saw Elisha climbing the ridge to sit where he could see Ephraim's house. Sure enough, Evelyn came into the yard and waved a handkerchief in Elisha's direction. Elisha wasted no time in going to the Harmon house and entering. Just as quickly, Ephraim returned to his home, peered through the window, and saw them in bed. As he burst into the room, Elisha jumped up and begged for his life, promising to end the affair. But, Ephraim was one step ahead, he ended the affair with a bullet under the right arm. Elisha lived only a minute or two. Ephraim's wife begged her husband to go tell Mrs. Trivette what had happened. Instead, Ephraim dragged the body down to the road, mutilated it with his pocketknife and placed the knife in the dead man's hand. That afternoon when Ephraim's children came home from school they found the body and reported it.

Here you may expect to hear of a trial concerning premeditated murder, crime of passion and all that. Not so fast. Ephraim was tried, convicted of murder and sentenced to be hanged. He got an appeal, and it appears, new evidence. Ephraim convinced Evelyn that if he could prove that she became pregnant while he was waiting to be hanged then he could show that she was a bad woman and this would give him just cause for killing her lover. Anyhow, the sentence was changed from hanging to life in prison and he was soon paroled.

Out on a Limb!

Genevieve Sherwood Henson

Told by Genevieve Sherwood Henson to Catherine Stokes Sheppard and Nannie Greene in 2003.

My Dad was often in his store till nine or ten o'clock at night. One winter night he got home around nine and Mama urged him to go out by the road and see what on earth the dog was barking at. She told Dad the dog had barked non-stop since about 5 P.M., which was dark at that time of year. Dad decided he would get no rest from the dog or Mama until he took a look.

He went outside with his flashlight, looked all around, and saw nothing until he shined the light up in a large tree in our front yard. There sat a terrified man. Now Dad was not only a merchant, he was also a magistrate. The man in the tree had a grievance he didn't want to air in the store so he intended to catch Dad at home. I guess the dog pretty well settled the problem because I don't recall that the man ever came back.

A Pottertown Tale

Council Main

Council Main lives in Vilas, N.C. His story was recorded in 2003.

Pottertown is located in the northern part of Western Watauga, joining Ashe County. Some might say it is far back. Today it is no longer isolated, but one hundred years ago, it was. Pottertown was a place that men sought if they wanted to be lost from society in general. Old stories handed down say that there were more men killed in Pottertown than in all of the rest of Watauga County. The use of alcohol was often the indirect cause of shootings.

One story tells about a man named Brooms who drifted into the community and took up residence. One day a group of men was drinking and Mr. Brooms must have felt that he controlled the world. He went in the yard, stretched out his arms and said, "I dare any man here to put a bullet between my eyes." Brooms should have known better than to challenge a man from Pottertown! Sure enough, some one did just as he requested. Wham! Mr. Brooms was no more.

Perhaps the most infamous murder was credited to Clarence Potter. The Potters were, in general, good law-abiding people. They were honest, good neighbors and hard working. But, they had violent tempers and if a man, never a woman or child, provoked them severely, their instinct was to kill.

Clarence Potter was a young man, seventeen years old. He was the son of Abraham and Salina Potter, respected people. One day he and his cousin Booney Potter were hauling logs to a sawmill. When their team of horses pulled in to the sawmill, a deputy sheriff was waiting to serve a warrant on Clarence for some misdemeanor. Clarence seemed humble enough and asked the deputy if he could go to his home and tell his father and put on clean clothes. The deputy refused. A scuffle ensued and Clarence backed up, picked up a stone and flung it at the deputy. It hit the deputy in his forehead just between the eyes. At about the same time Booney had got hold of a pistol and fired at the deputy. It was never determined who actually killed the officer. Booney fled to Wyoming and Clarence went to jail.

Jury selection was much more simple around the turn of the century than it is today. Someone went out on the street near the courthouse and solicited jurors. Legend says a man heard of this and volunteered, saying, "I've always wanted to hang a Potter." And sure enough, Clarence was found guilty.

The judge sentenced him to be hung one month from the present date, which would have been on Clarence's 18th birthday. The story goes that Clarence smiled at the judge and the entire courtroom wept. Then Clarence was taken to Hickory for incarceration. It seems the jail in Hickory was considered more secure than the one in Boone.

Clarence's lawyer appealed and he got a second trial. This time the jury acquitted him. Interestingly enough, Clarence's father recorded the name of each person on the jury and admonished his children that if any of these jurors ever needed help they were to assist him.

But, this does not end the tale of Clarence Potter. After he was in jail and had a second trial, he became a really rough man, always getting into scrapes. After a few years, he went to West Virginia and worked in the coal mines, where he continued to fight. However, he did save $3,500 and put it in the bank at Butler, Tennessee, the bank nearest to Pottertown. The year was 1929 and Clarence heard enough about banks closing that he took the train to Butler. He went to the bank and asked to draw out his money. The banker hesitated and talked in circles. Finally, Clarence put a pistol in the face of the banker and said, "You can give me my money or you can take a bullet from this pistol." Clarence walked away with his money and the next banking day the bank did not open.

Years later Clarence caught the train to Mountain City to pay his mother a Christmas visit. Two deputies were waiting for him at the station with a warrant for his arrest. As they approached him, they stated their business. Clarence very calmly said, "I am going to see my mother. You can try to shoot me but I can get one of you or maybe two before you get me. What will it be?" The men turned and left.

Clarence was a small man but women considered him very handsome. He married several times; in fact, he married one woman two times. It was reported that late in his life, he was hospitalized and nurses who attended him said that he had scars all over his body. He had been shot eight times in his life but it was rumored that he had killed thirteen men.

I understand why Pottertown had a bad reputation, but that reputation has haunted me most of my life. I always felt that people looked down on me because of where I came from, although I only lived there when I was a child. It did not help that my grandmother was a sister to Clarence Potter. Regardless of my heritage, I try to be a good citizen and contribute what I can to my community. The past is history, what I do today is what I am responsible for.

A Tuffy Tale

Carlton H. Swift

This story was submitted by Carlton H. Swift of McLean, Virginia, in 2002.

In the 1930s and '40s there lived not far from us a fellow who was the object of a great deal of derision and the source of much amusement in the neighborhood. He had the nickname "Tuffy" and was also sometimes called "Forty." I don't know his exact age but he was probably approaching 40 and still lived with his parents. Some felt he was a brick or two short of a load. I did not agree. While he had no job or visible means of support, he always seemed to find a way to buy some hooch and drank it with gusto. He told lots of tall tales and I, being a naïve teenager deficient in worldly wisdom, listened to and believed many of his lies. He was always kind to me and I liked him.

When Tuffy's parents passed away, he moved from the community and lived with a sister, I think. He acquired an old muffler-less "Model A" Ford and came back to our neighborhood from time to time, drunk more often than not. Between his drinking and his car without a muffler, his great nemesis was Highway Patrolman Miles Jones. They had a running battle and Tuffy outwitted or outran Jones many times.

Late one hot summer day my brother and I were outside when we heard the roar of the Model A and knew who it was before the vehicle drove into sight. It was running flat out and traversed the part of the highway in our view, perhaps more than a half mile, in record time. No sooner had it passed out of sight than Patrolman Jones came along, also running at high speed. The chase was on. After 10 to 15 minutes, we heard the mighty roar again, coming from the other direction. Presently the Model-A came flying up the road, having somehow eluded the patrolman. It slowed a bit, turned into our lane, crossed the bridge and quickly covered the two hundred yards to where my brother and I were standing. Tuffy flung open the door and jumped out, yelling, "Jones is after me, Jones is after me." Patrolman Jones sure enough was; he came back up the road, spotted the Model A and also turned into our drive.

Seeing this, Tuffy took off around the corner of our house and dove into the tall grass, weeds and brush at the back of the yard, close by an abandoned grape arbor. My brother ran in another direction. Before I could decide what to do, the lawman arrived and demanded, "Where's that #@# ?" "I don't know Sir," I stammered, "He ran that-a-way," pointing to a path leading to a gate to the neighboring farm. "You sure he didn't run into the house? Don't lie to me, boy." I told him no he didn't, that my mother was not home, and nobody was in the house, which was true. Officer Jones continued to grill me for a while and I continued to respond with truths, half-truths and lies. When he became convinced there was no one in the house, he strolled over to the grape arbor, unzipped and relieved himself only inches from where Tuffy was hiding. He said, "I'll get him next time," and left. After he had gone, Tuffy emerged from the bushes and said, "Man, the SOB almost peed on me!"

Another Tuffy Tale

Len Stokes

This story appears as told to Catherine Stokes Sheppard by Len Stokes, of Boone, N.C., in 2003.

Regardless of the calendar, it is often hard to tell when spring comes to Watauga County. Some judge the budding of leaves, others look at the birds, sometimes even the woolly worms get into the act. Some years we have to disregard the temperature because another cold spell may still be coming. But, quite a few years ago I learned the absolute way to tell.

As regular as the swallows come back to Capistrano, Tuffy would suddenly appear on the streets of Boone, usually in the vicinity of the courthouse. Sometime in the fall, we would realize we had not seen Tuffy for a while. Soon after that, the chill of winter would be in the air. Then one day Tuffy would reappear, year after year. Nobody knew where he had been but the spring day when he reappeared, you could put away the longhandles; spring was here to stay.

Schoolhouse Misdemeanors

Jerry Shull

Jerry Shull, who lives in Boone, shared this story in 2004.

Some of my school memories that started out as what looked like a great idea turned pretty sour. When I was about 12 years old, one of my buddies came to school one day with a one hundred dollar bill and announced to his close friends that we would eat Moon Pies and drink Pepsi today! About a half dozen of us ran with him to Tom Moody's store to help him enjoy his fortune. How he came by the money did not seem too important at that moment. He failed to mention that the money came from the pocket of his grandfather's overcoat. Few people of any age then had hundred dollar bills, but this grandfather was said to measure his corn by the gallon and therefore had cash.

Later in the morning, a very unhappy grandpa also went to Tom Moody's store and inquired of Mrs. Moody if anyone had given her a hundred dollar bill in trade. Tragically for us, her memory was excellent! Pretty soon the scene moved from the store to the elementary school where Tom Moody was principal. Mr. Moody lined us up and made us pull our pockets inside out. My pocket contained $4.60. The other young criminals had about the same except for the instigator. When the search ended, all the money was recovered except for $1.50. How nice it would have been if the story ended right there. Oh, no! As each of us bent over a desk, Mr. Moody administered justice as only he could with a large wooden paddle. To this day I am not sure how the responsibility of discipline became his. The crime was not committed on the school ground nor was the aiding and abetting. But, that is where the punishment occurred, and I had the blistered bottom to prove it.

I took part in another wayward plan that backfired and left us all with a sheepish grin and half scared to death. Under the old elementary school building, there was a tunnel of sorts. I do not know what it was used for or why it was there but we boys found it. The tunnel ran from one side of the building to the other. When we discovered it, we dared each other to crawl thru it. Neither danger nor dirty clothes ever entered our minds. Most of us got through the tunnel, but Johnny Mast decided it was not his cup of tea. Being the regular fellow he was, we dared him to go and he could not endure the shame if he did not. He got to the middle of the tunnel and had a panic attack. He cried out, "I am dying, I am dying! My body has swelled and I cannot move!" We knew right then that we were all in deep trouble. Someone ran and got a rope, another crawled in and tied the rope around Johnny's legs and we pulled him out. Once outside he was fine, but that ended our tunnel adventure.

A Slap in the Face

Len Stokes

Len Stokes of Boone, N.C., submitted this story in 2002.

My dad had strong opinions about his list of priorities. Among his priorities were his hunting dogs, playing checkers, and the Democratic Party. We kids learned early on not to challenge Dad about any of these subjects. One of the things he was not strong on was church attendance, nor was he fond of any work in the hot sunshine. I tell you this in order for you to understand the following story.

Toward the end of World War II, we had a young self-ordained minister move into our Phillips Branch community to pastor the small church near there. Back then, it was customary for the preachers to visit people and invite them to church. One hot July afternoon Mama had convinced Dad that if we ate he would have to raise a garden and so far, all we had was a patch of weeds.

Reluctantly, Dad was hoeing the garden and the sweat was pouring off his body. The new preacher arrived at the gate just in time to grant Dad a break. They sat on the ground in the shade near the house and made light conversation until the preacher expressed sadness for our family since one son had died in the Pacific and the next son was currently a POW. After Dad thanked him for his concern the preacher took off on how evil war was and then how bad the US government was, and how bad Franklin D. Roosevelt was. When Dad stood up, I guess the preacher took this as his cue to leave and he, too, stood up. He summed up his remarks with, "I believe that Adolf Hitler is a better man than Franklin D. Roosevelt." He had gone one step too far for Dad, who slapped the young man so hard that he hit the house. Mama came running out to see what had happened. By then the preacher was at the gate, rubbing his jaw.

The word reached us that the next Sunday the topic the young preacher chose for his sermon was: It Looks Like the Devil's People Are Trying to Kill Off the Lord's People.

Part 3: Western Watauga at War

The people of Western Watauga County are a law abiding, peace loving people. We are not the feuding mountaineers often portrayed in folklore. However, when duty calls our people do not hesitate to pick up arms. It has been said that men from the Southern Appalachians made good soldiers. These men are often outdoorsmen who have for generations enjoyed hunting; they are accustomed to being outside in all kinds of weather. They are used to making do with what is at hand; they can live on the land when it becomes necessary. They follow orders without question, they are generally family oriented and willing to fight for family and home. It is no wonder that so many people from our area have answered their nation's call in all major conflicts from the American Revolution to the War in Iraq.

If we could count the number of men and women who have served our nation in one capacity or another during only World War I, World War II, Korea, Vietnam, Desert Storm and Iraq, we would have a staggering number. We do not know how many men and women from Western Watauga have served in these conflicts but we have no doubt that we have sent our fair share.

In compiling this book, we are fortunate to have first-hand accounts from men who were in actual combat at Pearl Harbor, Korea, Germany, and Vietnam as well as on the high seas. We think it is unique that from this small rural area there were three men who fought at Pearl Harbor on the infamous date of December 7, 1941, and lived to tell their stories. We also have stories handed down from fathers to their children telling about experiences in World War I, as well as combat stories about World War II. We are able to tell personal glimpses of life at home during wartime.

The Korean conflict was a different type of war, and we learn that personal safety is not always the honorable route to take, tempting as it may have been. One seventy-five year old veteran smiles as he remembers how he chose combat over playing basketball for the army because he felt it was the right thing to do. Another Korean veteran admits that he still dreams about his high school buddy who died in Korea and sends money for a memorial to that friend. These stories help us to define who we are because of who has gone before us.

We would like to think that in generations to come there will be young people who will delight in saying, "Look! Here is a war story about an event in which my ancestor tells his story." Or, "Did you really have to ration shoes?" My one regret is that we could not find stories from Desert Storm and Iraq. At least actual encounters with the enemy have been recorded and visuals can be found in media centers, but these will have a hard time competing with first person narratives.

World War I

Three Who Served

My father was Ed Winebarger and he was in World War I. He was gassed while serving in France and for the rest of his life he had weak lungs. He used to tell us how they would load poisonous gas onto railroad cars and when the wind was blowing away from the US troops they would slip to these cars, in the cover of night, quietly roll the cars to the enemy lines, release the gas, and the Allied soldiers would run to safety. This worked pretty well except one night about the time they released the gas the wind shifted and Dad breathed it. Dad died at age 62 from lung cancer. Our family always thought that his war experience was a factor in his death. He also, at a different time, caught shrapnel in his foot and while it did not appear to bother his walking, that leg was always weak. (*Berlin Winebarger was interviewed by Catherine Stokes Sheppard in October 2000.*)

Luther Martin Bingham Sr. was my wife's father. I never knew him because he died when my wife, Geraldine Bingham, was only five years old. Consequently, I never heard him swap war stories with anyone. I do know that he was in World War I, served in France and won two Purple Hearts and a medal for marksmanship. He was also a victim of mustard gas, or "gassed" as the term was in those days. He died at age 36 from lung damage incurred in the war. He died in the National Sanatorium in Tennessee. I have no idea what the diagnosis would have been in 1936 or today. (*Blaine C. Miller submitted his recollections of the war in 2000.*)

Lionel Ward entered the military service September 18, 1917, which was only five months after the United States declared war on Germany. He received his training at Camp Sevier in Greenville, South Carolina. He was sent overseas in May 1918.

Five months later he wrote his parents, "I am sleeping on the ground, but … we are in a barn now. A barn seems like a hotel. We have slept on the ground and in it so much. I have slept in dugouts 40 feet under the ground. You bet it is the same bed, but we feel good under there when the big shells are falling." This letter was written less than one month before the end of the war. Lionel was fortunate to return home without a wound. He later served as Watauga's Veterans Service Officer. His twin sons John and Jack were in combat in World War II. (*Edna Ward Ellis, daughter of Lionel Ward, submitted her memories of her father in 2000.*)

World War II

A Mountain Boy Leaves Home

Berlin Winebarger

The following is from Catherine Stokes Sheppard's taped interview with Berlin Winebarger of the Mabel community in October 2000. We are very grateful to Berlin Winebarger for this interview. He was suffering from lung cancer and emphysema. He would frequently have to stop talking and cough or just rest. Catherine felt it was a strain on him, but he seemed to really want to be a part of this book. He passed away in November 2000.

I have been told that the first Winebargers came to this country from Germany. My ancestors settled in the Meat Camp area. My dad was nine years old when he came with his father to this area. My grandfather was in the sawmill business. All these mountains around here were logged out by them. They used steers to log with. My mother was raised right up the holler. Her family name is Moretz, that is also a German name. If you will notice the road sign in front of my house says Moretz Hollar. My parents lived up the hollar with their folks till they could build their house, which is our old home place across from me.

I was five years old when we moved down here. The state was re-building old Highway 421 at that time and my brothers and I would slip off and watch the men work. Now this was before convict labor was used. Later convicts from the prison in Boone worked the roads. The machinery was horse drawn scoops, picks and shovels. I don't remember any motor graders. They used heavy hammers to break up the rocks. There was a big rock crusher down the road and the state would pay farmers to haul in rocks from their fields to be crushed. The state did have trucks to haul the crushed rocks.

My family always kept horses and cows, hogs and chickens. You know, the farm had to be pretty self-sufficient back then. We always had plenty of food.

When I graduated from high school in 1940, I got in a NYA program. I worked in Claire Simpson's office. Robert Honeycutt and I were the only guys, the rest were girls. Then they sent me to the county school bus garage to work. While I was there, I heard about a training school in Wilmington shipyards where I could work and learn to weld. Walter Thompson, Blaine Fletcher and I went to Wilmington but they wouldn't accept me because I was too near draft age. (They didn't want to invest in me.) They did not tell me why I wasn't hired and I could not understand it; they were hiring everybody else. I came back home and heard about jobs at Ft. Bragg. I went to Ft. Bragg and hired on as a carpenter at 90 cents an hour. That was really a good wage at that time. A lot of people around here were going up north to work so I went to Cleveland, Ohio. I had been there six months when I got my draft notice. If I reported to the draft board in Ohio I would leave that same day, but if I came back home I would have 30 days to settle affairs. So, I came home and left from here. Nobody wanted to go into the service until they had to.

Berlin Winebarger was working in Cleveland, Ohio, in 1942 when he got his draft notice. He had 30 days to settle his affairs before entering the Navy. Most of his service time was spent training soldiers for beach landings. His only combat was spent in Okinawa. In 1946 he left service and returned home in Mabel (photograph furnished by Nancy Fletcher).

I went to Great Lakes Naval Training Center and was placed at Green Bay for my boot camp. They gave us an aptitude test and I was put in a group and sent to the University of Missouri to train to be a diesel mechanic. I was there for five or six months. These particular diesel engines were used on landing boats. Later I was sent to New York Navy Yard to learn to read the gyrocompass and maintain them. After that I was sent to Norfolk, Virginia, and then to Ft. Pierce, Florida, for about six months. The Navy chose twenty sailors and sent them to an Army camp. There we trained as soldiers for beach landings. I was in charge of maintaining the landing craft. I would train with one group, ship them out, and train with another group. This lasted seven months.

Then I was sent to Cambridge, Maryland, assigned to a regular crew and sent to the West Coast. There we picked up our ship and went to the Pacific. By then a lot of my military time had passed. Of the three and a half years I spent in the Navy most of it was right here in the USA. The only actual combat time I saw was in Okinawa. All the ships stopped in Hawaii and we also stopped briefly in Guam on our way to Okinawa. On the way back we stopped in Saipan and Tinian. This was where the planes left from to drop the bombs. Of course, we saw Japanese planes in the air all the time but we didn't pay much attention to them. We were more interested in the B-29's. They were the Super Fortress in the sky and were used to bomb Japan. I was on a beach landing craft and boy, could they haul a load! I used to watch them load those ships; tanks, and row after row of trucks. All that heavy equipment and all our men made me wonder, how can they move all that!

With all that equipment we had on board the ship and rough seas, it took us about three weeks to get from San Francisco to the Pacific site. The water was choppy and there were storms; not typhoons, just regular storms. There were a lot of men so sick, but I was lucky, I never got seasick. Looking back I know it was a good time in my life. I learned a lot and I know I developed skills that later helped me. But it wasn't so good that I wanted to re-enlist. When I got a chance to get out, I got out. I wasn't released until six or eight months after the war ended. Men were not released by seniority, but by jobs waiting. If a man owned a business or had a job waiting, he got out first. I got out in 1946 and Rosa Lee Warren and I got married three weeks after that.

I often wonder why I did not go back to Ohio when I got out of the Navy. I guess I was so happy just to get back home. I suppose there had to be a time for adjusting to civilian life too. Anyhow, Rosie's father had an empty house on his place and she was content living here. There was a farm-training program being taught by Mr. Robert Shipley at Cove Creek and I enrolled in that. I was entitled to three and one half years of training, and we were being paid to go. I soon realized farming was not for me and there were no diesel engines, not even a diesel truck in this area. In fact, there were few jobs and none paid much. So in 1950 we moved to Cleveland, Ohio. My sister Nancy and her husband Ernest Fletcher were living there so we had family in Cleveland. I went to work for Caterpillar Tractor. It was a good job and I enjoyed it. We stayed there for twenty-five years, moved back here, and built this house.

You asked me about my hopes for the future of the Mabel community. What I wish for cannot be and I know it. I would like to see this area stay just as it is today. But I know as time moves along things will have to change. Come with me to the front porch, I want to show you the view. [We walked out on his porch and the scenery was truly spectacular. The fall foliage was a rainbow of color and all seemed so serene. No wonder he would like to see it unchanged.] I hate to see all the hills developed into summer cottages. I am just glad I could come back home to retire and enjoy what we have here.

Navy Life, Laughs and Lingo

Louis Farthing

The following are excerpts from the memoirs of Louis Farthing as told to his cousin Glenn Farthing. We have included the preface by Glenn Farthing. Dixie Farthing Huff, sister of Louis Farthing, shared both writings with us.

Preface

Enlisting in the U.S. Navy in 1937 at age 17, Louis Farthing, my double first cousin, spent 33 remarkable years in the service of his country. He served on battleships, oilers, and many other ships, at naval bases and ports all over the world. At Pearl Harbor on December 7, 1941, he survived the sinking of the battleship U.S.S. *West Virginia* during the sneak attack by the Japanese. His heroic actions that morning saved the lives of many of his fellow sailors. At the time of his retirement in 1970, at an impressive ceremony at the Norfolk Naval Base, he was the Navy's highest-ranking chief warrant officer. It is entirely likely that no other U.S. sailor can match his range of experiences in both peacetime and wartime.

This chronicle is a sampling of his endless number of Navy stories and reminiscences as related to me over a period of years. It comes to an abrupt end because of Louis Farthing's death January 14, 1996. We had been working on it intermittently over the last three or four years as his deteriorating health permitted. We had hoped to complete the stories of his World War II experiences and then to include some of his more memorable Navy assignments subsequent to the war. But his numerous physical problems, including a running battle with colitis, electrolyte imbalances, and asthma so severe that he needed oxygen most of the time, combined to prevent our completing this remarkable journal.

As John Donne says in his classic poem "For Whom the Bell Tolls," we are all diminished by the loss of one such as Louis, but we are better for having known him.

My main reason for enlisting in the Navy in 1937 just after my 17th birthday was because of the travels that I would otherwise never experience and the promise of a steady job with good health and dental care. My starting pay was 70 cents per day and deducted from that would be 20 cents for health and hospital insurance. One must realize 55 years later that 70 cents per day along with free medical care, free food and an initial issue of clothing would be worth thousands of dollars today. Of course, we had to purchase replacement attire from our own pockets. Sailors' white "Dixie

Cup" hats were 90 cents, a pair of Dexter trademark black shoes was $3.27, under pants and skive shirts were 60 cents, blue uniform was $14, white blouse and trousers were about $5.

My first training took place in Norfolk, Virginia. The Navy had only two training stations, with the other one being Great Lakes, Minnesota. During our three months of basic training, we learned how to wash and care for our clothing. Putting a "spit" shine on shoes was a training and learning exercise that required much effort and "know-how." Later, when I became an officer, I had a personal valet who cared for my room, bed, uniforms and shoe-shines. He would also help prepare and serve meals to the officers. We ate in an area called the "ward room," and it was always separate from the crew's eating areas.

Louis Farthing enlisted in the Navy in 1937 when he was 17 years old. He thoroughly enjoyed his life as a sailor although he never acquired "sea legs," even after 30 years of sea duty. During his prewar years he participated in sports events such as sailboats, rowboats, swimming and running. He enjoyed competition. Louis studied on his own and received an associate degree in military law and justice and "Laws of the High Seas" (photograph furnished by Ben Farthing).

Each sailor was required to purchase and shine his own personal wash bucket. Three padlocks and keys were required for each sailor—one for his wash bucket, one to secure his personal "pea jacket," and one lock for his personal clothing locker. Stealing among sailors was not very common, but "just borrowing" was a common practice. It was against Navy regulations to loan another sailor property or money.

My bucket was used for washing clothes, bathing and also my personal "puke" bucket. I never did acquire "sea legs" and could puke a greater distance, even after 30 years of sea duty, than the newest raw recruit. I am told that the famous task force 51 commander, Admiral "Bull" Halsey, also never gained puke-proof sea legs.

My Navy chief retired brother, Raymond Farthing, also never conquered seasickness. "Up-chucking" and being seasick was not a valid excuse for not standing a proper watch. There were many times when I prayed to die I was so miserable. After the big war, a few sailors were discharged, with no disability, for chronic motion illness.

On a few occasions, I was placed on

"the report" for some minor infraction where my reported offense would be excused. Every one charged with any infraction would be required to make an appearance before the executive officers' mast. The XO could excuse the offense or order extra duties or restriction from liberty for minor offenses. Serious offenses calling for brig time, bread and water, or reduction in rating, would be decided at "Captain's Mast." The captain was not only judge and jury but also defense counsel as well as trial counsel. He was God in four persons. He would order 30 days bread and water in solitary confinement, reduction in rating, or recommend trial by courts-martial. After becoming commissioned, I studied on my own and received an associate degree in military law and justice and "Laws of the High Seas." During my 28 years as an officer, I was involved in many, many law cases in the Navy. I enjoyed this collateral duty which most of us were required to perform. There were many times when my collateral duties required more time than did my professional duties.

Here is an example of a collateral duty. In late 1958, I was on medical limited duty, having been released from a naval hospital after several surgical procedures. I was getting radium treatments for an undetermined length of time, and I needed weekly evaluations. I started researching the driving habits of Navy personnel and, after extensive letter writing to various military hospitals and other commands, what I learned was absolutely appalling, alarming and a disgrace. I assembled all of the data I had obtained and was fortunate to get an actual movie from the Mississippi State Highway Patrol taken at scenes of bloody vehicle accidents. I put together an hour lecture and a 45-minute movie showing our Navy personnel and their deplorable driving record. After only about a half dozen lectures, every ship and station wanted to see the records and the movie. Soon I was involved most every day doing my "Drive Safe" program. My program showed an improvement in military driving in the 5th Naval District within a few short months. I am proud that my efforts did make a favorable difference.

Earlier I commented on the military justice system. Here is a true story. After much of the Pacific battle fleet was transferred to the mid–Pacific, each ship was required to establish an armed surface patrol around each ship at anchor. During early 1940, the battleship *West Virginia* was anchored along with several other battlewagons in Lahaina Road, Maui, Hawaii. My motor launch was designated the armed patrol from 8:00 P.M. until daylight the following day. Each patrol boat had machine guns, rifles, three enlisted men and one officer. During the long hours of patrolling around the ship, time was very boring. On one of our patrols, I attempted to break the monotony by telling our ensign boat officer, son of a well-known admiral, a simple story of an officer and a sailor getting haircuts in the ship's barbershop.

When the officer's hair was cut, his barber asked: "Sir, shall I put some hair tonic on you?" The ensign replied, "You'd better not because my wife will smell it, and she'll think I've been in a whorehouse." Just at that moment, the adjoining barber had finished the sailor's haircut and asked, "Sailor, shall I put some tonic on your hair?" The sailor said, "Yeah, go ahead and put some on me. My wife has never been in a whorehouse." Suffice it to say, I was placed on the report for "becoming too familiar with an officer and a gentleman." Usually my charges were "unbecoming conduct." That charge covers every angle.

You can damn well bet I enjoyed every day I was in the Navy—even in Athens, Greece, when I had to explain how I got the chaplain into a Greek house of ill repute. That story cannot be told here.

In 1939, the Pacific wagons joined the Atlantic battleships for competitive gunnery, engineering and seamanship evaluations. We would anchor off Puerto Rico or Havana, Cuba, for liberty and recreation. We did this anchoring on just a few occasions. While at anchor, we would compete in sailboats, rowboats, swimming, and a few sport events ashore. My first year to row or sail in the champion crew was in 1939. After we won the World Military Rowing Event, the captain of the *West Virginia* selected me as coxswain of his private boat, called a "gig." On one of my first trips to take the "old man" ashore, we were in trouble returning him to the ship later that night. Not only was the old man in his "cups," but the weather and winds were very rough. All of us were half-drowned, and the old man had "thrown up" all over his white formal uniform. Officers don't get the "clap," they get "non-specific weatheritis"; officers don't "puke," they "throw-up." When we reached the ship and helped him on board, he told the OD to place me on report for puking on his uniform. The next morning, the skipper called the XO and suggested I not be punished. The XO was adamant and said, "Captain, Farthing is in the brig, and he will stay there because he not only puked on you, but when we undressed you and put you to bed, he had also s—in your pants." A day in the life of a sea-going sailor is never dull.

We did not see any reserve officers until early 1941. Robert Montgomery was a savvy and learned personality. Douglas Fairbanks was another one. I attended invasion briefing by Henry Fonda in early 1944. He was another sharp reserve officer. Our academy officers were extremely smart and alert, but some were what we sailors called "pricks." One such officer placed a sailor on report for purportedly calling him an "SOB." The captain was investigating the charges, and he asked the accused, "Son, you're charged with calling Ensign Smith a son-of-a-bitch. Did you call him that?" The sailor replied, "No, Sir, I did not!" The captain turned to a sailor witness to be absolutely sure because this was a very serious charge.

And he said, "You heard the accused deny that he called Mr. Smith an SOB, how can you be so sure that he did?" The witness said, "I am sure of my answer because Ensign Smith was the only son-of-a-bitch standing there when he said it!"

There were many different personalities and cultures that comprised the 80,000 persons who were serving in the pre-war, peacetime Navy. Navy officer positions were handed down "family style" in those lean years after World War I. Officers' sons had automatic appointments to the Naval Academy at Annapolis. I was fortunate to obtain my chance to enter the academy because the president had 100 appointments to be given to those of us who had no political connections or had no ancestors who were graduates. Unfortunately, even after intensive schooling in ships anchor windlass class room, I could not pass the entrance exam because the math requirements far surpassed my feeble command of arithmetic.

During my almost 33 years of active duty, I had many good tours but one especially rotten tour. My Uncle Greer Glenn had some tough years from his peers. He told me about being "teacher's pet" and how much he had to suffer because of envy and jealousy from less fortunate students. I had the same tough time on a ship named for a sound in North Carolina.

Finally, I wrote my own orders to the hospital for surgery and later radiation treatments were ordered for me by that medical facility. Being teacher's pet can be a disaster, and during my career, I made positive that I would not show partiality. I always had an excellent rapport with my superiors but favoritism can be a disaster and can actually ruin a person's professional career.

During my prewar enlisted service, I attempted to participate in every military exercise or evolution, and I attempted to challenge every vacancy in recreation functions. I knew in my career's infancy that I wanted to become a warrant officer and stay in the Navy forever. During my early years on the *West Virginia*, BB48, I was assigned to the 1st division. Divisions one through six were deck department forces. We were the operators and caretakers of the topside areas—guns, boats, anchors and cargo handling. Several below deck spaces were also the responsibility of the deck department. Odd numbered divisions were responsible to the starboard side and even numbers the port side. The "WeeVee," as she was affectionately named, was our newest battlewagon. The 1st division manned turret one for battle stations. Second division, turret two—and on down through turrets three and four. The 5th division manned several 5-inch 51 caliber broadsides and several 3-inch 50 caliber anti-aircraft weapons supported by 40 mm, 20 mm, and smaller anti-aircraft weapons. My high school classmate, Howard Rowe, was a member of the 6th division on the port side. Howard would later have to abandon the ill-fated aircraft carrier USS *Lex-*

ington in the Midway battle in mid–1942. In that engagement, he was recognized for bravery in operating a ship's boat through fire and brimstone to rescue many men in the water. Sherman was quoted as agreeing with me, "War is hell." I was a little more fortunate in not losing my second ship until February 1944, in the Battle for the Marshall Islands.

The *West Virginia*, along with several other ships home-ported in San Pedro and Long Beach, California, was assigned to the mid–Pacific fleet many months prior to December 1941. Included in the Hawaiian detachment were heavy and light cruisers, many tin cans and submarines, as well as troop transports, tankers, supply ships, and smaller support craft. We spent most of our time at sea engaging in damage control and gunnery exercises, fueling at sea as well as re-provisioning ammunition and food supplies. Other drills practiced were towing other ships, being towed, man overboard, and sending fire and rescue teams to other ships disabled or in distress.

After each 10-day exercise, the task force would enter and moor in Pearl Harbor or anchor in Lahaina Roads, Maui Island, for rest and recuperation. This period of R&R would normally be for five to seven days, and then the revolution would be repeated. Much of my recreation time was spent playing football on the ship's team, boxing, rowing in the world's champion (military) whaleboat crew, and as sailing crew member that was undefeated for three years. My boxing expertise was worse than "blah." I soon learned that getting punched and hit would hurt badly the next day, and I retired after a half dozen bouts. I was not good enough to play basketball or baseball, and I nearly got killed attempting to wrestle. I did well at long-distance running and swimming. I did my share in helping the ship's crew win the coveted "E" against 12 other battleships for '39 and '40. The year '41 had not been completed and no award was given for 1941.

Shipboard life was routine during peacetime. Except for exercising at battle problems and training in engineering and seamanship drills, each day and week would be planned in advance with few changes from month to month. Each meal from week to week and day to day was always the same. For example, every Thursday the evening meal would be liver, onions, fried potatoes, water and coffee. Saturday breakfast was always powdered milk, called KLIM, corn flakes, navy beans and cornbread. Sunday noon would be chicken (seagull), navy bean soup, cornbread, potatoes and green beans. Because of a lack of refrigeration, most foods were dehydrated or canned. Fresh milk would be served in limited portions when the ship was in port. Fish was always served for Friday noon meal, with cold cuts, olives and sliced cheeses for the evening meal. In the pre–World War II Navy, the supply officer was allowed 33 cents per day per man for food and drink. Wow!

"Reveille" was a simple order to obey because the ship had no bunks for the crew, and the crew could not eat until hammocks and cots were dismantled and stored in the hammock netting spaces in order to set up the mess tables. They were stored in the overhead when not in use. Later most ships were equipped with built-in bunks and meals were served cafeteria style.

When weather and operating schedules permitted, an inspection of material and cleanliness of ship's condition would be performed every other Saturday morning at 1000 hours, with personnel inspection the following Saturday at 1000 hours. Such was the routine on Saturday, 6 December 1941. I had recently been accepted on the master at arms force and was in charge of the ship's 100 mess cooks, spud locker and scullery crews. As a collateral duty, I was also the ship's brig master. This experience in dealing with and handling prisoners was a credit to my service record 16 years later when I would be assigned as the discipline officer at a naval prison with a population of 1200. That is an entirely different "sea story."

After Saturday's personnel inspection, liberty for one-fourth of the crew was granted and commenced at 11:30. All of us used to accuse the "old man" and the supply officer of letting 450 men off the ship just before lunch so they could pocket the profits saved by feeding a smaller crew. There was never a shortage of "scuttlebutt" among us sailors.

The crew was divided into four sections for duty purposes and for liberty. The starboard watch consisted of sections one and three, which was approximately one-half the total complement. The port watch was made up of sections two and four. Since early September 1941, the battle fleet had taken extra security measures, hence the small number of crewmembers granted liberty simultaneously. Further, unless a crewmember could provide a bona fide address ashore, he had to be back aboard at midnight. This was called "Cinderella" liberty.

Louis Farthing died (see page 99) before this memoir could be completed.

Pearl Harbor: December 7, 1941

Louis Farthing

The following is part of Louis Farthing's wartime memoirs, as told to his cousin Glenn Farthing. Louis' sister, Dixie Farthing Huff, shared his memoirs with us.

Just a few remarks to preface my remembrances of the Japs' "sneak" attack on Pearl Harbor, December 7, 1941. Some persons erroneously refer to the conflagration as a "surprise" attack. This expression is deplored and aggravates the hell out of Pearl Harbor persons who were at Pearl Harbor proper. No act of war had been declared, however, archive records now point to the fact that FDR and his henchmen in D.C. obviously knew more than we did in the Pacific Fleet at that time. I agree that we were remiss to a certain extent by not taking defensive action earlier that morning when the tin can USS *Ward* observed and shot at an unidentified submarine just a few miles off the entrance to Pearl Harbor. We also had another chance to prepare for an air attack when two army enlisted men observed many "blips" on their radar scope nearly an hour before the actual attack, which commenced at 0755 hours. We also ignored a report from the supply ship USS *Antares* indicating an underwater object appeared to be following her as she approached the net which guarded the entrance to the harbor. Records later proved it was a two-man Jap sub and that it hit the beach rather than the harbor entrance. Its skipper was the first Jap POW. His crewmember drowned.

The events of 6 December 1941 were routine except for the duty section. They had boats to operate, communications, both radio and visual, to maintain, paint work to scrub, boiler fires and machinery to tend, and hundreds of other tasks to perform. A busy crew creates less problems of a disciplinary nature than an idle, lubberly crew does. The "WeeVee" was a smart, alert and busy ship, manned by 1500 men who were in the Navy because each wanted to be a sailor. Our brig hardly ever counted more than 10 inhabitants. This fact alone proved the old Navy adage, "A busy and well-fed crew can do anything required of them." Saturday, 6 December, was a routine and uneventful day in the life of an average battlewagon sailor. In addition to being the ship's brig master and in charge of the mess cooks, I also had to inspect all lower decks, minus engineering spaces. Checking for fire hazards and insuring watertight integrity had been set at 1700 and was being maintained. I would also assist the DOD in inspecting returning liberty parties. This duty would terminate at 2400, and I would "turn in," sleeping in the brig lobby. There was always an armed Marine sentry just outside the brig.

Reveille for me usually arrived too soon at 0530. All deck divisions had reveille at 0530 except on Sunday, when "rise and shine" would be 0600 for the entire ship's crew.

Sunday, 7 December 1941, began no differently from any other Sunday. I arose at my customary hour, shaved, dressed and was ready to perform my routine assigned chores, which included checking each mess cook and his utensils, plates, bowls, coffee cups and silverware.

The Japanese attack force was commanded by Vice-Admiral Nagumo and consisted of 33 ships, i.e., 6 fleet carriers, 2 battleships, 2 heavy cruisers, 1 light cruiser, 11 destroyers, 3 submarines and 8 tankers. On 22 November, the task force had assembled in complete secrecy at Tankan Bay in the Kurile Islands.

At 0600, 26 November, this task force sorted and headed by devious routes to a standby point—latitude 42°N and longitude 170°W. This force awaited word from Admiral Yamamoto whether to go to war or not. The final decision was "yes," and the order was delivered to Admiral Nagumo on 2 December 1941. The date was set for 8 December at 0700 (US date was 7 December 0700). The course was altered to southeast, and at 1130 6 December, it turned due south and increased speed to 24 knots to arrive at 600 next day 200 miles north of the island of Oahu.

The first wave, under the command of Commander Fuchida, was launched and consisted of 183 planes—49 high-level bombers, 51 dive-bombers, 40 torpedo planes and 43 Zero fighters. Each bomber carried one 1,760-pound armor-piercing bomb; each torpedo plane carried one 1,760-pound torpedo. One hour and 40 minutes after launching, the pilots observed breaking surf on the north side of Oahu. At 0753, Commander Fuchida sent the message "Tora, tora, tora" (attack) to Admiral Nagumo, commander of the task force.

The torpedo planes approached battleship row from the direction of Diamond Head and downtown Honolulu. To our knowledge the *Ogalala*, flagship of the Pacific fleet commander, Admiral Kimmel, was the first ship sunk. She was moored alongside the cruiser *Helena* at 10–10 dock. The torpedo ran underneath the *Ogalala* and hit the *Helena*, a heavy cruiser. The resulting explosion caved in the thin skin of the *Ogalala*'s hull, and she sank very quickly. The DOD on the *West Virginia* observed the explosion and rang the alarm: "Away the fire and rescue party." The time was about 0755. Before I could reach my fire and rescue station, the general alarm was sounded: "General quarters, general quarters. All hands man your battle stations. We are being attacked by the Japs. This is no s—."

The word was passed a second time followed by a torpedo explosion. Those of us who were "double timing" to our battle stations were not knocked off our feet on the main deck but were shaken and staggered as the ship shook and shuddered. I suspected a torpedo hit because we felt no concussion on the main deck. The main deck of any ship is the first complete deck that extends from stem to stern. I was the gun captain on the No. 1, 16-inch gun located on the starboard side of turret 1. The entry point to my station was on the 01 level under the overhang of the turret. Before I reached my battle station, an aerial torpedo hit us again. Soon the ship began to list to port, which indicated our port hull had been penetrated, permitting the ocean to flood the lower decks. My gun crew consisted of gun captain, trayman, powder car operator, two persons to operate the 16" shell hoist, pointer, trainer and firing pointer, fire control officer, turret officer plus many men below operating shell and powder hoists. One final position in my gun crew was the primer man who would insert a 30–30 size primer into the breech, as the rest of us were busy loading a 2,200-pound projectile with 500 pounds of powder contained in five Chinese silk bags. We could load this 15-mile range weapon in 12 seconds, resulting in a fairly accurate rate of fire of four per minute. There was no radar but three OS2U Kingfisher plane pilots in clear weather would provide range beyond 10 miles to us. These planes could be catapulted from atop Turret No. 3 or from the main deck fantail tracked catapult.

Our turret officer, Lt. E. R. King from Memphis, had been transferred to assist the damage control officer. "White Meat" Chamblee from Columbia, South Carolina, had replaced him. My rammer man was 'Webfoot" Jack Barret from Cincinnati, Ohio. The powder car operator was "Slapsie" Max Bennett from Cytheana, Kentucky, who died of cancer in 1964. I still correspond with his brother Pat who saw many surface engagements later in the South Pacific. The primer man, unknown to me at the time, would die that day along with more than a hundred others.

As my gun crew in turret one, along with many others, awaited orders to load, Chamblee was on the sound-powered phone circuit monitoring damage control reports. He kept us advised of the damage to which the ship was being subjected. I counted seven explosions as we continued to list to port.

Just after 0800, we felt an enormous and pronounced jolt, which seemed to lift the *West Virginia* upward and forward. We were to learn later that the *Arizona*'s powder magazine had exploded. She was moored about 40 feet astern of the *West Virginia*. Many times my crew and I heard and felt explosions, which were not as dramatic as when our ship would be hit. Our turret officer King and the damage control officer, Claude Ricketts, who many years later became chief of naval operations, counter-flooded the starboard side to offset the 35° to 40° port list. This prevented the *West Virginia* from turning "topsy turvy" as did the *Oklahoma*, moored just 40 feet forward of us. The high-level bombers were not challenged, neither were the Zero fighters. The Japs had a field day strafing our exposed 3-inch 50 cal. anti-aircraft gun crews and our 5-inch 51 cal. broad side gun crews. The gun crews suffered many casualties, as did our engineering and electrical department personnel. The port side of the ship was to suffer nine torpedo hits and the super-structure would suffer armor piercing aerial bombs, resulting in severe personnel injuries and structural damage.

The lull commenced about 0845, but our reverie would be sobered by the second wave, which started a short time after 0900.

We learned later that at 0845, the second wave, commanded by Lt. Commander Shimazaki, was fast approaching with 170 planes consisting of 54 high level bombers, 80 type 99 bombers, and 36 Zero fighters, all of them loaded for bear. Most of the second wave was to attack airfields and other shore installations. However, their orders were to also attack any ships which appeared to be unscathed and functional.

The *West Virginia*, which had attained a 40° list, appeared to us in the turret to be settling on a less severe port list. The 16 inch guns were useless in such confined waters and with shore installations in close proximity. Chamblee, the acting turret captain, kept us advised as to estimated damage.

At about 1000, Chamblee announced, "All hands abandon ship." No second notice was needed by any of us. We scrambled through the overhang hatch, and all of us were stunned by what we observed. Having been inside the ship at battle stations, we were not aware of the extent of the attack. We were shocked and speechless. The *Oklahoma*, just 40 feet ahead of us, was almost upside down with the starboard side of the underwater hull showing above the water line. The *Arizona*, 40 feet astern, had exploded and settled to the bottom on an even keel. Her foremast was bent and lying almost flat toward her bow. Except on her forward section, fires were everywhere on the *West Virginia* from turret one to her stern. I ran to the bow, climbed over the life lines and lowered myself to the starboard anchor. As soon as the water below me was clear of swimmers, I dived in, made like a torpedo, and swam around the bow of the *Tennessee* and made a record-breaking swim to Ford Island. Upon reaching the beach, I met a fellow boatswain's mate, Billingsley, 5th Division, from Portland, Oregon. We were in close proximity to Ford Island's crash boat shed, and simultaneously, without a word, we ran to the deserted shed and commandeered a 45-foot high-speed crash boat. Our mission was to rescue men who were frantically swimming through thick oil and fires to distance themselves from the burning and sinking ships. Many boat crews were involved in this process. We worked the area east, toward the Navy yard and fleet landing, in our recovery efforts. All of the men were covered with black oil and many were burned. As we would fill the topside spaces with survivors, they would be taken to the Naval Air Station boat shed area and offloaded. We would continue our efforts until about 1200. We secured the oil-covered crash boat and reported to an officer who was making a survivor muster list near the boat shed. I was issued a .45-caliber Navy pistol and ammunition which I turned in the next day. Sunday afternoon was spent looking for friends and worrying about the expected Jap invasion.

Sometime after dark most of the survivors on Ford Island were ordered to go to the ferry landing and proceed to Black Recreation center near the submarine base and fleet landing—a distance of three or four sea miles. Without incident, several of us did just that. We had been without food since early morning and our growing hunger pains would continue for another 12 hours. About 2300, or 11:00 P.M., volunteer fire fighters were transported back to Ford Island to assist in fighting the shipboard fires. Of course, the *West Virginia* was my choice, and we volunteers assisted as best we knew how to fight the fires. A short time after we started relieving those men who had been at their stations for many hours, a group of high altitude planes flew over the burning ships and Ford Island proper. Every operable gun in all directions commenced firing. The sky was a greater spectacle than we would see 49 years later over Desert Storm and Iraq on TV screens around the world. Sadly, we learned later that the planes and pilots were American and had been launched by our carrier, the USS *Enterprise*. Many planes were downed and the pilots killed. The expected invasion by the Jap Navy and Army never did materialize, much to our surprise and good fortune.

Louis Farthing was a crewman on the battleship *West Virginia* anchored at Pearl Harbor on December 7, 1941. He was gun captain on No. 1, 16 inch gun. The attack began at 0755. At about 1000 they got the announcement, "All hands abandon ship." The *West Virginia* sank. Louis helped save many lives that day. He spent 33 years in the service of his country. At his retirement ceremony he was recognized as the Navy's highest-ranking chief warrant officer (photograph furnished by Ben Farthing).

A couple of days later, the survivors of sunken or severely damaged ships were assigned to various ships present which were sea-worthy and operable. I was assigned to the USS *Tangier*, a seaplane tender, which was moored west of Ford Island and had escaped serious damage. When I reported on board, the ship was moored at a Navy yard pier and all hands were just completing loading supplies and ammunition for our Marine defenders on Wake Island.

About 10 days later, as we were in communicating distance of Wake, we learned that the Marine defenders were in doubt as to their ability to successfully defend the island. The island fell one day before we were scheduled to arrive to replenish their supplies.

A few days after the Pearl Harbor Blitz, I was assigned, along with "Gasoline" Alley, from Chattanooga, Tennessee, to guard the eastern street near Admiral Kimmel's house. He was the Pacific fleet commander, and there was a common belief that the Hawaiian Japs would attempt to kill or kidnap him and his family. No one was to pass our roadblock without permission from us. Our first night on duty, a darkened auto approached and did not stop after repeated challenges from Alley and me to stop and be identified. After the auto passed, we both dropped on one knee — as we had been trained — and together counted one, two, and three — fire. One of us hit the driver in his left hip area, and the bullet exited his left leg near his knee. He was an expectant Marine father taking his pregnant wife to the nearby Naval Hospital. Suffice it to say, this was our last armed guard at the admiral's house! Next day I was assigned to harbor craft night patrol until my transfer to the *Tangier*.

After my venture aboard the seaplane tender *Tangier*, I was ordered to organize and train mine and bomb security in and around Pearl Harbor and all of the various locks. I had passed the exam for boatswain's mate first class in November 1941 and was advanced to first class on 1 February, 1942. Lt. Glenn, from upstate New York and a survivor from the USS *Utah*, and I plotted stations for the security watches in and around Pearl, and we also designed small concrete houses that could be formed and poured to function as small protective shelters for three men. They had two bunks so the three-man crew would have to "hot" bunk it. An azimuth circle with sighting vane was installed in each station covering magnetic points of the compass for their respective areas. Visually, we needed 20 stations and 60 men to cover all water areas 24 hours each day.

Six months after inauguration and intensive training of the crews, I was assigned as the petty officer in charge (POinC) of a yacht 60 feet in length with twin engines and a four-man crew not counting me — the HNIC. We would spend 10 days at sea and two days in port for upkeep, refueling and replenishing supplies. We had underwater listening gear, depth charges and three 50-caliber machine guns — one on the bow, one atop the flying bridge, and one aft in the stern sheets. We had six bunks, one seawater-flushing commode, a three-burner stove and a very small refrigerator. Each 24-hour period we would spend in a different area around Oahu. Sixty miles was our limit from Pearl Harbor proper. We probably depth charged a few whales during the next year. We caught enough yellow fin tuna to feed a battleship, but we could use only one tuna per catch. We soon learned 17 ways to prepare and cook tuna. Because of restricted refrigeration space, most of our food was canned. Fresh vegetables would keep for two or three days and fresh meats were rare. Our assigned areas required us to keep constant surface and underwater vigilance. Frequently our uneasiness would play tricks, and all of us would swear we were hearing submarine sounds and noises. A shark fin cutting the surface was surely a Jap periscope. Our cat Elmer was death on roaches, which he never ate. He did catch one mouse which we threw overboard, and it was devoured instantly by a large shark! Wow!! We had a ladder for climbing aboard after a swim. Needless to say, after the mouse incident, we never let go of the ladder as we cooled off on those sultry afternoons. We were credited with finding and reporting two unidentified underwater mechanical devices during my year of duty on the yacht.

The *Oklahoma* was rolled over and re-floated late in 1942 but was scrapped. The *West Virginia* was patched and re-floated in October 1942 and was modernized in Bremerton Navy Yard on Puget Sound near Seattle, Washington. She was returned to duty in time for our invasion and capture of Iwo Jima and Okinawa.

My appointment to warrant officer by the president of the United States came through in November 1943, when I was assigned as skipper of a small Navy refrigeration ship, the USS *Evonne Louise*. I lost her to a Jap submarine in the Marshall Islands in February 1944. I returned to San Francisco in March and was given 30 days' survivor leave. I traveled to North Carolina, where I saw my parents for the first time since 1938.

At the end of my leave, I reported to Terminal Island, off Long Beach, California, and was assigned as the minesweeping officer of the USS *Counsel AM165* which was to commission in Portland, Oregon, May 1944. I received two weeks of schooling in minesweeping at Santa Barbara, California, and then went by train and club car to Portland early May 1944.

Survivors of Pearl Harbor

Catherine Stokes Sheppard

The information about William R. Whittington was printed in the Watauga Democrat *on May 28, 2001.The article was written by John O'Dowd.*

It seems unique that Western Watauga sent three men to Pearl Harbor. There may have been more but we have been able to locate accounts of three and those three were survivors. In a preceding story, Louis Farthing gave his account of his day at Pearl Harbor.

The Cove Creek High School class of 1937 had two graduates at Pearl Harbor and both were on the battleship *West Virginia*: Louis Farthing and Howard Rowe. After the *West Virginia* was lost Howard was assigned to the aircraft carrier *Lexington*. Six months after losing the *West Virginia* the *Lexington* was mortally wounded in the Battle of the Coral Sea. Fortunately, Howard Rowe was one of the 2700 men rescued by U.S. destroyers. He, too, made a career of the Navy and chose to live in California after he retired. He died in the year 2004.

William R. Whittington was one of the three men we learned about who survived the December 7, 1941, attack on Pearl Harbor. William was there on the USS *Antares* only to deliver food and supplies to the ships that were anchored there. The tugs opened the submarine net to let them enter the harbor, but a Japanese sub followed them through. Louis Farthing and Howard Rowe were both assigned to the battleship *West Virginia*, which sank about ten o'clock that morning. All three men survived (photograph furnished by Cleveland Whittington).

Because William R. Whittington disliked farming, he convinced his father to allow him to join the Navy when he turned eighteen. That is how the Valle Crucis youth found himself on an oil tanker for a year before being transferred to the USS *Antares*. The *Antares* was a refrigeration ship that delivered food and supplies to other ships. They had been at sea for a while when they were ordered to Pearl Harbor to resupply.

"The tugs opened the submarine net and we sailed into harbor," he said. "It was Sunday morning, and we all came up on deck to get our first look at Hawaii. I looked across Oahu and saw about 300 planes coming across the island. We thought they were ours until they started strafing and bombing our planes and ships.

"One of those Japanese mini-subs followed us thru the net," he said. "The captain dropped depth charges on it. I don't know if we hit it. We were a food ship, but we still carried depth charges and a couple of five-inch guns. The captain ordered us below and told us to lay down so bomb concussions wouldn't break our legs and knees," he said.

Whittington laughed as he described how he stayed in a push-up position the whole time below decks. "Some of the boys who laid flat on the metal deck broke some ribs," he said. "We stayed below for about 20 minutes until the captain called us up. Everything was on fire. The Antares was not hurt that bad."

He remembered spending the rest of the day "doing my job. I was a cook, so I cooked. We got food ready for the crew but nobody had much of an appetite."

After the attack at Pearl Harbor, Whittington said, the crew loaded up and went out to supply ships. "It was a war and they never told us where we were going, but I know we went to New Caledonia and the New Hebrides," he said.

Whittington stayed with his ship until war's end. He then returned to Vilas and later moved to Boone, where he lived quietly until his death July 12, 2003.

Blaine Miller, Merchant Marine

Blaine Miller

Blaine Miller submitted this story to us in 2000.

It was the summer of 1941. I had just completed my sophomore year at the then Appalachian State Teachers College. Hitler's tanks were already in Poland. Boys my age were wondering how they would look in uniform. I knew I did not want to be a teacher. One might say it was the season of indecision for many fellows my age. Without a great deal of thought, I simply boarded a Greyhound bus one Saturday morning and went to Chicago and later Sheepshead, New York, to begin my training for becoming a crewmember of a liberty ship for the Merchant Marines. It was here that a whole new world unfurled in front of me.

Most people's perception of a ship is related to a Navy ship or a cruise ship, crowded with people. The Navy ship is an offensive weapon, a floating arsenal where only the senior officers ever have any privacy, men take turns sometimes sleeping in the same bed, sleeping in hammocks, assigned to certain areas, forbidden in others, always regimented and subject to the authority of the entire chain of command. On cruise ships, most crewmembers live in crowded, restricted quarters. A cruise ship with a 1000 passenger capacity will probably carry a crew of 800. A liberty ship operated by the Navy usually carried some 300 to 350 crewmembers.

The merchant ships were entirely different. To begin with, they existed only to carry cargo, like a truck on the highway. In peacetime, they move oil, automobiles, food, and fertilizer — everything imaginable. In time of war, it is the merchant ship that carries the trucks, locomotives, tanks, bulldozers, the food, the clothes, the guns, the ammunition, and the bombs for the Air Force, everything the armed forces need to fight the war. As for armament, there were usually four 20mm antiaircraft guns, a small 2 or 3 foot gun mounted on the bow, another on the stern, a few depth charges at the rail at the stern of the ship. A good half of the crew had private staterooms; others had two or three bunks to a stateroom. We had six inch mattress, a large locker and I was free to go anywhere on the ship anytime. I didn't hesitate to use the purser's typewriter when he was not using it. I could spend time in the radio shack with Sparks, or go to the chief engineer's quarters for technical help or sometimes to just talk.

The eight officers had a mess hall of their own; the 22 regular crewmen had another. When we were underway six of us would be on watch, another six might be sleeping and another six reading, playing cards or whatever. The baker worked nights, but the steward, cooks, mess boys, bosun, deck engineer, and purser (he kept the books, manifest lists, and all the paperwork) worked days. The radio operator slept near his equipment and was on call all the time. The captain and chief engineer were always available but usually worked days. Everyone had plenty of opportunities to get to know everyone else. There was always a poker game, chess or a bridge game in progress. In my years in the Merchant Marine, I never saw anyone pull rank. I never saw a problem that the crewmembers didn't settle. If a man came aboard drunk, friends (and remember there was never a time when everyone would be ashore at the same time) would do whatever necessary to take care of him, throw him in the shower or stand his watch. Contrary to popular belief, there was rarely any trouble.

Perhaps the biggest advantage to being in the Merchant Marine was the food. We had a menu typed by the purser under the direction of the steward every meal. Breakfast was a choice of eggs any style, bacon or ham, French toast, pancakes, toast, jelly, juice, sometimes chipped beef on toast and always croissants, bagels and so on. Lunch was a choice of two meats, six vegetables and a salad. Dinner had a similar selection, usually one choice baked, or fried. The reason the baker worked nights was so he could make not only fresh bread each night but also bake pies and cakes. Each mess hall had a large coffee urn, a refrigerator with a supply of lunchmeat, peanut butter, and snack food along with tea bags and so on, pretty much like home. As for dress, the only requirement was a clean shirt, clean hands, combed hair, shoes and socks in the mess hall. The purser would open a little store once a week for the purchase of cigarettes, toothpaste, tee shirts, and toiletries. The 2nd mate served as a doctor/nurse for an aspirin, Band-aid or toothache.

Every ship I was on had a similar crew. There would be about 15 Americans, a couple of Swedes, a Norwegian, a Frenchman, an Italian, a Dane, a Scotsman, a Filipino, and at least one Greek. The captains and the chief engineers were invariably older men, sixties, sometimes seventy. The other officers were usually in their thirties or forties. Bosuns, deck engineers, were all older men. Mess boys, ordinary seamen, radio operators were always young. We seldom referred to anyone by name, preferring 3rd for third mate, bosun, Ole for a Norwegian Sparks, Cap'n, and so on. I was always called Carolina. Many crewmen were physically impaired. I sailed with men with one leg, diabetics who had to keep their insulin in the mess hall refrigerator, and a one-eyed Frenchy.

Roc was one of the men who will ever remain in my memory. We called him Roc because even the Italian boys couldn't pronounce his name, full of consonants. He was from Pittsburgh and looked like a gorilla, went right instead of left and we all liked him even if he was a loud mouth. He often saw me at the typewriter and always asked the same question, "Writing your sweetie, Carolina?" One day he saw that I was licking stamps and disappeared for a few minutes, returning with a sheet of stationery in his hand. I said, "What cha doing, Roc, writing your sweetie?" "Want to. Don't know how. Help me, Carolina, I'll pay you." Then and there I developed my new career. Roc had scribbled, "Dear Darlin, How are you I am fine. Please write me." After several questions, we wrote a few lines about boot camp, just as I had written to Gerry. Then we asked several questions about school, her family, and friends. I explained, "That makes it easy for her to reply with a long letter. Don't ask questions she can answer with a yes or a no. Then tell her you need to write to someone who will have news of the old gang, someone you wish you had spent more time with before you left home." And yes, there was a long letter by return mail. Roc whooped and hollered so much that I had customers galore. We even had a special table, though most of the letters were almost the same. My shoes stayed shined, my hair was always cut and I got my share of homemade cookies. Oddly enough, the fellows were willing to share some pretty risky secrets. I developed some close friendships in a short time, especially with Roc.

Another friendship that I cherished was that of Papa John, who was somewhere around sixty, a little man, by that I mean he was short but he had a huge stomach, a thick neck, little hands and feet, a very bald head, and terribly thick spectacles. He was from a place near Linz, Bavaria, on the Danube River. He spoke with a heavy German accent and I truly believe he was the most intelligent man I have ever known. He was also one of the best. We shared a stateroom on more than one ship, and shared our books.

He shared his knowledge with me; I had nothing to offer him in that department. Everyone called him Papa because it was convenient. I called him Papa because he was like a father to me. When Hitler's troops took over his part of the world Papa John made his way down the river (it empties into the Black Sea), had gone to Greece and ultimately found his way to the U.S. His papers called for Deck Engineer, which meant he worked days at sea and was very busy in port.

I don't remember anyone ever telling him to do anything. He seemed to have an insight as to problem areas, and took care of things before problems developed. Sometimes I accused him of thinking I was a piece of deck machinery. He would explain to me what we would find in any port we happened to visit. He would acquaint me with the history, the customs, what to look for in the way of museums or palaces, caution me about the dangers, what to drink and eat. We had an agreement; we would go ashore, he would take me to native areas, select the restaurants or bars, show me everything worth seeing and I would see that no one stole his money or slipped him a Mickey and also made sure he got back to the ship no matter how much he drank. One trip ashore in any one port was usually his limit. He mailed letters at every opportunity yet never received a single one. He even sent some by way of Switzerland but like those of other shipmates from the heart of Europe, the letters just died somewhere. Papa John could speak Latin, Italian, French, Spanish, German, and Slavic and pretty darned good English.

That is a lot to say about anyone but there's more. As a young man somewhat familiar with a few Protestant churches suddenly exposed to the many sects and faiths of the Mediterranean, I was full of questions. Papa John grew up in the land native to Martin Luther, knew the significance of Catholic symbolism, the history of the Greek Orthodoxy, the ritual of the Jewish Synagogue, and the philosophy of Mohammed. On the ships with such diverse nationalities, different age groups and various levels of education, there had to be many disputes. When anything came up where these was a disagreement one of the disputants would say, "Let's ask Papa John." His matter of fact answers would almost always settle the matter.

We were civilian employees very much into the war. We signed a contract called articles when we went aboard ship, turning in our seaman's passport and U.S. Coast Guard papers, which certified our competency to perform the duties of our position. We could arrange for an allotment to be sent to a wife, family member or a bank. And within twenty-four hours of returning to a U.S. port we were to be paid in full. We and "they" had the option of remaining on the same ship. A tour of duty was usually two to three months. In my case, I had to take another ship within a week or so or else be subject to Navy active duty. Most of the foreigners, other than the Scotsmen and Filipino, were from German occupied countries, which meant no mail, no way to know about their families. We were a real polyglot of men with only one thing in common; we hated Adolf and Benito.

The floor plates in the engine room were 30 to 40 feet below water level depending on how loaded the ship might be. It was also the target of German U-boat captains because a torpedo exploding there would disable and sink the ship. I want to say just this once that at no time did I ever see any man run out of an engine room or any shipmate express a desire to be somewhere else no matter what the circumstances. I did see old chief engineers as well as many younger men rush down into the engine room to stand by the fire pumps, the generators or the boiler in case more help was needed. And, remember, no merchant mariner had to be there; all were volunteers.

As for the men themselves, they were from all levels of society, all levels of education. Most of the older men had little or at least no important family ties. But, there was a communal spirit that was hard to explain. It was certainly pure accident that I became a merchant seaman but it was the right place for me considering my ability, my interests and my independent nature. And, I was exposed to conditions "over there" and "back home" each voyage.

All liberty ships, more than three thousand of them, were identical. Their maximum speed was about 12 knots unless the safety valves were tied down. They were of welded steel construction and had five holds for cargo. Each cargo had an upper and a lower section. And, almost all ships were loaded in a similar fashion so if one was sunk there would be no total shortage of the goods aboard. Extremely heavy items like a locomotive were carried in the very bottom, and food, clothes, or whatever, filled up the hold. The upper space was usually saved for ammunition of various sorts, including bombs. Then items like tanks, trucks, rolling guns and so on would be welded on deck. A full load was some 10,000 tons, about 150 train carloads. In those days, we had no radar, no sonar, just binoculars. No lights of any kind were allowed, not even a match or a lighted cigarette. When traveling in convoy every ship had the right and responsibility to shoot out any light emanating from another ship.

We traveled in groups called convoys with as many as 100 ships constantly zigzagging and changing the overall course. In those days, torpedoes could be aimed only by repositioning the submarine, which was a slow process. Another standing order was, "You don't stop for anything. If another ship breaks down, if it is hit, if a man is overboard, you don't stop." It was sensible because the enemy was sure to still be in the area, and your ship was more valuable than a few men or a ship in distress. I learned all of these things and more on my first voyage.

The ten-hour trip from Savannah to Charleston under cover of darkness was uneventful. We went to the weapons station to load ammunition and then to the Army docks for deck cargo. Five ships left Charleston late one afternoon. One, an old English freighter, was sunk within sight of Sullivan's Island. We continued at full speed, my ship in front, to Cape Lookout, North Carolina, where we stayed behind a steel mesh submarine net for more than a week. We could see the sub on the surface way out to sea. The old timers said he was charging his batteries. Finally, one dark night we took off for Norfolk. More ships joined us and we went up the Chesapeake, joined more ships out of Baltimore, then tugs had to pull us through the C&D Canal. We scraped bottom several times when we went down Delaware Bay to New York, up the East River, through Long Island Sound, through Cape Cod Canal. We joined more ships out of Boston. We had a blimp escort from there to Halifax, Nova Scotia, but we had to anchor outside the harbor. A cargo ship loaded with ammunition had been hit in the Halifax harbor during World War I and most of the city had been destroyed. A lot more ships joined us there flying Canadian, English and all sorts of flags. Soon after we left Halifax, the blimp escort left us.

My ship was on the starboard side of the convoy toward the rear. I can't say how many ships there were. We were so stretched out that the lead ships and those on the far side were out of sight. There were more than eighty, probably a hundred. And, almost every day one would fall back because of engine or boiler trouble. Some of those ships had been confiscated from the enemy; some had been brought out of mothballs. Most were oilfired but some burned coal. All, I suppose, were overloaded. Somewhere off Iceland, way up there in iceberg waters, first one and then another would be sunk. One of them left me with a memory.

When it is early spring and one is that far north, even the brightest day seems like dusk. Life at sea, especially where you could see the dull luminous shape of that huge white mountain, a mountain the book said was only one eighth of the total mass, was so new to me that I would frequently go on deck just to see the tossing ships, the gray water, the bigness of the world I was in. As I stood there holding on to the lifeline, a cable stretched tautly from forecastle to the stern, the ship dipped and a huge wave rose, carrying the swirling foam along the rail beside me. On that foam, only a few feet away, was a form. It was a Count Mourner Suit, a black rubber thing carried on ships to be donned by crewmen during an emergency. It completely covered the body, rubber boots, gloves, pants, coat, even one's head except for the face, all one piece and all of them were one size. When worn it would keep a man afloat indefinitely. The suit surged, mounted the crest of the wave, rolled toward me, and the fixed stare of a young man, a very white face in that black rubber hood, met my gaze, eye for eye. Then, just as quickly as it had appeared, the Count Mourner Suit slid down the face of the wave and disappeared forever from my view. The suit disappeared, the face stayed with me.

By the time we got to the area just north of Sweden, we knew we were headed for Murmansk. Our destination was no longer a secret. There was no other place in that direction to go. Murmansk was one of the main ports during World War II for supplies reaching the USSR from the West. The sea route to Murmansk was known as "suicide run" because of the many allied ships sunk by German submarines along its path. God, it was cold on deck! I was glad I was a fireman and could sit between the nice warm boilers. Suddenly all hell broke loose. I had personally seen 32 ships hit and I believe they all went down. Then the convoy broke up, ships scattered in all directions. Eight others and mine headed south. Seven of our ships made it to London where there was at least one air raid every few hours. You know, I was never really afraid that my ship would be hit, it would always be one of those others. But, I sure hated cold weather, couldn't bear the thoughts of going into that frigid water. Somehow, I learned that ships loading out of Charleston would more than likely go to the Mediterranean by the southern route. For the next three years, I sailed out of Charleston. Of course, there was much action that way too, especially at Gibraltar. Now this may sound strange but men do crazy things in wartime. Invariably there would be some joker who would get up a pool. The names of ships in the convoy would be placed in a hat; we would each bid on a name of a ship. A ship traveling to one side of the convoy and in a rear position would demand the highest price. Then the money was placed in a pot. The fellow holding the name of the first ship to be sunk won the pot. Of course, our own ship's name was never included. You wouldn't be around to spend the money anyway.

One of my most vivid war experiences occurred sometime in late '43. I had signed aboard a ship in Charleston and was stowing my gear when I heard a familiar voice singing as he came along the companionway. It was old big mouth, very likable, Roc from Pittsburgh himself. While I hung my clothes in the locker, he told me the latest about his "sweetie" and then ran to get her letters and read them all to me. And, no wonder he saved them. She wrote all the right things, even said he was handsome, the man of her dreams. What a nightmare for most folks!

The next two weeks were routine; beautiful weather, smooth seas. Even the no moon phase was right as we approached Gibraltar. I want to digress a bit to explain why Gibraltar was so important. First of all the Straits are only about ten miles wide. It is the only western entrance to the Mediterranean; the water is very, very deep. The surface current is always easterly into the Mediterranean. Deep down it moves to the west. The Rock, a British

Fortress, dominates the sea, but the adjacent mountains dominate the Rock and are a part of Spain. While Spain wasn't a big factor in the war, it was pro–Nazi. The Germans had super observation posts in those mountains, well hidden in the many cliffs, and could report any activity within a half-day's run for a slow convoy to a submarine base or air field. An allied armada would then be subject to high-flying bombers, low-flying torpedo bombers, submarine attack, and sometimes all three depending largely on the weather. Consequently, every effort was made to arrive there on a dark and stormy day or at least before daylight. Men show their nervousness in different ways, the captain stayed glued to his stool in the bridge house, the bosun took the tarps off the lifeboats, the 1st assistant paced the floor plates, Roc and I talked about our sweeties.

But, nothing happened, absolutely nothing. The Navy had sent a few gunners aboard that ship. They manned the 20mm antiaircraft guns, stationed a bow watch, and bragged about what they would do if any damned periscope showed its ugly head. But we moved ahead in fine fashion on an unusually calm sea, all that day and night. I got off watch at 0800; Roc served me hotcakes, juice and lots of bacon. When he finished clearing the table we went to the flying bridge, and helped the bosun spread the tarpaulin over a lifeboat. Another ship was close by on our starboard side. Suddenly there was the sound of metal, a sharp rattle and I don't really remember what else. When I turned toward the ship to starboard there was an airplane swooping over its funnel and then it dived into the water probably fifty yards away from me. Next there was the sound of antiaircraft fire from somewhere and a dull thud. And Roc wasn't there.

The 3rd Mate came running to the flying bridge, the Navy man screamed. They all, including the bosun, ran to the funnel. Roc was shoved up against it. When they rolled him over it was just awful. After a while, I went to the stern of the ship. I could see the fellows on the ship to the starboard launching their lifeboats and start rowing for the Morocco coast. They were lucky, the sea was calm and the coast was in sight. The ship was sinking. The plane had already sunk. The pilot had obviously flown low from Spain, made a big circle and approached us from the south. He had dropped his torpedo, swooped over the target ship and dropped low again as he approached us. Either his machine guns or 20 mm shells from the attacked ship had strafed our deck; some said both, because the Navy man only had a shoulder wound, not serious at all. Roc was torn apart.

That night I managed to write Roc's sweetie a letter. When I took it to the captain the next morning, I asked him if he would mail it so it would arrive at the proper time, "About when President Roosevelt's letter would be delivered to Roc's parents," he said. "But Carolina, I'll have to read it, censor regulation." The captain had bought a farm outside Richmond,

Virginia, and had lived there since he retired in the early thirties. "Son, why don't you write another letter to his folks? I'll be on the bridge for an hour or so. Use my desk and here's my pen." The captain mailed the letters in Mostaganem, Allied African Headquarters, a little town just east of Oran, Algeria.

In the early spring of 1945, I was back in Charleston waiting for my next tour. My Sweetie, Geraldine Bingham, came down from Greensboro, N.C., for the weekend and we were married March 2. Gerry went back to her college and I headed west. My ship, along with every other ship in the free world, it seemed, was on its way to invade Japan. However, we had engine trouble and were diverted to Frisco. The crew was sent back to Charleston to pick up another ship, yet to go through sea trials. By now it was the last of May. Gerry's school term ended May 30, so we had a two-month honeymoon in Charleston, sort of a honeymoon. I had to report in every morning and learn everything there was to know about the engine room. This was pretty intense training because I knew we were heading into war conditions. As first assistant, I had to know every valve, every switch and be able to find them in the dark if necessary. I had to verify that spare parts and supplies were on board. Gerry had little more to do than do her nails and fix her hair. After all, we were fortunate to find one room and a bath. Then I left again. The orders read, "To proceed to Borneo or port or ports unknown for a period of one year or more or return to a recognized U.S. port as directed by the War Shipping Administration."

So many ships were lined up to go through the Panama Canal that we were assigned anchorage and were able to go ashore for brief periods several times. On one of these trips ashore, I purchased a Christmas gift for Gerry and wrote her a note about how much I would miss her at Christmas. Of course, these were sent with all kinds of "Do not open 'til Christmas" notes. On the way back to the ship, some fellows were talking about an atomic bomb. "What in the hell is an atomic bomb?" "Dammed if I know, but it must be big." "Yeah! They went all the way to Japan and only dropped one." Art Bently, the chief engineer, and I were the only ones on the ship who had any idea what an atom was. I had seen an exhibit at the Chicago Museum of Science and Industry and I knew about the danger of splitting the atom and setting off a chain reaction that would destroy every atom in our part of the universe. When Art went to the crew's mess to explain the theory we could see that no one, including the Danish captain, had any idea what he was talking about. Never mind, we went thru the canal as scheduled and then headed for Salina Cruz, a tiny primitive Mexican village not far from Guatemala, to await orders. We stayed, we stayed, and we stayed! Finally, I went from Salino Cruz to San Francisco. I had more than enough points for an immediate discharge so I was shipped back to Charleston in late December and was home for Christmas. So ended my war!

The Romingers

Helen Smith Rominger

As told to Nannie Greene in 2005.

No text on Western Watauga at war could overlook the Romingers.

Manuel and Annie Shoemaker Rominger had eleven children. This in itself was not unusual. However, when seven brothers are serving in the armed forces at the same time, that is occasion for pause. In 1945, the governor of North Carolina honored Mrs. Rominger for her contribution to the war effort. She was given the All American Mother's Award. Fortunately, all the brothers came home! One can only imagine the number of prayers that were said for this family.

Of the eleven children, the seven who served were Charlie, Clyde, Grady, Johnnie, Dexter, Howard, and Richard. By 1945 they had served a total of 54 years, and they served overseas a total of 14 years and 5 months of that time. Six of them were overseas at the same time. Clyde was the only one who retired from service. The two boys who did not serve were Fred and Ernest. The last two children were girls, Mae and Edith. In 2005 the only child still living is Mae.

Fourteen Down, Eleven to Go

Ralph Stokes

Ralph Stokes declares that he was a man without a title. Although he was detained in Switzerland he could not be designated as a prisoner of war because Switzerland was not at war. The U.S. classified him as a POW since he was detained. International law referred to him as an internee. Mail sent to him was addressed to POW Ralph Stokes.

Today he states that he has no ill will toward his "hosts" in Switzerland. He was not mistreated. The internees were not well fed, but neither were the Swiss people. They were all victims of war and it could have been much worse.

Ralph Stokes lives in Chilhowie, Virginia. He submitted this text in 2003.

Did you get shot? Did you ever run? How many Germans did you kill? Were you scared? Did you see any German girls? Did you ever see Flanders Field?

Our high school junior class was peppering Mr. Horton with these questions and others of similar nature. Mr. S.F. Horton was principal of Cove Creek High School and was substituting for an absent teacher this day. The year was 1940 and World War II was breaking out all over the patch but none of us realized the size of the patch. We did know, however, that Mr. Horton was a veteran of World War 1, which ended about 20 years before. He answered questions but offered nothing on his own. He much preferred scanning his newspaper and then dozing, telling us to use the time studying. That's exactly what we did — studying the girls, that is. They, in turn, were probably studying the boys, so we had a very amiable class.

We knew that war was close at hand and yet, it seemed so far away. None of us could have realized how close it really was because, within two years, most of the boys would be in some branch of military service.

Finishing fourth in our graduating class of 1941 gave me the false impression that my education was over. It didn't take long for me to discover that I was an educated fool, and that I had to run like the dickens just trying to keep up.

A light dusting of snow covered the ground, and the brisk air accommodated a few snowflakes on that late November morning in 1942. I flagged a Greyhound bus across the creek from the Stokes house, and a journey into the unknown had begun. The home folks were told that I would be back that night — that I was merely going to investigate joining the Armed Forces. However, I had confided to a younger brother, Bill, that if I were accepted, I would not be back for a little while. (In reality, that "little while" amounted to two years, two months before I again saw Cove Creek.)

Looking back, I now see that first Greyhound bus trip as the beginning of a series of events much too large and complicated for me to understand. Within a week, I had been sworn into the Army at Fort Bragg, and a week later, I had taken my first train ride and was in Biloxi, Mississippi. By then I was in the Army Air Corps, because the Air Force was not a separate service in 1942.

I'm sure my basic training program was nothing compared to what most of the boys had to endure, but it was time consuming. Out of the sack, or cot, at 5:30 and everything from then until 3 in the afternoon was called basic. Then, it was airplane mechanic classes until 11, which completed our day. Of course, it was repeated next morning, six days a week and lasted for five months.

May 4, 1943, was graduation and departure was made the same day for Laredo, Texas, and Aerial Gunnery School. Basic training was behind but a full schedule was maintained in Laredo. However, all classroom and flying instructions were conducted during daylight hours.

After graduating from Aerial Gunnery School, and getting my silver wings, it was on to Salt Lake City, Utah, where we were introduced to our own weapon of war — the B-24 heavy bomber. A crew of ten was formed and living as a troop was begun. Individualism was cast aside as we ate, slept, and flew as a unit and our only duty was flying.

Almost daily we flew as we moved from Salt Lake City to Boise, Idaho, and then on to Riverside, California. We believed that Riverside would be our last training site, and so it was. By the middle of December, training was over and so was my first year of Army life. A backward glance brought relief that it was over, but anxiety ruled supreme as we pondered what lay ahead.

Our crew, and other crews, went to an aircraft manufacturing plant in San Francisco and left with a new B-24 Liberator bomber. We immediately christened ours *Portland Ann*, honoring our pilot who came from Portland, Oregon, and whose wife was named Ann. After a fuel consumption flight out over the Pacific, we were on our way.

There didn't seem to be any rush as we made several overnight stops before reaching West Palm Beach, Florida, about a week later. Then, it was good-bye United States and hello Central and South America. The ocean was crossed between Natal, Brazil, and Dakar, Africa. Two days later, we landed in Wales, Great Britain, and there we stayed for ten days, awaiting our support group who came over by boat. Then it was on to Old Buckingham, England, and our home away from home.

Suddenly, it dawned on everyone that this war was nigh at hand. Each night, we listened to Axis Sally, German propaganda broadcaster, and she properly identified and welcomed our group the day we landed.

We learned that we were expected to fly 25 combat missions before being relieved, and that actual losses were averaging around 10 percent for each mission flown. One airman interrupted the general who was doing the briefing, saying he didn't like the odds because he was expected to fly 25 missions, but he would be history after flying ten raids. The general explained that replacement crews would be coming in and that the percentages were for each individual raid.

The moment of truth arrived for our crew the first Sunday in February 1944 as we bombed a German air field in Abbeville, France. An engine was shot out so we came back on three and landed in southern England. An oil line was replaced, and we flew back to our base, on four, the next day. The countdown had begun, and it was one down with 24 to go.

Our daily living soon developed into a routine pattern, depending on the schedule of the day. There were no wake-up calls on non-flying days.

Much of the day was spent just lying around and doing nothing in the line of duty. All flying was now limited to actual combat missions. The leisure time was most welcomed because breathing oxygen for an extended period of time drained one's strength, resulting in a sluggish feeling. In fact, the heart had to be speeded back into its natural rhythm after each mission. This was accomplished by drinking "a shot" of scotch whiskey as soon as the plane taxied to a stop. Being a non-drinker, I obtained the same result by jogging around the plane a couple of times. Of course, there were arguments about who would get my "shot."

We always knew the night before when we were scheduled to fly. Wake-up was around 2:30 with the truck coming for us at 3. Several grumblings of "to hell with Hitler" could be heard as already tired bodies tried to awaken. Sometimes it took a violent shake to awaken a sleepyhead, but we were always ready by truck time.

First order of business was the mess hall, but who in the world could eat powdered eggs and powdered milk at 3:00 in the morning? Besides, we had an ace in the hole. Next, it was the sideshow building where we exchanged our clothing for our flying apparel. The exchange was made right on the spot, each airman putting his regular clothing, except shoes and leather jacket, into his own "pigeon hole" from whence his flying clothes had come. The exchange, in reverse, would be made when we got back and were de-briefed. The change of clothing was absolutely necessary because the temperature at our flying altitude (4 miles) was between 40 and 45 degrees below zero. Resembling long-handle underwear, our first layer of clothing was interlaced with electric wires. There were receptacles for shoes and gloves, which were also electric. A flying suit resembling coveralls was next, finished off with flying helmet, oxygen mask, parachute, and one's own leather coat. Shoes were carried in a duffle bag in case of a bailout—electric shoes were no good for walking.

Now, it was off to the briefing room and revelation, for the first time, of today's target. A lot of pertinent information was discussed and the base chaplain offered a prayer. Trucks hauled the crews to their planes that were loaded with bombs, thousands of 50 cal. machine gun rounds and topped-off fuel tanks. However, only the engineer was allowed inside the plane just then, and he had already been there for about an hour.

Day was just breaking and an enjoyable ritual was about to commence. Remember the "ace in the hole?" The ace was a concentrated chocolate candy bar and the hole was the knee pocket of the flying suit. The candy was put there for every mission and was capable of providing energy for eight days if eaten as directed (one square each day). Of course, it would be a useful aid in case of a bailout. Without any hesitation, whatsoever, each of us opened the candy bar and didn't stop eating until all eight squares were "down the hatch." (There's no wonder that we weren't hungry for a day or two after that.)

To make our assignment of 25 raids seem more attainable, we adopted three major goals. The first one was to complete three combat missions. Anything less than three and it was assumed by Washington Brass that Hitler had won this battle of economics. We were very happy when our first goal was reached. We didn't want Hitler to win anything; also our hides were still intact.

It was now time to think about our second goal, and it, too, meant very much to us. Doctors had determined that combat readiness was very difficult to maintain over the span of 25 missions. In an effort to remedy the situation, a two-week break or vacation was granted around the middle of the tour. So the countdown toward 13 was eagerly recorded. Most of the crews went to Scotland and we could hardly wait.

Of course, after accomplishing number two would come number three. That would be completion of 25 and returning to the States, knowing, never again, would we have to fly a combat bomber raid.

April 24, 1944, gave cause for celebration, but we dared not indulge until we got back to England and were safely on the ground. Today's mission was our thirteenth, which meant that we had reached goal number two. Of course, there were twelve more to go but, right now, there was nothing on our minds except Scotland and a two-week rest period. I had saved $139 for such an event, but I had no intention of spending the whole bundle.

Nightfall was in the process of capturing the day when Al, our tail gunner, announced that he was going to amble over to the dayroom and pick up our passes, if they were ready. This was good because it would be the first step in our getaway.

We didn't like the look on Al's face and his empty hands when he returned about thirty minutes later. "Where's the passes?" he was asked. "Aren't they ready yet?"

"No, and they'll not be ready in the morning," was his reply.

"You mean we are not going anywhere tomorrow?" and his looks and actions were making half-believers of us.

"Yeah, we are going somewhere, all right. We are scheduled to fly tomorrow."

"You are lying, Al Bocchino, and this is no joking matter."

"I'm not joking, boys. You'll see soon as the boogerman gets here." (Boogerman was the nickname for the fellow who came to alert us about the next day's flight.)

It wasn't long until the boogerman came and Al's message was confirmed. "Crew 70 [ours] will be flying tomorrow. Wake-up at 2:30. Your passes will be ready when you get back. You can leave tomorrow night, if you wish." Knowing there were no appeals, we soon "turned in," amid grumblings of "to hell with Hitler, to hell with Hitler."

Sgt. Ralph Stokes and his crew buddies were scheduled for a two-week rest period in Scotland. Instead, they were assigned to fly one more bombing mission in Germany, but ended up in Switzerland in a damaged plane. The entire crew became prisoners of war. Ralph's internment in Switzerland lasted six months before he and a friend escaped into France. They were flown back to their home base in England and then back to the U.S.A. He was discharged in October 1945, after the war had ended (photograph furnished by Ralph Stokes).

Early next morning, April 25, 1944, found us once again winging our way toward Hitler's Fortress, Europe. Germany occupied just about all of Western Europe at the time and even shot at us from flak boats that operated in the English Channel and on the North Sea. But, even at that, Germany was not considered to be the formidable foe that the "early boys" had faced. We flew deeper into Germany than they did, but we had more and better escorts. While the flak was still fierce, the German fighter planes were not nearly the threat that they had been, but still it was something to be feared. In 1943, the 8th Air Force (we were in the 8th) lost 1261 bombers. We were glad that we were flying in 1944.

As we reached the French coast, there was a reminder (if we needed one) that this game was being played for "keeps." Two heavy bombers were observed plummeting toward the ground. Apparently, they had collided in their close formation; no enemy fighters were sighted and there didn't seem to be any flak. Shortly afterwards, another bomber, close to our echelon but not in our group, was seen tumbling from the sky. It had been hit by flak and was burning. We, too, were hit but our damage was minimal and we continued on. There was a general feeling, however, that the events so far did not have the markings of a good day.

Flak continued just about all the way to our target, which was a ball-bearing manufacturing plant in Mannheim, Germany. Several severe "jolts" were indications of near misses by German shells, but enemy fighter planes appeared to be absent this day. For this, we were thankful.

Amid a heavy barrage of flak, our plane lurched upward as the bombs were released. It was 11:30 A.M. and time to get out of there. We knew we would be facing a strong head wind going home, but we could handle that, so we thought, because we were now several thousand pounds lighter. But, it was not to be. Shortly afterwards, the gun turrets refused to respond, and our guns refused to fire. A call was made to the pilot to advise of the malfunction, but the mikes were, strangely, silent. A quick inspection revealed our problem. All four-voltage regulators were dead and this meant big trouble for Crew 70. All internal power was gone with no hopes of recovery. We could deal with most of the problems, including no heat, although it was 45 degrees below zero, but there was no way to compensate for the fuel in the wing-tip tanks that we absolutely had to have, but could not get. This fuel had to be pumped into the main tanks, but we had no power for the pumps. The plane had taken a shellacking all day from the flak, but it was still airworthy (barely). (I still think we would have made it back had we been able to get that fuel.)

We were 90 miles from Switzerland and chose to fly there, rather than back into France, bail out, and then try to escape the Germans by walking to Switzerland.

Our internment in Switzerland was nothing compared to what it would have been in a German or Japanese prisoner of war camp. There were certain restrictions, but we were not housed behind barbed wire. We were not confined to our building and we were allowed to browse around in the community. I was in three different camps; two were in small communities and one had no community. The guards were friendly enough and so were the people. An incident comes to mind that might be worthy of mention.

The second day there our crew of ten plus two guards were passengers on a train and headed for our first internment camp. The train was very crowded and we were standing in the center aisle, holding on to an overhead anchor rope. A few miles out of the station, the passengers began conversing with our guards, but they were speaking German, so we knew not what was being said. And then, an amazing thing happened. Those people who were sitting near us arose and offered their seats. We refused, but gestured our thanks. Then, a lady, probably around 50 years of age and sitting next to where I was standing, grasped my free hand and, squeezing it, repeated over and over again, "Americana, Americana." This 21-year-old airman didn't know how to react, so I patted the back of her hand when she released mine.

We were able to keep up with the war efforts through a rented radio. The Allies had occupied Southern Italy and we picked up an Allied broadcasting station. We heard the news of the Allied landing on Normandy on D-Day as it happened. We had been interned for six weeks and had already been moved to a second camp. From a certain direction, the sky was very red one night. When queried the next day, our guards said it was Munich, Germany, burning. We asked why and they answered that American bombers had bombed the city off the face of the earth. We rejoiced, inwardly, but dared not gloat. However, we watched with great satisfaction the reddened sky for a second night in a row.

The mail service was nothing to write home about, and the mail probably wouldn't have got through, anyway. We were allowed to write one letter a month. I was interned for eight months and received four letters. The first one was received five months after it was written. (Guess they had never heard of the "Pony Express.")

The United States maintained diplomatic relations with Switzerland during the war and had an embassy in Bern. A military attaché from the embassy came to our camp each month and paid our regular salary. I usually kept about $25 and wired or cabled the rest of it home.

The summer allowed itself to drift into fall and then winter was threatening to crash the party. My buddy and I could think of a lot of places where we would rather spend the winter than in Switzerland. Southern France had been liberated and, not wanting to wear our welcome out in Switzerland, we decided to try an escape. But, there were a few little matters that had to be rectified first.

A favorite guard was bribed for some civilian clothes. They were a sight to behold, but I wasn't going to a fashion show, anyway. Hilda Graf, a 29-year-old shopkeeper in a little store, was given a package containing the four letters that I had received and a back-up diary that was just about up to date. Also, some pictures that I had accumulated in the three camps. She was given money to mail this package to my home address in North Carolina. I knew I could not carry this material with me in an escape attempt. (Hilda held true to her promise but it took a while and then, she mailed it to a former internee who was living in Colorado. We did not know each other in camp but he eventually made contact and mailed it to me. It took Hilda 51 years to mail the package and she was 80 years of age by then.)

Faking a toothache, which enabled us to buy a train ticket to Bern, we were on our way "to get that blasted molar fixed." A few nights later, as we crossed the border into France, we marveled at how easy it had been. "Did the Swiss not care if we did get away?" we wondered. "After all, they wouldn't have to feed us since we were gone."

The house on the mountainside didn't look too inviting, but it was no time to be choosy. It was 2:30 in the morning and we were tired, hungry, and cold so we rapped on the door. Several raps finally aroused a Frenchman from his warm bed, and I'm not too sure that he was glad to see us. Finally, after we repeated "Americana" several times, he stepped aside and allowed us to go inside. We helped ourselves to an uncovered bowl of milk and observed a cat doing the same thing a few minutes later.

A lady and a girl in her early teens then made an appearance. They left the room shortly but returned a few minutes later with a loaf of bread. The man left before daybreak, gesturing for us to stay. We didn't trust him and left a few minutes later, amid protests from the women.

Around 10 that morning, we saw what we had been looking for. Two cars, a star painted on their tops, were approaching and we knew they were coming for us. Never again did we see the Frenchman, but he had done us a very good deed.

Two days later we were flown from Lyons, France, to London and "the show had hit the road." A short trip to Old Buckingham (my home base) and then a flight from Glasgow, Scotland, to New York; a train to Fort Bragg, N.C., and a 30-day furlough (my first time home after two years, 2 months). Then, to a rest camp in Coral Gables, Florida, for 4 and a half months. Laredo, Texas; Savannah, Georgia; and Goldsboro, North Carolina, finished it up. The war ended September 2, 1945, and I was discharged in October.

Looking back, I can see that my contribution toward the war effort was very insignificant, and I realize that this story is hardly worthy of print. Nevertheless, I am proud that I was privileged to serve, and I consider my honorable discharge to be one of my most prized possessions. I believed then, and I believe now, that being born an American is my greatest blessing.

Luther Martin Bingham

Catherine Stokes Sheppard

This profile is based on information submitted by Blaine Miller, brother-in-law of Luther Martin Bingham, in 2001.

Luther Martin Bingham was a happy-go-lucky kid whose loves in life were playing basketball, hunting and fishing, and playing cards. As soon as he graduated from high school in 1944, he joined the Navy. After boot camp he went to boatswain school to learn about the operation of landing craft.

In October 1944, the Kamikaze (divine wind) planes began their suicide attacks on the U.S. Navy. These planes, loaded with explosives for one-way missions to crash into U.S. ships, wreaked much havoc on ships in the Okinawa area. Luther Martin was on one such ship.

Somewhere near Okinawa a kamikaze pilot was sighted and the general alarm was initiated. Luther Martin was running through an open hatch when the ship was hit. The steel hatch cover (door) with heavy steel handles slammed shut. One of the handles (dogs) had struck him in the head. He suffered a severe skull fracture. The injury was not treatable aboard the ship or any readily available medical facility. He was strapped to a stretcher and flown to Fort Worth, Texas. He did not respond to treatment or even regain consciousness for several weeks. The doctors gave no prognosis because they simply did not know if he would ever regain his mental faculties.

About a year later, someone suggested that a trip home might stimulate his mind to some degree of normalcy. There were brief periods of excellent mental function. Luther Martin enrolled at Appalachian, played bridge and poker, fished a bit, but after a few moments of anything, he would throw up his hands and walk the floor. Another year passed and his mother received a letter from the Veteran's Administration suggesting a treatment with a new drug called Thorazine. The VA believed the new drug would provide Luther Martin with a few years of normal mental function, but the letter warned that a most certain side effect would be severe damage to his heart. He could be expected to have a severe heart attack at some point of time.

Luther Martin Bingham, Jr., joined the Navy in 1944. He was on a ship near Okinawa when a kamikaze pilot crashed into his U.S. ship. Luther Martin was severely injured and was flown to Fort Worth, Texas, where he remained in a coma for several weeks. These injuries plagued him the rest of his life (photograph furnished by Blaine Miller).

Luther Martin's family felt that a few good normal years were better than a long life of the condition he was in. Strangely enough, he responded to the medication favorably. He bought a service station, worked long hours, made money, and gave it away to the church or to anyone who needed it. Then for some unknown reason the VA reduced the dosage of the medicine. He functioned in a semi-normal state and then had what they called a massive heart attack.

Cruel and unfair as it may be, many families in our nation have experienced the same loss of a father and a son, both causalities of war, one generation apart. Although neither was killed in battle, both died from having served.

The Home Front

Catherine Stokes Sheppard

World War II changed the world forever. It certainly had an impact on Western Watauga County. Not only did many of the young men (and some not so young) go off to war, but many civilians left also.

Most of the people of Western Watauga County earned their livelihood from farming. There were few job opportunities off the farm. After Pearl Harbor, many factories converted to building war materials, but these were mostly in the North. So many men were drafted that the call went out to women to come and work in the factories. For the first time in their lives, women had a chance to work outside the home and be well paid. Men not eligible for the draft also went to places like Norfolk, Cleveland, or Detroit. It was not unusual for entire families to move to the industrial cities. Young women who were proficient in typing readily found employment in Washington, D.C.

A home front memory that is still poignant in my mind was the small flags in the windows of homes where sons and husbands were away at war. The flags were about six inches square, white background, smaller blue square inside the white and a star in the center. The number of stars indicated the number of men in service from that household. If the star was gold, it meant that a man from the home had given his life. The other stars were silver. Very few windows did not have a flag.

Although rationing was an inconvenience, most did not consider it a hardship. After all, we had lived through a Depression; certainly, we could cope with not having chocolate or coffee. Since my family had always had a garden and had canned vegetables as well as meat, we did not suffer. Mother made lots of gingerbread with molasses rather than cake. My parents did have a problem with the coffee that was mostly chicory, but they drank it. Our ration covered what we needed. We did not have a car, only a truck, and Dad drove so slowly that he could not use much gas.

I was disappointed that we could not have basketball games that were very far from our school. Other school activities were canceled or limited if they required travel. We walked to most places in the neighborhood or rode the Greyhound bus to places too far away to walk. When someone would complain about the short supply of anything, he could count on someone countering with, "There is a war going on, have you not heard?"

Metals of all kinds were scarce commodities during World War II. Individuals would go through the country and buy scrap metal which they would sell to a foundry to be recycled into war materials.

We all wrote letters to the people in service. The War Department urged us to write in order to keep up the morale of the fighting men. We even wrote to people we did not know. Another way we tried to help was to invite soldiers into our homes for a home cooked meal. If a soldier was hitchhiking, no one thought of passing him and not stopping. If it was mealtime, he was invited into the drivers' home for a meal. We bought all the War Bonds (U.S. Savings Bonds) we could afford.

In many communities, ladies met at churches or schools and rolled bandages for the war effort. My Aunt Blanche Stokes knitted several sweaters, olive drab, in a variety of sizes. I recall that when she purled her mouth twisted to one side, when she knit her mouth went in the other direction. Sometimes I watch an old war movie and note the soldiers wearing a sweater. I do wonder if one of those was hand made by my Aunt Blanche Stokes. These are but a few examples of how civilians wanted to contribute whatever they could to help the war effort.

The people in Western Watauga, as in the entire United States, were united as never before. Their politics may have been different, but all wanted the war to end and our men to come home.

We saw newsreels and read magazines about the celebrations in the cities when the war did end. Our joy was pure but we were much more sedate. Cove Creek High School's Junior–Senior Banquet was in progress when the war in Europe ended. We had expected the ending and someone had taken a radio to the banquet. When we heard the news for a few moments there was complete silence, then applause. It was as though the world had heaved a giant sigh. After all, the war in the Pacific was still in progress.

When the Pacific war was over there was a feeling of relief, but I recall no celebrations. When the men came home, slowly we realized we were no more emotionally prepared for their return than we were for their leaving. Boys were sent to war, men returned. The veterans felt misplaced and the families did not know how to react. It was truly a time of adjustment for all.

Rationing During World War II

Reba C. Farthing

This was submitted by Reba C. Farthing in 2000.

During World War II, I recall the rationing of consumer goods, which caused hardships for families. The United States Armed Services had first priority on all products. Sugar, coffee, shoes, gasoline and tires were some of the important things that I remember were on the rationed list. Many other products for civilian use may not have been rationed but were of short supply. Coupons were issued for each family to use to buy the rationed items.

The rationing of sugar was difficult because it was needed in cooking, canning and preserving foods. In a large family it was important for the canning and preserving many kinds of foods to be used not only for the winter months but also for year around use.

Shoe coupons were issued for one or two pairs per individual per year. If one family member did not need new shoes, the coupon could be used for another member of the family.

Gasoline and tires were also in short supply and were on the rationed list. Farm families may have been allowed as little as three gallons of gasoline per week. A coupon was used for this also and no doubt, this was very hard for farmers and people who had to rely on gasoline for their type of work. A rationing sticker was placed on the windshield of each vehicle to show how much gasoline was allowed.

Rationing started in 1941 and lasted until 1945 as I recall. I was 11 years old and I remember my family being very concerned, and how they struggled to make things last or go as far as possible. They planned ahead and used the rationed items conservatively. It was a very hectic time.

Victory Gardens

Nannie Greene

World War II brought circumstances to the home front that seem unrealistic to those too young to remember that time. One of those circumstances was a shortage of food. Rationing assured that each family could obtain their fair share of the available food items but often items were not on the shelves of grocery stores.

The federal government encouraged everyone to grow all the food they could. Those who lived in towns and cities were urged to grow Victory Gardens on their vacant lots. The wife of the governor of North Carolina planted a garden on the grounds of the Governor's Mansion and was photographed with the many jars of vegetables she had put up. This was to encourage the women of the state to do likewise.

The term Victory Garden was a morale builder as well as a source of produce; everyone was doing his part. People in the cities grew small vegetables in window boxes or patio planters. Landowners were asked to share plots of land for gardens. In the industrial cities, many workers had come in from the farms for jobs and they had the know-how for making a garden.

The USA not only had troops to feed, but friendly countries that had been bombarded had people who needed to be fed. It was not unusual for a farm boy to be exempt from the draft because he was sorely needed on the farm. People who had never worked on the farm were now enlisted for such work. Near Mountain City, there were large fields of green beans planted. High school students, old men and even men in jail went to those fields to pick beans. The pay was good for this backbreaking job.

Western Watauga County was not too impressed with the term Victory Garden. Here we all had gardens as large as we could cultivate anyhow. And we were accustomed to giving vegetables to our cousins in the city. Gardening and sharing was a way of life for mountain people. However, we often referred to our garden as a Victory Garden (victory over weeds) and felt we were helping the war effort.

My Wartime Job

Baxter G. Farthing

This reminiscence of going to work during wartime was submitted by Baxter G. Farthing in 2000.

In the spring of 1943, the National Carbon Company started construction on a large facility near Morganton, North Carolina, in Burke County. The purpose of the plant was to manufacture or process carbon for use in batteries and for other purposes.

The United States had become embroiled in World War II when the naval base at Pearl Harbor was bombed by the Japanese on December 7, 1941. Many of our factories in the United States had shifted over full-time to production of war materials to use in the war effort. Carbon was also needed in this effort.

The contractor that was building the carbon plant recruited truck owners from several counties, including Watauga, to transport workers to the plant site each day. My brother-in-law, Ralph Church, had a large truck, and he was one of the truck owners who signed up to haul men to the job site each day. Two other truck owners from western Watauga County also signed up for the project. They were Howard Simpson of Phillip's Branch and Ferris Bumgarner of Zionville. It is my recollection that Ralph Critcher usually drove the Bumgarner vehicle.

Truck owners were responsible for going out in their communities and locating workers who were willing to go to Morganton each day to work in building of the plant. I had just finished the tenth grade at Cove Creek, and I decided to work the four months' school vacation period at the plant construction site. The pay scale was forty cents per hour for common labor, and for that time period, that was a rather large wage even though it meant riding in the back of a truck for two and a half hours or more each morning and evening going to and from the job site.

That summer, I stayed with my sister, Laura, and her husband, Ralph Church, and rode the truck each day to Morganton. We would leave their home at Vilas at 5:00 A.M., and we would drive to Valle Crucis and up to Matney where we would pick up several men. We would backtrack to Valle Crucis, then to Shulls Mills and Foscoe, picking up men all along the route. We would then go to Blowing Rock where we would hit the hard surfaced road and proceed on to the job site in Burke County. (The road from Valle Crucis through Foscoe and on to Blowing Rock was gravel.)

Several large kilns were constructed for use in the carbon baking process. A number of bricklayers were employed to build the kilns. My job was to carry brick and keep the brick masons supplied with the various types of brick that were used in the construction of the kilns. Other men also did various jobs around the construction site, such as mixing mortar for the brick masons, unloading freight cars, etc. The truck owners would also use their vehicles throughout the day transporting various materials as needed around the job site.

We would usually return to Vilas about 7:30 each evening after letting off the workmen at their homes in the various communities.

We worked six full days a week and about July the contractor gave all of us men a ten-cent raise to fifty cents per hour. I thought I had finally hit the big time. I quit the job that fall at the beginning of the new school year so I could finish high school at Cove Creek.

The truck owners continued to transport men to the job site until about December 1943, at which time the construction job was completed.

Korea

World War II and Korean War Memoirs

Glenn Farthing

Glenn Farthing and wife Martha still live in Greensboro, N.C. He submitted this piece in January 2005.

I, Glenn Farthing, son of Richard Aubyn Farthing and Hazel Glenn Farthing, was born June 24, 1922, in Valle Crucis, Watauga County, North Carolina. I attended grades 1 through 7 in a 3-room schoolhouse in Valle Crucis where I built the fires in the three wood stoves when I was in the 7th grade. I attended Cove Creek High School, grades 8 through11, and graduated valedictorian in 1939. I graduated from N.C. State College, BS in engineering with honors, in 1943. Having had four years of ROTC at State, the Army sent me to Officers Candidate School, Ft. Benning, Ga. I was commissioned an Infantry 2nd Lieutenant in December 1943.

I returned to Watauga County on leave and married my high school sweetheart, Martha Rachel Harris, December 31, 1943. She was the Cove Creek High School salutatorian, 1939, and graduated from Woman's College, now University of North Carolina at Greensboro, in 1943.

After attending Officer's Motor Course at Fort Benning and serving a few months at Camp Hood, Texas, and Camp Carson, Colorado Springs, Colorado, I was sent to Europe with about 15,000 other replacements. We sailed to Glasgow aboard the Dutch liner the *Nieuw Amsterdam*. We went by rail to Southampton, then by landing craft across the English Channel. We went into France across Omaha Beach, September 1944. I drove an Army 6x6 truck loaded with troops to the front line in eastern France at the request of the truck driver who was in severe pain with a swollen jaw from an abscessed tooth.

Near Luneville, I joined the 36th Infantry Division as a platoon leader in "I" company. The 36th Division was a part of the 6th corps of the US 7th Army and was on the front lines in combat with the German forces in eastern France. Some of my combat experiences remembered vividly follow.

Seeing Germans in woods to our front, I called by field phone to company headquarters and asked the artillery forward observer to come up to my platoon position to adjust artillery fire into the woods. Tree bursts would be especially effective against the German soldiers. He said, "Lieutenant, do you have your area map?" I replied that I had it, and identified the wooded area for him. He then said, "Well, there's no need for me to come up there. You go ahead and adjust fire for me." After his battery fired a couple of rounds, we had the guns zeroed in, and I told him to "fire for effect." We did not go through the woods, as our line of advance was south of them, so we did not actually see the result of our artillery fire, but we did not meet any resistance from the area.

We were taking some prisoners as we advanced, and I remember one soldier approaching us with his hands held high. We kept him covered, of course, and as he came closer he said, "Nicht schiessen, me polski (Don't shoot, I am a Pole)." He was a Polish citizen who had been forced by the Germans to serve in their Army. He had taken the first opportunity to lay down his arms and surrender.

Another time a German medic with a Red Cross arm band was surrendering to me and one of my battle-hardened squad sergeants. In searching him, we found that he had a pistol stuck in his belt. My sergeant was furious; the medic had, in effect, tricked us, as we knew by his Red Cross arm band that he was unarmed. The sergeant leveled his submachine gun at him and said, "Stand back, Lieutenant, I'm going to let him have it!" I pushed his gun barrel away saying, "No, George, he's just a boy. We'll send him back with the other prisoners." He was probably seventeen or eighteen and not very well trained. Of course, the sergeant and I were old men of twenty and twenty-one. As for the sergeant's actions, combat hardens men to the point where human life means little, and he knew the medic could have taken us out before another of my men could have killed him.

By this time, we were in the Vosges Mountains of eastern France, November 1944, with very cold weather and snow on the ground. In such weather, men in the front lines are hard put to avoid frostbitten toes. Feet are at the greatest risk as they are continuously exposed for days at a time, cold and wet. They become numb, and the solider suffers the frostbite before he realizes what's happening. Medics would not take men out of combat for minor frostbite, but it was painful enough to cause men to moan in their sleep.

"I" company was ordered to take the French village of La Nolle and Mariemont, and our intelligence said the Germans had departed. We decided to undertake the assignment after dark, and Lieutenant Lachenmaier's platoon assigned to take La Nolle soon found that the Germans had indeed pulled out. So, I took half-dozen men to reconnoiter Mariemont. We were moving across snow-covered fields by moonlight and went around the village to come in from the east. As I moved toward the road going east, suddenly I became aware of a sizable line of Germans marching single file going east on the road. I squatted motionless in the snow beside the road as about 30 Germans marched by. My submachine gun was on my knees, not cocked. The last man in the line stopped, swung his rifle off his shoulder, pointed at me and said, "Was ist los? (What's the matter?)" Not daring to try answering, I simply motioned him to go on, my heart in my throat. He turned and went on after his men, to my great relief.

We figured they must have been the occupying troops evacuating the village, so I brought the rest of my platoon up and began to check it out. We soon found that we were wrong about all the Germans having left Mariemont. We came under fire, and I felt a bullet hit my neck. Falling down in the snow, I realized blood was dripping into the snow, and I wondered if my jugular vein had been hit. I was also spitting up blood, but did not pass out. When I got back to my CP, my aid man put sulfa powder on the two holes in my neck and wrapped a bandage around it. I found my voice box wouldn't work. I could make no sound at all! The next day I was taken to a field hospital where they decided to send me to a hospital in Cirencester, England. I flew to London in a C-47 full of wounded GI's, all hurt much worse than I, many in great pain. I felt guilty to be walking around with no obvious wound and in no pain. I couldn't even talk to explain why I was aboard! The specialists at Cirencester knew of no solution for my lack of voice, but in about two weeks my vocal chords began to function again, and soon were normal. Oh, happy day! Christmas in the hospital was pretty bleak, but it was made a lot better by my vocal chords slowly coming back.

My return to the continent and the 36th Div. was upsetting when my barracks bag with all my belongings, including my spare pair of spectacles, was stolen just before I left England. Upon arriving back in France, I reported to the clinic for a pair of spectacles, as was required for nearsighted soldiers. When the optometrist, Captain Gettelfinger, saw the prescription for my glasses, he asked, "How did you get in the infantry with such badly nearsighted eyes?" I had to admit to having memorized enough of the eye chart to pass my physical for OCS at Fort Benning, the Army Infantry School. He said, "Well, you're not going back to the 36th Division. I'm sending you to the transportation section of the 7th Army Headquarters." He had apparently noted my attendance at the Officer's Motor Course at Fort Benning. Can you imagine how upset I was? Oh, happy day!

Shortly after I joined the 7th Army Headquarters in Kaiserslautern, Germany, in the Kaiser Wilhelm Kaserne, I was assigned to find suitable quarters for our transportation section in Darmstadt, Germany. Arriving there, I found the entire center of the city destroyed and learned that our Air Force had conducted a saturation bombing of the city in response to the German Luftwaffe having firebombed the city of Coventry, England. In order to get adequate space for our section I had to go into the suburbs and evict Germans from three large homes. My orders to them were, "Sie mussen bei Mittwoch rausmit (You must be out by Wednesday)." There was no dissent at all; they were happy to realize the war was about over. I soon was promoted to 1st lieutenant and became traffic control officer for 7th Army area. We had men stationed at key road junctions, called Traffic Control Points (TCPs), and at major German army installations, which we utilized as stops for convoys and for major troop movements.

I had a Lieutenant Paul in charge of the Kaiser Wilhelm Kaserne in Kaiserslautern, and the city was also the headquarters of the French troops from Tunisia, the 4th Regiment of Tiralleurs Tunisien (4th RTT). The French had invited the native ruler, the Bey of Tunis, to review his subjects in Kaiserslautern. They threw a big banquet for the bey and invited Lieutenant Paul and me. Of course, we accepted, along with a couple of lieutenant colonels from Eisenhower's headquarters near Frankfurt. The French put on quite a party, and the next day they took the bey to see the Rhine River at Ludwigshaven. His troops were stationed every two or three hundred yards along the way, saluting him as he passed. I was part of the convoy as I returned to Mannheim in my jeep. Mannheim is across the Rhine from Ludwigshaven.

Moving east through Bavaria, southern Germany, we used the Autobahns, Hitler's invention of super highways to facilitate movement of both business and military units around the country. We found fighter aircraft, powered by the first jet engines, parked in revetments along the Autobahn so they could use it for takeoffs and landings. Most of the planes had been strafed by our fighters and were inoperative. My driver and I took pictures of each other in the pilot's seat of one of them. At that time, they were very odd-looking to us, as they had no propellers.

Shortly after we moved 7th Army Headquarters to Augsburg in April 1945, we heard that our 45th Infantry Division had liberated the concentration camp of Dachau, a few kilometers east of Augsburg. We had heard of concentration camps but knew very little about them. I mentioned this to Col. Littell, chief of the Transportation Section, and asked if I should check it out. He said, "By all means. Go over there and see what you can find out." My driver and I took a jeep and went to Dachau the day after the 45th had moved through and gone on east (about April 30). We were the only Americans there that morning and were amazed and shocked by what we found. We went through the entrance gate with the words "Arbeit Macht Frei (Work Makes Free)" in wrought iron over it. We saw the huge guard dogs lying dead where our troops had shot them the day before. Then we went into the headquarters building which was littered with paper and trash from the Germans' hasty departure. I picked up a rubber stamp and an SS sergeant's manual from a desk. He had signed it Sgt. Schultz. Then at the crematorium, a huge furnace shut down the day before, we found a large pile of naked bodies, fifty or more, just skin and bones, probably having starved to death. Their clothes and shoes were stacked in neat piles. On the nearby rail siding, we found a number of boxcars containing hundreds of bodies, apparently shipped in from other camps for cremation. We saw thousands of prisoners in prison garb, many in the last stages of malnutrition walking around like zombies. Later we learned that they were dying at a rate of 25–30 per day. We started to go into one of the barracks buildings, but the stench was so bad, we stopped.

With no prior information, it was impossible to grasp the significance of what we were seeing. Only later did we learn of Hitler's plan to eliminate a whole race of people, the Jews, in his "Ultimate Solution." He had also targeted for elimination many categories of people, so-called "undesirables;" gypsies, homosexuals, Jehovah's Witnesses, mentally retarded, handicapped, etc. The extent to which he succeeded, in the cold-blooded murder of over 11 million men, women, children, in an educated and civilized country, is incredible and frightening.

The Americans who took over management of the Dachau death camp found that the German people in the village of Dachau denied any knowledge of the horror taking place at the camp. The Americans then made the local farmers bring their large horse-drawn farm wagons, load them with the emaciated bodies and drive them through the village. Did this gruesome parade accomplish anything?

Soon after VE day, May 8, 1945, I was sent to Berlin to help with the redeployment of the 82nd Airborne Division to the States to prepare for the upcoming invasion of Japan. They were the garrison troops for the American sector of the 4-way divided city of Berlin, with Russian, British, and French troops in the other three sectors. Basically, it was the Russians in East Berlin and the Allies in West Berlin. While in Berlin, my driver and I went into the underground bunker where Hitler and his lover, Eva Braun, and the Paul Joseph Goebbels family all committed suicide as the Russians were entering the city. We could travel anywhere in the city, so we saw the Reichstag, the Brandenburg Gate and other points of interest.

One evening we went to Freidrichs Platz, in the Russian sector, to see the huge black market operation. This was happening because the Russian soldiers were loaded with invasion marks, the temporary money of exchange. The soldiers of all four countries were paid in invasion marks, all very similar except for identification letters and serial numbers. In fact, I've been told that President Roosevelt and Treasury Secretary Morgenthau agreed to allow our printing plates to be used by the Russians to print their marks. Allied soldiers could convert their marks to their own country's money, in our case dollars, and send it home, up to the amount we were paid. But the Russians were not allowed to convert their marks to rubles and send it home. Also, most of them had been paid in a lump sum for long periods of service, many for years. So, they were frantically trying to buy anything of value, and small, to carry back to Russia. Watches and jewelry were much in demand, and the Germans were selling anything small they could bring, including door knobs! As we watched, all of a sudden some Russian soldiers, with their submachine guns leveled at us, motioned us to come with them. Two GIs, captured by the Russians in Berlin! They took us to a small cellar room, lighted by a single light bulb hung from the ceiling. An elderly German interpreter assisted a Russian major in charge. After some time cooling our heels and wondering if we'd ever be heard from again, we learned that we were being charged with participating in the black market. We denied the charge, but thought, so what? Were they so determined to restrict its activity for the benefit of the Russian soldiers? We had initially been unable to communicate, as the German did not speak English, and we didn't speak much German. But I found that the German spoke pretty good French, and I did too. But we weren't getting anywhere with the major. Finally, after a few tense minutes, my driver pulled out his cigarettes and fortunately had three left. With the Russian major, the German interpreter, and the American GI lighting up, the tension broke, and the major signaled for us to be gone! Their little game was a typical Russian maneuver of intimidation. They were letting the Allied soldiers know who was in charge!

Later, they tried the same trick by closing all the roads to Berlin, hoping to starve the Allies out and take over the whole city. Fortunately, we had access to Tempelhof Airdrome, and President Truman ordered the Berlin Airlift which supplied West Berlin until the State Department (or the War Department) got it straightened out.

During a little more than a year in the Army of Occupation and being promoted to captain in December 1945, I was fortunate to travel in Europe quite a bit. On a Swiss-Rome tour, Captain Jess Dall and I drove a jeep to Paris for a couple of days. We then drove to Basel, Switzerland, to join the tour. We visited Zurich, Thun, and Lucerne in Switzerland. In Lucerne (or possibly Thun), I made a deal with a jewelry shop owner for a couple of fine Swiss watches, the latest thing in calendar watches, a Movado, for me, and a fine gold lady's watch for Martha. We had been restricted by the Swiss government as to the amount of money we could bring in (something about upsetting their economy if they allowed the thousands of GI tourists to bring in unlimited funds) so I did not have enough Swiss francs to pay for them. But a practically new officer's trench coat swung the deal! Apparently, the war had limited the supply of textiles in Switzerland.

While in Switzerland, I had the opportunity to make a telephone call to Martha in Greensboro, courtesy of the American Red Cross. Overseas calls were quite a rarity at that time so the Vick Chemical Company telephone operator got pretty excited. She hollered, "I've got a call from Switzerland on my line for Martha!" Mr. McNeil, the accounting department chief, told Martha to take the call in his office. He was a very considerate southern gentleman. Martha and I were thrilled to hear each other's voice after almost two years of separation. I also called my mother in Valle Crucis, in the North Carolina mountains. This was noteworthy enough that it was reported in the *Watauga Democrat*, Boone's weekly newspaper, and Mother was quoted as saying she could hear me quite clearly, all the way from Switzerland!

We went by rail to Rome via Milan. In Milan, we saw the Esso Station where the Italian partisans hanged Mussolini and his paramour, Clara Petacci. We also saw Michelangelo's *Last Supper* which he had painted in a small church. One evening in Rome while having dinner in the Hotel Maestoso, who should I see coming down the aisle but my old college buddy from North Carolina State University, Captain Bill Corbin of the Corps of Engineers. I have a picture of us made at that time.

Riding on the Autobahn one afternoon, Captain Hank Blackwell and I came across a GI Harley-Davidson motorcycle with its unit identification painted out. It was out of gas. An AWOL GI had probably stolen it. When we got back to Mannheim, we asked our motor pool sergeant to take a truck and bring it back. He did so and put our unit designation on it. It became, unofficially, Captain Farthing's and Captain Blackwell's motorcycle. We enjoyed riding our "hog" around Mannheim and on the Autobahn. One of the few pictures I have of me during this time is of me astride our motorcycle.

Shortly after VE day, May 8, 1945, I took a trip into the Black Forest, an area known for the work of German craftsmen: cuckoo clocks, music boxes, etc. With a local boy as my guide, we went to a small plant that made a singing bird in a gilded cage. The owner was out of business and had only two units left. One was his shop model, the other belonged to his wife, and he would not sell either. My guide suggested we pick up a nice alarm clock at another shop, and then wait at the train station for the *Orient Express* train, which had recently resumed operation. We traded the clock to a dining car steward for a kilo of butter, which had not been available in Germany for a long time. With the butter added to a generous offer of marks, we made the deal. I don't know which of the two models I got, but 60 years later, it still works. The tail feathers and the bird's beak move as it sings. It will sing continuously or intermittently in a very natural manner.

One of my jeep trips in Bavaria took me to the prison in Bad Tolz where Hitler had been imprisoned in the 1920s. I made a point of going

Captain Glenn Farthing enjoyed many rides on this GI Harley-Davidson motorcycle in France. He and a friend found the motorcycle abandoned on the Autobahn, so they confiscated it. Glenn, a Valle Crucis native, married his high school sweetheart, Martha Harris, on December 31, 1943. By September 1944 he was crossing Omaha Beach into France. He returned to Martha and in December 2004 Glenn and Martha celebrated 61 years of marriage (photograph furnished by Glenn Farthing).

into his cell where he wrote his life's story and spelled out his philosophy in *Mein Kampf* [*My Struggle*]. This was about the time he changed his name from Adolf Schickelgruber to Adolf Hitler. No doubt he was impressed by Josef Dugashvili having changed his name to Joseph Stalin some time earlier. Both ruthless tyrants understood the power of public image.

Heidelberg was the only German city of any size that I spent some time in that was never bombed or shelled. It is an old university city which had no targets of military significance. Its only wartime scar was the center span of the Neckar River Bridge which the Germans dropped as they retreated.

Shortly after my 24th birthday, June 24, 1946, I received orders to report to Bremerhaven, Germany, in order to return to the States. Hallelujah! Finally! Arriving there, I was put in charge of a packet of about 250 men also happily anticipating a short trip home. With three other packets, we boarded the *Mahanoy City* Liberty Ship in mid–July and set sail for the good ole USA. The ship's speed was only 10–12 knots so it was a slow passage across the North Atlantic. Each morning I had to inspect my men's quarters below decks, then find a spot on deck where Lieutenant Jack Reinhart and I would play cribbage with Captain Art Holst and Lieutenant Bill Flynn. I still have the cribbage board on which we kept score, and it shows that Farthing and Reinhart beat Flynn 67 games to 56 during our slow voyage from Bremerhaven to New York July 8th to 17th, 1946.

Martha and her dad, Stanley A. Harris, were on the dock when our little vessel tied up, and I waved to them from the ship's rail before my packet disembarked. Oh, happy day!

During Army Separation procedures at Camp Kilmer, New Jersey, I elected to stay in the Army Reserves. Five years later in May 1951, I was recalled to duty during the Korean War. By that time, Martha and I had two children, and the third was on the way. Had he already been born, I would have had four dependents, the number which allowed a reserve officer to decline the honor of serving again. I reported to the Transportation School at Fort Eustis, Virginia, where I was assigned to the Combined Arms Section. Rick was born a few months later in the base hospital, but that wasn't good for a discharge. I was already on active duty. My section taught officer classes all the subjects not specifically relating to transportation, infantry, artillery, armored, etc. I had an engineering degree from North Carolina State University, so I became instructor of atomic, biological, chemical, and radiological warfare. Since we had ended World War II by dropping atomic bombs on Hiroshima and Nagasaki, Japan, my main focus was on atomic and radiological warfare. At that time, 1951, we were hard at work on the H-Bomb, and I was allowed to mention to field grade officer classes, majors, and colonels, the possibility of a bomb far more powerful than the A-Bomb.

Our year and a half at Fort Eustis allowed us to visit some very important sites from our country's earlier years, Jamestown, Yorktown, Williamsburg, Mt. Vernon, Richmond, and others.

In November 1952, I was discharged and returned to Greensboro, N.C., where I resumed my career in the engineering department at Burlington Industries, soon to become the largest textiles manufacturing company in the world.

A remarkable coincidence occurred at the birth of our first child, Edwin, in July 1947. During her pregnancy, Martha had been under the care of Dr. Frank Sharp, one of Greensboro's leading obstetricians. When her labor pains started, I took her to Wesley Long Hospital, across the street from our apartments at 369 North Elm Street. She had called Dr. Sharp's office and was informed that a young doctor recently added to Dr. Sharp's practice would take over as Dr. Sharp, president of the North Carolina Medical Association, was out of town at the annual AMA convention. She was a little upset but had no choice. When Dr. Reed Wood showed up at the hospital to examine Martha, she noticed that an unusual look showed on his face and on mine when we first saw each other. She was even more concerned about this stranger having to take over at the last minute. He and I left the room and were gone for some time. The issue was happily resolved when I returned to tell her that I was renewing acquaintance with Dr. Wood, who was one of the Army doctors who had treated me in the hospital in England. He wanted to see the scars on my neck from my bullet wound in Mariemont, France.

Ed's birth proceeded normally under Dr. Wood's supervision, and a week later, I used a wheelchair to take Martha across the street, accompanied by Martha's mother, Mary Harris, carrying the baby.

Sometime early in my life, a Chinese fortune cookie had predicted that I would set foot on the land of many countries. How did they know? In World War II, I was in many countries in Europe. With Burlington, I have been in many countries in Europe, Central America, and Asia. The total number is now over 40 countries and counting! How did they know?

Martha and I have been so marvelously blessed by the good Lord above who has given us four wonderful children, Eddie, Betsy, Rick, and Stan, ten beautiful grandchildren, and a little charmer of a great-granddaughter. December 2004 we celebrated 61 years of wedded bliss, and counting!

Basketball or Bullets

Len Stokes

As told to Catherine Stokes Sheppard in July 2000.

After I finished high school I attended ASU for two and a half years. I suppose I had what is called the sophomore slumps. Anyhow, I thought I would like to see the world so I joined the army. Soon I was looking at the world of Ft. Jackson, South Carolina. I had played basketball in high school and college and really loved the sport. Pretty soon I found my feet taking me pretty often to the gym at Ft. Jackson and shooting a few hoops or scrimmaging a little. One day an officer approached me in the gym, talked a little sports chatter, and then asked me if I would like to be on Ft. Jackson's team. I was shocked and I suppose a little flattered. Anyhow, he told me that if I would come by his office the next day and sign some papers I could stay at Ft. Jackson and play basketball until my tour was up. This sounded almost too good to be true! I went back to my barracks with my head spinning.

The following day I set out for his office, which was at the far end of the base from my barracks. Strolling Ft. Jackson in the hot summer sun and sand is not something you do for fun. Anyhow, I got to the building and learned that his office was at the end of the hall about as far as I could see. Oh, well! What a break, what the heck. I got almost to his office and I got hit with the biggest streak of patriotism (or it could have been guilt) you can imagine. I thought about how my brother, Roger, had died in the South Pacific; my brother Ralph had been a prisoner in Europe; my brother Bill had just come home from Japan; and my brother Landon was still in Korea. How would I be able to face these brothers? Then and there I made a decision. I turned around and went back the long journey I had just come.

Pretty soon I was on my way to Korea and when I was in the trenches and the bullets were flying around my head all I could think about was what an utter idiot I was. I could still be at Ft. Jackson, playing basketball, going home every weekend and living like a real person. I often said to myself, "Len, you may not be the best soldier in the U.S. Army, but you sure are the biggest fool." If somebody asked me what I thought about when I was under fire I could answer in one word. "Basketball!"

Richard Minton Remembered

Nannie Greene

This profile of Richard Minton was compiled after conversations with Willis Farthing in 2005.

Willis Farthing and Richard "Shorty" Minton were good friends in the 1940s at Cove Creek High School. Shorty was anything but short; he played center on the basketball team where he and Willis were teammates. In high school they enjoyed hanging out together and they both graduated in 1947. After graduation, they worked long enough to draw unemployment benefits during their second summer out of school. They became even closer friends after that.

Richard and Willis were drafted into service and both ended up in Korea in 1952. Willis's mother wrote Willis about Richard's whereabouts and gave him the address, but they were never able to get together. By the time Willis located Richard's unit, he found out that Richard had been killed by Chinese machine fire. Losing his friend was extremely painful for Willis.

In the fall of 2002, Willis had a dream about Shorty, and he felt sad for days. During this time, Willis received a notice about his high school class reunion. This notice also included information about the new windows needed for the now historic Cove Creek High School. Willis decided that buying a window would be a perfect memorial for Richard, his high school buddy and Army pal. The plaque under the window will be a lasting testi-

Lifetime friendships are often begun in high school. A team sport always strengthens such friendships. Willis Farthing and Richard Minton were on the Cove Creek High School basketball team in 1947, and they were good friends. From the left are Coach Sam Osborne, Willis Farthing, Richard Minton, Jimmy Mast, Len Stokes and Lee Greene (photograph furnished by Nannie Greene).

mony of their friendship and a memory of the supreme sacrifice Richard made for his country.

Jackie "Deacon" Mast

Nannie Greene

From an interview with Jackie "Deacon" Mast in 2004.

Jackie Mast left the Cove Creek community where he lived with his grandparents, Myrtie and Lee Mast, in October 1950. He joined the army and was assigned to the 45th Division of Company G in the 180th Infantry. He received his basic training in Louisiana at Camp Polk, now known as Fort Polk. It was there on a training mission that he earned his nickname, which followed him all the way through his army career. This is the way he says it happened:

> We marched out into a field where we had our classes. We had class for 50 minutes and then we had a 10-minute break. During one of these classes I had made

> a silver cross from a paper in a cigarette pack. I taped it on my helmet like I had seen on a Chaplain's helmet. Now I was a not so smart 17 year old and a very young soldier. When I saw the platform there for the instructor and his charts, it reminded me of a pulpit. So during the break after class, I jumped up on that platform and I said, "Let me have your attention, please." I took out a little New Testament that I was carrying in my pocket and read a couple of paragraphs. I continued with my speech. "Guys, we have been hearing a lot about the war in Korea, how they are going in there and clean up that mess, and then get out, but I don't know about that. Something is telling me that is not what is going to happen, and that we are going to be right in the middle of it. Now the chances are that a lot of us won't be coming home. When I was 15 years old, I was saved, and the Lord told me then that He would look after me, and I believe him. So if you will put your trust in Jesus Christ, He will take care of you, too. Even if you don't get back, you will be all right because you will be in a better place than you are right now." It was then that the instructor walked up behind me and said, "O.K., Deacon, your time is up." From that time on, everybody called me Deacon as long as I was in the Army.

Jackie and the 45th Division of Company G arrived in Korea in October of 1951. His duty was to man the 57 mm recoilless rifle. This was a heavy rifle about 5 feet long. One assistant, Merlyn Reed, was assigned to him and they became best friends. There were also 3 ammo bearers and each carried six rounds for the rifle at a time. The maximum range of the recoilless rifle was 4800 yards with an effective range of about half that. It was definitely an accurate weapon, but when he learned to use the scope, it became deadly. It was the instant artillery for the company.

A picture of Jackie and his friend Merlyn with the recoilless rifle hangs in a museum in Oklahoma City, Oklahoma. There is snow on the ground in that picture.

His company spent the winter in the mountains of North Korea, about 10 to 15 miles above the 38th Parallel. Sometimes it was 30 degrees below zero. He spent time on several hills there. The first one was Old Baldy where they lost forty-some men, and then Bunker Hill. Kelly Hill was next and that was where they spent most of the winter. They moved on to Pork Chop Hill before going to T-Bone Hill where their company was completely destroyed. Records show they saw combat 147 consecutive days.

T-Bone Hill was farther north than any of their other outposts. The Chinese had an outpost there and they kept moving in more and more equipment, and they were firing directly at our lines. The American general officers decided to put a stop to that. So on June 12, 1952, Company G was given the task of taking over that outpost. At 9 o'clock they pulled out from their camp and by 12:00 noon the Americas had control of that hill, or so they thought. What they did not know was that about 3,000 Chinese had encircled the hill and had completely cut them off. The Chinese started coming down in waves, one group right after another. All afternoon they came. About 4 o'clock, when the Americans were all out of ammunition, everything became quiet, and the Chinese started going away. They thought everyone was dead. That day only 18 of the 200 men in Company G walked away. Those 18 men went back to their MLR (Main Line Resistance.) The next day Company E went back to T-Bone Hill. On the second day the 18 survivors of Company G joined Company E on T-Bone Hill, where they stayed for a week without anyone relieving them. All their commanding officers had been killed, so they had no leader. If they had left their post they would have been considered deserters. That turned out to be a disaster. In other areas of North Korea there were American Marines and troops from the Philippines, Greece, and Turkey, but they didn't run into each other.

The first casualty of the battle was the commander of their company. He was walking along with Jackie, who was carrying the recoilless rifle. The enemy was after that gun. They didn't get the gun, but the commander was killed. They went on without their company commander because they had a job to do, and they did it. Jackie had trusted the Lord to take care of him and so far he had done it. He said he knew the enemy was after that gun all the time, but something kept telling him when to move and when to stay put. There were times when he had just moved from a spot and it would blow up the next minute. He felt very blessed that God let him get out of that country alive. He said that after the T-Bone massacre, he and many of his soldier friends had given up any hope of getting out alive.

Jackie started looking for the machine gun that had killed the commander. He could see where the fire was coming from, but he was not in a position to get to it. Their company was on one hill and the machine gun was on a hill on the other side of a valley between them. Alone, with the gun on his shoulder and the ammunition in his hand Jackie zigzagged across that valley (about 100 yards) and kept going until he got behind a little knoll. He laid his weapon down, loaded it and locked it in, and then put it on his shoulder. He could see where the machine gun was, so he fired. The first shell went over the bunker. He adjusted his sight and fired again. The second shot hit the bunker, but just for good measure, he fired the third shot. That time he saw nothing except a white mushroom cloud and he knew he had succeeded. His company was already moving forward so he joined them in the rear.

For that deed, Jackie received a Bronze Star with a V for valor. When asked who pinned it on him, he said a division general did. He received two other Bronze Stars for distinguished Korean service, and 10 recognitions in all. Jackie was most impressed by the Combat Infantryman Badge given to the members of the 180th Regiment for the 147 consecutive days of contact with the enemy. He was also issued a Presidential Citation. Jackie says that winning medals was never on his mind. He was kept busy trying to stay alive.

After the T-Bone Hill battle, he went back to South Korea, where they formed a new company from basic trainees, casualties and leftovers. Jackie was made platoon sergeant of this heavy weapon platoon. He was in charge of two other sergeants and they trained 36 men. He personally trained the men how to use the recoilless rifle because of his hands-on experience with it. He worked with that platoon until he left Korea.

Jackie returned to the States in October of 1952. He was sent to Fort Benning, Georgia, where he was an OCS instructor. He trained men to use the recoilless rifles because of his knowledge of that weapon. Jackie thinks the recoilless rifle was the best weapon the Army had, but they discontinued using it. They thought the weapon was inconvenient to carry, and it was hard to keep ammunition to it if you were on the move. It was definitely an accurate weapon. Jackie was an instructor at Ft. Benning until October of 1953, when he came home.

Jackie's best friend, Merlyn Reed, got hepatitis while he was in Korea and was sent to the hospital in Japan. They never saw each other again. After Jackie came home, he tried to contact Merlyn in his home in Louisiana, but he could never find him. A few years ago, Rev. Doug Robinson moved to Cove Creek, next door to Jackie. One week Doug was going to the same town where Merlyn had lived, and Jackie asked him to try to find out what had happened to his buddy. Doug found Merlyn's widow, but she had never heard him mention Jackie Mast. Finally Doug said, "Well, did you ever hear him mention Deacon?" "Oh, yes! It was Deacon this and Deacon that." She said that Merlyn had died of a heart attack at the age of 47. Later Jackie gave her a call personally. At last he had found news of his friend after 50 years.

Jackie, for a little boy from this small Cove Creek community, you did a man-sized job for which we all want to thank you. We, too, are thankful you came home safely.

Vietnam

John Adams in Vietnam

John Adams

This reminiscence was recorded by Catherine Stokes Sheppard in 2000. John Adams lives in Vilas.

I was 22 years old when I went into the Navy in 1968. A short while after my basic training I was in Vietnam, where I was assigned to a river gunboat. These gunboats were 36 feet long. We were a crew of five and I was the gunner. However, we were each trained to do any job that was required on the gunboat. After all, if one of us was in any way incapacitated the job still had to be done.

Our job was to patrol the river and try to prevent arms and other military supplies from getting to the Viet Cong. We stopped everything from junks to large fishing boats. Part of my training had been alongside Navy Seals. Consequently, when a large vessel came along I had to swim under it to see if contraband was carried there. We often boarded a craft that looked like a harmless family of fishermen (wife and children) only to find that they, too, were smuggling arms.

Part 4: People Who Made a Difference

It is a very common practice for adults at sometime in their lives to reflect on past events that have shaped their lives. In so doing these individuals often realize that certain people have had a memorable impact on them. Sometimes the person remembered may have been a parent, a teacher, a religious leader or simply someone in the community who had the respect of many. With this in mind when we began our endeavor to glean stories, we asked in our brochure for people to tell about persons in our area that had made a difference in the lives of others.

As we read the stories we were impressed not only with how many people in our Western Watauga area were deemed important, but also what a wide variety of interests were represented. Certainly it was not difficult to find stories about influential citizens.

Interesting, though not surprising, is the fact that many that are remembered as having made a difference were in the field of education. One man recalled was a farm youth who literally worked his way through college and went on to become a county superintendent of schools at age twenty-eight. The boy who had never been stopped by lack of funds became the man who at the height of the Depression launched a gigantic building program of school buildings. Soon his innovative projects had resulted in pulling Watauga County Schools from the state's lowest rank to near the top. Other educators remembered were teachers of agriculture who were able to introduce their students to the outside world as well as to ways to improve their farms. A teacher of the language arts inspired her students to be proud of the storytelling legacy from their forefathers. She inspired her students to want to read and to love knowledge. But perhaps no teacher inspired students more than a dedicated basketball coach. Several former students gave statements regarding the influence they felt from a man who taught them life skills. From him they learned discipline, team work, fairness, mutual respect, and constructive solutions.

Some community leaders are remembered as helping to mold the lives of young people. One was a Sunday school teacher and church youth leader; another was a nurse who rose in the ranks to become a first Ph.D. in nursing. She was a tremendous influence on her siblings and cousins. One lady probably changed the lives of many people who never knew her. She willingly allowed herself to use a trial medication which later was widely used to treat cancer.

The evolution of a community is a slow, silent process but it is the people in the community who work for the betterment of all that keep the process moving forward. We see in this chapter how it is the small, un-noticed deeds in the day to day grind of living that often make such an impact on many people.

Miss Jennie Love

Ben Mast

Ben Mast lives in Washington, D.C. This story was submitted in 2003.

Cove Creek High School was blessed with many fine teachers from the beginning. But generations of admiring students agree that one of the finest was Jennie Dare Love, or simply "Miss Love," who began her thirty-nine-year teaching career at Cove Creek in 1934. In defining the mysterious alchemy of truly great teaching, both Emerson and Dostoyevsky believed, "It is not the intellect that matters most but the character that guides it."

Some of Miss Love's distinguishing traits—spirited determination, dedication, modesty, and love of knowledge—can be traced to her Appalachian Mountain roots. Also, because her life spanned much of the twentieth century, her outlook was profoundly tempered by the epochal events of those times: Depression and poverty, bloody world conflicts, nuclear confrontation, and Cold War.

"I am a part of all that I have met," Jennie quotes Tennyson in crediting others for her accomplishments, especially her close-knit family. She was born in 1910 on Rush Branch in the Laurel Creek Township of western Watauga County. Her father, Dr. Jack Love, taught her names of Appalachian flora and fauna as he took her on horseback to make house calls along tributaries of the Watauga River. He also encouraged her studies at the local one-room elementary school on Ivy Ridge, and later, because roads were primitive, provided room and board so she could attend high school at Cove Creek.

Jennie Love was a good student and rose to become class valedictorian and editor of *The Coveteer*, the Cove Creek yearbook. An entry by her senior classmates in the 1930 annual attested to other hallmarks of character that distinguished Jennie Love both as student and teacher: " [She] has a personality that wins with everybody. She is quiet, unassuming and dignified. She does her work in a superior manner and never shirks."

Although describing herself as "green as grass and nearly as poor as the proverbial church mouse," Jennie rode a bus from Boone to Greensboro and enrolled at the Woman's College of the University of North Carolina, where she earned the nickname "Love from Sugar Grove, Kraut country." But with grit and determination to succeed, she made top grades as an English and French major. A literature professor commended her essay on Robert Browning as the best in all his years of teaching. In it she admired the poet's abiding optimism and faith in one's capacity to grow:

Jennie Love, a Cove Creek High School graduate, returned to teach there for more than 30 years. She was an excellent teacher of French and English and also established one of the finest libraries in the county. She was the sponsor of the school newspaper, ***The Wachovian***, and the school year book, ***The Coveteer***. Many years she was director of the commencement exercises and directed numerous dramas. This photo was made in July 1996. Her nephew, Doug Love, brought Miss Love back to CCHS for a school reunion and one of her rare visits to the school since she left there in 1965 (photograph furnished by Nannie Greene).

"Man must pass from old to new, / From vain to real; from mistake to fact; / From what seemed good to what now proves best."

Following graduation in 1934 she began her teaching career at Cove Creek High School, whose principal was then S.F. Horton. Her main subjects were English and library science, but she was given additional classroom and extracurricular assignments. Her classes were unencumbered by pedagogical formalism or rigid lesson plans based on what today's educators call "standards-based, constructivist, collaborative learning." Instead, the daily lesson plan was often the point of departure for a free-ranging exploration of human triumph and tragedy not only as reflected in great literature, but also in topics of current interest.

From the outset, her senior high school subjects seemed awed by what they described as Miss Love's "quiet dignity" and "decorous composure," and so there were virtually no problems with unruly students. "There was a certain presence about me that made for great respect, an awareness that there were limits that all of my pupils were aware of.... Maybe that's the reason I had no discipline problems to speak of," she later reminisced.

However, that "presence" was nothing short of charisma as the ancient Greeks defined it: a special gift divinely conferred on one to inspire the minds of the many. Underneath Jennie's seemingly stern persona was a gentle style that compelled students, even the most jaded, to lean forward to catch the nuanced phrasing of her daily discourse. As George Farquhar put it, "Charming women can true converts make, / We loved the precepts for the teacher's sake." Miss Love's fervent devotion to teaching instilled in us a lifelong respect for learning.

Among her storehouse of "teacher's aids" was Jennie's unique gift of humor. She drew upon the jocularity of Chaucer or Shakespeare, the irony of Dickens, the satire of Goldsmith, and the sarcasm of Swift to spice up discussion. Whether in the form of riposte or acerbic commentary, her sense of humor could be urbane and literary but also laced with frontier drollery.

Sometimes Miss Love's wit morphed into Socratic irony, of which I was once recipient. One morning our classroom was warmed by the pyrotechnics of Jonathan Edwards' *Sinners in the Hands of an Angry God:*

> O sinner! Consider the fearful danger you are in: It is a great furnace of wrath, that you are held over in the hand of that God, whose wrath is provoked and incensed as much against you, as against many of the damned in hell.

When she asked what we thought hell was like, I volunteered: "It's a 'fiery pit,' just as Edwards says...." "But how do you know?" she shot back. "Have you been there?" The class dissolved in laughter.

In addition to the red pencil, Jennie also used humor to illuminate the tricky mechanics of English grammar. For example, she gave us quotes by people in the local community and asked us to unscramble the misplaced modifiers: "Hand me that little black pan with the handle hanging on the wall." Also, "That boy was beating my old hen with a stick that was ready to hatch!"

Beyond technique and form, Miss Love encouraged us to probe the mind of the writer. Why was April for T.S. Eliot "the cruelest month?" What was behind Jonathan Swift's savage irony in *Gulliver's Travels*? What passions moved Emily Dickinson to versify that "Parting is all we know of heaven and all we need of hell"? Suddenly we were as one with the author, sensing the exultation, sorrow, affection, loathing, humor, or despair which fueled such outpourings.

Miss Jennie's teaching also was suffused with a strong sense of humanity and compassion, and she did not hesitate to speak out against prejudice. She voiced indignation at hearing of ethnic slurs against one of her most brilliant students, whose father had moved to Watauga County from another part of the country. After quoting from this girl's Haiku-like assignment, "Snowflake ballerinas all in white, / They've pirouetted out of sight," Miss Love commented with a pained expression, "How could anyone make ugly remarks against the composer of such divine works?"

Jennie Love rekindled in her high school students the childhood curiosity so often lost during the boisterous, "know everything" teen years. She made the study of literature, especially poetry, come alive by unraveling the mysteries of writing techniques, introducing us to such magic words as "iambic pentameter" and "onomatopoeia," then having us exercise what we had learned. One class compiled its own version of Canterbury Tales; another chronicled diary entries in the piquant manner of Samuel Pepys. These compositions have been dug out of trunks and reread many times over the years with fond memories.

An imaginative teacher, Miss Love organized special dramatizations, simulated radio broadcasts, and used other innovations that made each student feel important and want to offer his or her talents. She also invited speakers to make presentations. One memorable guest was storyteller Ray Hicks, who was then unknown to the outside world and of such modest means Miss Love paid for his transportation to the school. Hicks was a sensational success, so much so other high school audiences demanded to hear his spellbinding folk tales. Who knows? Perhaps his rise to legendary "national treasure" status began with Miss Jennie's early recognition of him as a unique part of our local literary fabric.

Jennie Love was scholarly but certainly did not live in an ivory tower; her upbringing and frontier spirit would never allow that. She was erudite without being bookish, yet her love of books served her well as probably the finest public school librarian in Watauga County. A very private person, Jennie was, in her own quiet way, a "woman's libber" long before the phrase found coinage. She marched to her own drummer—not an easy feat in surroundings which beg conformity. The pole star by which she set her compass stood for moral integrity, sincerity, fairness—exceptional attributes for any professional woman, especially a teacher.

The bond forged between a great teacher and inspired student endures long beyond school days. Countless CCHS alumni have paid homage to Miss Love over the years with letters and visits expressing gratitude and reliving poignant memories. "Forty years after we graduated," one admirer wrote in tribute, she and her reunited classmates "quoted passages of literature we had learned in Senior English" even though they had not been required!

After a long absence I returned to the beloved mountains wondering if Miss Jennie would recall my name or even wish to see me. After all, I had been what she called "an erratic student." I had also let her down as Cove Creek's debater in the state contest. (Maybe that's why she inserted a quote by Demosthenes in my commencement address; he'd also had a shaky start as an orator!)

When I telephoned and asked how she was faring, Miss Love summoned words from *As You Like It*: "Oh," she chuckled, "I guess I'm in Shakespeare's 'seventh age' of 'mere oblivion,'—'Sans teeth, sans eyes, sans taste,'" she said with a chuckle, displaying her famous gift for the apposite turn of phrase. "But I carry on," she added, remembering Edna St. Vincent Millay's verse: " 'Life must go on; I forget just why.' " She also very much remembered me. "I have followed your accomplishments—and those of other students of mine—very closely," she said, and began asking questions about my travels. We amused each other with anecdotes and quips as if our conversation had not been broken by the hiatus of a half-century.

"Learning," said Aristotle, "is an ornament in prosperity, a refuge in adversity, and a provision in old age." Jennie Love lives in quiet retirement at the edge of her beloved "woods dark and deep," and despite the ravages of age and afflictions, holds her head high with Browning's "wholesome outlook." Her mind is as keen as ever, and like the "gray spirit" of Tennyson's Ulysses, "yearning in desire to follow knowledge like a sinking star, beyond the utmost bound of human thought." She reads widely, follows world, national, and local news, and watches sports events on TV.

Goethe wrote, "A teacher who can arouse a feeling for one single good action, for one single good poem, accomplishes more than he who fills our memory with rows on rows of natural objects, classified with name and form." So it was with Jennie Love, who made an immense difference in our lives because she instilled an appreciation not only of literature and language, but also of the eternal verities that undergird them. A quote from

Robert Frost that might apply to her own life recalls how Miss Love inspired greatness in the many generations fortunate enough to have sat in her classroom. She would have each of her students be able to say of his or her life: "I took the road less traveled by, and that has made all the difference."

W.R. Trivett: Appalachian Pictureman

Ralph E. Lentz II

Ralph E. Lentz II, author of W.R. Trivett, Appalachian Pictureman: Photography of a Bygone Time *(McFarland, 2000), submitted text and photographs in 2001.*

The death of W. R. Trivett on August 3, 1966, took up little more than nine lines in Avery County's only newspaper, *The Avery Journal*: "Willie R. Trivett, 81, of Elk Park, Rt. 1, was dead on arrival at a Marion Hospital last Wednesday night after suffering a heart attack. Mr. Trivett was a native of Watauga County and a retired farmer. Surviving are the widow...."

W. R. Trivette was a self-taught professional photographer who lived in Western Watauga County through his teen years. His family moved only a few miles away, but it was in Avery County. Mr. Trivette left a legacy of images that are windows into the early history of Watauga County (photograph furnished by Ralph Lentz).

His life, however, filled up an entire book—*W. R. Trivett, Appalachian Pictureman*—published in the first year of the new millennium. This "retired farmer" from Watauga County was also a "pictureman"—one of many self-taught professional photographers who lived in the

W. R. Trivette took pictures that reflect the history of Western Watauga County early in the twentieth century. He was called the Pictureman. This photo shows the aftermath of the flood of 1916 (photograph furnished by Ralph Lentz).

Appalachian region in the first half of the twentieth century. Over 400 glass plate negatives of photographs that Trivett took between 1907 and the late 1940s in rural Avery and Watauga counties survive, and these are to historians W. R. Trivett's greatest legacy.

Born in the Laurel Creek Township of Watauga County (present day Bethel community) in 1884 to Goulder and Martha (Harmon) Trivett, W. R. lived in western Watauga County through the early teens. It was here that he met, wooed, and married the love of his life, Mertie Weaver (1890–1976), also of the Laurel Creek township. In 1917 Willie and Mertie moved to the Flat Springs community of Old Beech Mountain in Avery County. By all accounts W. R. Trivett was a quiet, unassuming man, but he did not live a dull life. In 1934 he was made a deputy sheriff by one of Avery County's legendary sheriffs, W. H. Hughes. Trivett also served as Flat Springs' resident dentist, or at least resident tooth-puller.

The photographs of W. R. Trivett are invaluable windows into western Watauga County's history in the early twentieth century. Among his many images can be found scenes of important local history, one of which records the aftermath of the cataclysmic flood of July 15 and 16, 1916. Taken on Saturday, July 16, on the banks of the Watauga River, the photograph gives a hint of the destruction wrought by the deluge. Watauga County suffered an estimated $200,000 in ruined crops, roads, and property, but no one lost their life.

Perhaps most importantly, Willie's photographs show that the people of western Watauga County were not the isolated, backwards "hillbillies" so often portrayed in the popular mass media. His images show young mountain couples who dressed and acted like other typical Americans of the early twentieth century. As a "pictureman" W. R. Trivett became an unintentional historian, providing us with realistic views of Appalachia and the people who live there.

W. R. Trivett was a man whose life warmly touched all those who knew him, and he left behind a legacy of images that will continue to make a difference to the people of Appalachia for many years to come.

The Golden Girl

Blaine Miller

Blaine Miller shared memories of his wife in this loving tribute, written in 2000.

Geraldine Bingham was never ever a girl who could be described as typical or average. She was a child born with a zest for living and the drive to make things happen. When she was still a small child her father died from injuries sustained in World War I. Although the family received a meager pension it was never enough for more than a modest livelihood. Lack of money never kept Geraldine from pursuing her goals. Among her natural attributes was self-confidence. When she wanted something it never occurred to her that if she worked hard she would not win. So work she did! She was captain of the girls' basketball team, drum major in the band and co-valedictorian of her senior class at Cove Creek High School in 1942.

Months before graduation Gerry was applying for college scholarships. Her academic record and letters from community leaders aided her in being granted a small scholarship to attend Woman's College, University of North Carolina. The ink was hardly dry on her high school diploma when she went to Washington, D.C., to work as a file clerk in the War Department. In the fall she went to Greensboro to enter college and got a job waiting tables in the school dining room. She made it a point to learn the names of all the students in her dorm and her class. She also learned the names of all the professors with whom she came in contact. She, to the utter dismay of

Geraldine Bingham had big dreams and was never afraid of a challenge. To become a part of the first band at Cove Creek High School, Geraldine became its only majorette. This photo was taken in 1942. On the first row, left to right, are Geraldine Bingham, Kathryn Horton, Mary Martha Bingham, Carlton Swift, W. T. Payne, Jr., Bernice Badgett, Carleen Mast, and Mrs. Margaret Fletcher, the band organizer and director. Second row: Fuller Horton, Robert Atkins, Jack Presnell, Tommy Holloway, Jerry Adams, Frank Mast, and Bobby Sherwood. Third row: Grey Bingham, Betty Collins, Mary Hazel Farthing, Mary Frances Church, Bonita Rominger, Rebecca Moore, and Joyce Collins. Fourth row: Ted Eller, Earl Rowe, unidentified, Ross Winebarger, Junior Townsend, David Love, and Leo Mast. Back row: Billy Billings, H.W. Mast, and Jimmy Billings (photograph furnished by Leo Mast).

some, organized a bridge club, made the varsity golf team, and made excellent grades.

In later years Gerry would reminisce about the strict rules at WC (the accepted abbreviation for Woman's College, UNC). The theory was that WC was training young women to be the future leaders of society, setting standards for social advancement. The truth is, they were doing exactly that. The girls had to wear a hat and hose to go out to eat. They had to carry a handbag when shopping and were forbidden to patronize many crummy restaurants in Greensboro. They had to be accompanied by another girl or an escort to leave campus. Marriage was cause for dorm dismissal, along with drinking or similar behavior. It so happens that Geraldine Bingham was the first girl to get married and be allowed to continue as a dorm student. A month later another girl enjoyed the same privilege.

In the summer of 1941 Geraldine met the man who was to become the love of her life. Blaine Miller had gone to Cove Creek to be interviewed for a position as assistant band director at the school. Blaine was still a student at Appalachian State Teachers College when Gerry happened by the home of the principal where the interview was in progress. Although he was quite taken by Gerry, Blaine did not take the job nor ask for a date until December of 1942. What took him so long? Merchant Marines duty, he said.

Dates and partings were always on short notice during those turbulent war years. Soon Gerry became the center for information for her and Blaine's many friends in the service. The service men would write to her and she would relay their news to others. (She may have been the forerunner of Internet!) Also when the guys passed through Greensboro they could count on Gerry to get them a date. She claimed that was her contribution to the war effort! Gerry and Blaine were married March 2, 1945, in Charleston, S.C., just as he was about to be shipped out for parts unknown. A wedding and a honeymoon all in one weekend was fairly common practice during World War II.

While Geraldine was attractive she was not by common definition a great beauty, but she was stunning. Her poise and her self-assurance grabbed and held one's attention. It is not surprising that she was elected as a marshal in her senior year at WC. The following is an excerpt from a letter she wrote to her new husband in September of her senior year:

> Mrs. Roosevelt is coming next week, I can't wait. Hope she is nice. Oh, I didn't tell you. I've been elected Marshal. At WC we don't have a beauty pageant or anything like that, just two senior girls for marshals. The students elect us from a small group previously selected by faculty. Grades play a part but mostly it's 'having those characteristics most becoming to a graduate of WC,' you know, poise, knowing which fork to use and all. The two of us greet celebrities when they arrive, take them to the guesthouse, then chaperone. Can you imagine me chaperoning Mrs. Roosevelt or Mrs. Luce [Clara Booth Luce, U.S. Senate]? Mrs. Luce comes in December, and we introduce the faculty and student leaders to them at the reception. We also usher celebrities in the Art Center and places like that. Graduation isn't for a long time yet but I know you will be proud of me.... I'm so happy.

Gerry's drive to accomplish goals did not end with her college days. When she was about 30 years old she and her husband were living in Spruce Pine, N.C. Their daughter had vision problems and for several months they took her weekly to Johnson City, Tennessee, to the eye specialist that was nearest to them. During this time their son Ron developed severe abdominal pain and had to be rushed to Asheville to the nearest hospital. Johnson City and Asheville just happen to be in opposite directions from Spruce Pine.

Shortly after these events Gerry was in a meeting of the Junior Women's Club. The agenda called for a discussion of projects for the coming year. After much had been said and nothing done, Geraldine Miller stood up and startled the group by saying, "Damn it, what this town needs is a hospital!" The shocked ladies snickered and responded, "It couldn't happen in such a small town!"

Livid by such complacency, Gerry came home more determined than ever. Her husband reports that before she went to bed that night she was heard to say, "By damn, I'll see a hospital built and if anyone of those girls ever needs a hospital, I'll tell them to go to Asheville and stop by hell on the way!" And she meant every word she said.

The next morning Gerry started telephoning during breakfast. She called the mayor, the editor of the *Tri-County News*, the president of the Senior Women's Club, the owner of the textile mill, the state representative and several others and told them there would be a meeting at the club house and they should cancel anything else they might have scheduled and be present. Within three weeks Sid Montague had written a check for $5,000 to cover organizational expenses and to retain a professional fundraiser. My lady lived and breathed hospital, spent countless hours on the phone to Raleigh and Washington as well as to local people. One year later contracts were let for construction and a year after that we had a brand new, fully equipped sixty-bed hospital and I sorta got my wife back. I no longer had to baby-sit five or six nights a week.

Our son Mark was born about midnight in January of 1958 in the new hospital. It was considered an easy birthing and before long Gerry settled in for a good winter's nap. But what do you know, about 30 minutes later (actually it was four hours later) the head nurse was waking her for a morning bath, change of sheets, etc. I won't bother to quote the new mother; it would be censored anyway. But the thing I want to tell you is that the dominant lady on the new board of trustees asked, some said demanded, that the new administrator be brought before the board immediately where he was given a lecture on new motherhood, the trials and tribulations of having a baby, and the lack of any need for a bath when you had been bathed four hours before. As long as we continued to live in Spruce Pine new mothers could sleep late the morning after and could instruct the nurse if they wanted early morning attention during their entire stay.

Come to think of it, I don't remember the head nurse ever speaking to my wife after that, not even in church. As for my girls, they advanced to the Senior Women's Club where they reminded everyone that the idea for a new hospital originated in the Junior Women's Club, and were an active group, you know! Anyway, Geraldine Miller's name is on the plaque that hangs on the wall of the hospital in Spruce Pine.

Today Geraldine Bingham Miller lives quietly on Sullivan's Island (as quietly as one can on an island prone to hurricane attacks) with her husband, who lovingly cares for her every need. Her health, both physically and mentally, is very frail. As Gerry's health began to fail and before any dementia set in, she slipped a note into her husband's income tax records. In it she says: "Please do not grieve for me. I have had a very good life and outlived everyone in my family. I was born wanted, loved, white, bright, attractive, surrounded by aunts, uncles, cousins, who loved me. Blaine and I have had a good marriage, few bad times. We have had you three wonderful kids, two grands, and great in-laws.... I love all of you."

Gerry, Mom

Truly, one person can make a difference. This golden girl did!

Early Recollections of Nora Mast Wilson

Nora Mast Wilson

We compiled the following in 2004 from taped interviews with Nora Mast Wilson and personal acquaintances.

I started to school at Silverstone when I was five years old, a few weeks before my sixth birthday. I walked about a mile, though not alone. As we walked along other children would join in and by the time we arrived at school there would be a big group of us. I attended the Silverstone School which was a two-room school with grades one through seven. For the eighth grade I went to Valle Crucis and boarded with the Finley Mast family. (Today this same house is the Mast Farm Inn.) Several girls boarded there while the boys boarded elsewhere. The school was located near the present Valle Crucis Methodist Church. Back then cash was scarce, so to pay our board we girls helped with the housework and washed dishes, etc. This supplemented the cash payments.

The next year when I was 14 years old I went off to Boone to live in a dormitory and enter ninth grade. By then there was a school at Cove Creek but there was no transportation and I lived too far to walk. (Many Cove Creek students did board in private homes.) My uncle John Mast knew the Dougherty brothers and felt that I should attend their school. I enjoyed my four years at the Appalachian Training School. I found life in a dormitory very different and very interesting. At that time there was one dorm for girls. We ate family style and one teacher sat at each table. We were taught manners as we ate. Boys and girls did not sit together unless they were athletes. Since I played basketball I sat at a long table with girls at one end and boys on the other. Boys and girls did not have much chance to talk to each other so they wrote notes. Because I ate with the boys I became the letter carrier.

The diet was different for the athletes. For instance, athletes were not allowed to eat Karo syrup because it was believed it would alter their breathing. When we finished our meal we had to carry our dirty plates to the kitchen. If there was food left in the kitchen we could have another helping.

I loved sports and I played basketball and was on the tennis team. The girls' basketball uniforms were white middy blouses and black bloomers, black stockings and high top tennis shoes. The tennis uniforms were not too different from today's except for the black stockings.

Mrs. Nora Wilson was always active and usually a leader in community organizations and their projects. She has represented the Cove Creek community well on the local, county, and state levels, and has received many kinds of recognition from all levels. She was one of the first women in the county to own a car, which she drove to school from Zionville to Boone. In her mid-nineties, she was still driving and mowing her own yard, where she grew beautiful flowers that she loved to share (photograph from C.C. Grange collection).

In 1925 I graduated from the then Appalachian Training School. That fall I was 17 years old and I had learned to drive a car. This was most unusual for a woman at that time. I lived at home and drove to Boone to attend Appalachian State Normal School. In the mid–1920s the roads were pretty bad even in good weather. So for the winter quarter I lived again in the dorm. I graduated in 1928 with a two-year Grammar School Certificate. This was the best available credential until two more years were added and the school became Appalachian State Teachers College.

My first teaching job was at Silverstone where I taught grades three and four. There were three teachers in this school. My salary was $75 a month which was considered a very good salary. The school term was six months. Later I taught at Mabel and had grades five, six, and seven.

By the 1930s times were getting harder and I soon noticed that several children never brought anything for lunch. I began to ponder what I could do to remedy that. I knew they had milk and cornbread at home. So I began to bring a jar of milk and crumble cornbread into it for my lunch. In no time the students all brought something for lunch, many brought milk and bread. We had running water that came from a cool mountain spring, and we would put our milk in this water to keep it cool.

After I married Odes Wilson I only taught a half-year because I was needed on the farm. In general married women back then did not work outside the home.

The Rest of The Story

We believe we would be remiss if we allowed Mrs. Wilson's story to end with only what she told here. We have both known her since we were teenage girls and we are convinced that what she did not tell is just as important as what she did tell!

Nora Wilson has been active in church and community affairs that have been far reaching. She has been a stalwart member of the Cove Creek Baptist Church since she was a young woman. She has taught every age group in Sunday school and received a plaque of appreciation in 1979 for over 17 years of dedicated service as church training director. But her greatest love was working with Women's Missionary Union. Her church recognized this and showed their appreciation for her ministry as WMU director from 1968 to 1997. The Three Forks Association recognized her as the "First Lady of Missions." She also directed Bible school, as she said, "For years and years." She provided and arranged flowers that decorated the sanctuary and other areas of her church many, many Sunday mornings.

When visiting ministers came to Cove Creek there was no question about lodging for the minister and his family; with Nora Wilson, of course. Few churches could boast such a complete set of records as those of the Cove Creek Baptist. In Nora's basement, we are told, there are files that contain a copy of every bulletin or printed program ever produced in that church. Each is filed by date and is easily accessible.

Miss Nora, as she is affectionately called, is a name known throughout Watauga County. In western Watauga there are few who have not known her or have not been influenced by her labors. On December 7, 1988, she was chosen as January's Woman of the Year. She was honored for being council treas-

urer from 1978 to 2000. She was grand marshal in the Cove Creek antique car parade at Farm Heritage Days and also for the Boone Christmas Parade. In 1993 Blue Ridge Electric Membership Corporation gave her a "Certificate of Outstanding Community Service of the Doer's Council in recognition of wise and generous use of abilities and example set in a personal sense of responsibility in society."

Mrs. Wilson even received acknowledgment from the state's governor, James B. Hunt, Jr., for her dedication to providing volunteer service in North Carolina's greatest source, her people. From Northwest North Carolina Development Association she received a scroll in appreciation for outstanding volunteer for Family Living Division in Watauga County.

Another love in Nora's life has always been flowers. She has been an enthusiastic member of the Garden Club. Anyone who enjoys the flower beds beside the intersection at highways 321 and 421 has Mrs. Wilson to thank. In the summer the lane that leads from the highway to Nora's home is a blaze of color from the lilies and other perennials lovingly tended by Nora herself. By the way, in her early 90s she was still driving her lawn and garden tractor, as well as her car.

Not only have her church and garden club benefited from Nora's talents, so has the Extension Homemaker's Club. We are told she has filed complete records of this also. She has been a member of and has kept the "Cove Creek Extension Book" since July of 1932. She has been recognized as an Outstanding Extension Homemaker and for 40 years of outstanding leadership to Farm-City Banquet. She received the volunteer award for "managerial and leadership skills in the Watauga County Cooperative Extension Service."

Nora's life has been full and productive. At 94 she still drives to church every Sunday, attends Grange meetings once a month, and is in charge of part of the Farm-City Banquet program once a year. She is the one people call on when they want to know about the past. Nora is an amazing lady who loves her church, her community, and her independence. What an example she sets!

Newton Banner

Nannie Greene

This profile is based on personal acquaintance and stories from the Banner grandchildren.

It would be unrealistic to have stories of Western Watauga County and not mention Newton Banner (1842–1941). Only official documents would refer to Mr. Banner as Newton. He was called Uncle Newt or Grandpa by most of the local population.

The first Banners came to North Carolina from Wales in the early 1700s. A few years before the Civil War several brothers settled in the area that is now known as Banner Elk. It seems that a man named Banner killed the last elk seen in that region, thus the name Banner's Elk.

Newton Banner was born October 8, 1842 and lived until 1941. When he was a young man Newton and his brother walked to Kentucky to join the army. The Confederate Army would not accept Newton because he was so small. When he presented himself to the Union Army they told him he could join if could whip the biggest man in their outfit. He accepted their challenge, fought the largest man, won, and became a Union soldier. At the end of the war Newt and his brother, who had fought for the South, located each other and began the journey home together. The brother was ill and died on the way home. His boots were much better than Newt's, so Newt took the better boots and brought his brother's body home.

After the war Newt came to Cove Creek met and married Sophronia Mast, whom he always called Fronie. Sophronia was from a prominent Mast family in the area. In 1871 Newt and Fronie set out on a journey to Oregon in a covered wagon (with their cow walking behind the wagon). The trip took three months. None of the family seems to remember why they did not stay in Oregon or how long they were gone. But they did return to Cove Creek and built a house on the George's Gap road in 1890.

To say that Uncle Newt was a colorful character is a gross understatement of fact. Although he was small of stature, he was big of heart. His grandchildren remember his kindness, goodness, and joviality. To mention his name to those who knew him is a sure way to get a funny story. He loved people and loved to entertain them. In his old age he would sit on the front porch and if he saw someone walking on the road he would insist that they come in and eat with him. His grandchildren tell the story about two preachers who were eating with him and he passed them beef tongue. One declined, saying, "I couldn't possibly eat anything that came from the mouth of an animal!" Uncle Newt immediately turned to his wife and said, "Fronie, fry 'em a couple of eggs."

Uncle Newt was a strong Republican, but he decided to attend a Democratic precinct meeting out of curiosity. When a neighbor asked how he felt among all those Democrats he replied, "I felt just like a grain of rice in a barrel of rat turds." Uncle Newt had quite a collection of canes. In his later years, before beginning his walk to the store one day, he reached for one of his canes. By the time he reached a neighbor's house he found himself walking rather unsteadily and he wound up in the ditch. He held up his cane and said, "I should have known this was a Democratic cane!"

Newton Banner built his own house on George's Gap Road in 1890 where he and his wife, Sophronia, reared their children. Newt built houses after he spent four years in military service and received an honorable discharge. On a trip to Gettysburg, Pennsylvania, for a reunion of Civil War soldiers, Newt and his brother, Lum, went to the White House, where they demonstrated buck dancing for President Franklin D. Roosevelt. Newt loved having fun and encouraged others to join him in playing many kinds of games. He enjoyed life as long as he lived, and that was more than 99 years (photograph furnished by the Banner family).

Playing cards was a favorite pastime for Uncle Newt; Rook, Rummy, Pinochle, Poker, or his all-time favorite, Setback. Neighbors were often invited to the Banner home to play Setback. He would play as long as he could get them to stay. But card playing was not condoned by everyone in the community. Some of the elders in the church hinted that they might have to "church" Newt for his card playing. His response was, "Good Luck. If you have any trouble, let me know and I'll hire a lawyer to help ya' out." Checkers was another game Uncle Newt enjoyed playing. The checker table usually sat on the front porch, ready and waiting for any takers.

Helen, his granddaughter, recalls many times of observing his generosity. Some members of Helen's high school class were going on a trip to Washington, D.C. When Uncle Newt found out that she was not going because she did not have the money, he paid for the trip so she would not have to miss it. Once she was driving him along a back road and he saw a little girl who looked very poor. He had Helen stop the car, back up and speak to the child. He reached in his pocket, gave the little girl some money and told her to have her mama buy some cloth and make her a dress. Then he added, "See to it that you go to Sunday school." Helen noted that Grandpa never went to church.

Because Newt was a veteran of the Union Army he received a small pension. This was at a time when few people had pocket money and he had many opportunities to loan money. He had one pocket in his pants that he referred to as "the World." He never carried money in that pocket. If someone asked to borrow money he would show the empty pocket and say, "I don't have a cent in the world." Because everybody knew about his pension he was often approached by people asking for a loan. This prompted him to place a sign in his front yard that stayed there for years. It read thus: "Don't ask me to go your security. Life is one damn thing after another."

Newton Banner loved life. He loved to have people around him and he loved the shot of whiskey he drank every night before retiring. He lived almost 100 years and he lived life to the fullest.

Luther Oliver

Frankie O. Stokes

This profile is based on information given to Catherine Stokes Sheppard by Frankie Oliver Stokes, daughter of Luther Oliver (1904–1987), in 2000.

If anyone had ever asked Luther Oliver to describe himself he probably would have answered modestly, "I'm just an ordinary man." To those who knew him well, he was anything but ordinary.

Luther Oliver grew up in the Mabel community one of three children. In his childhood and youth, times were hard and mountain people learned to make do with what they had. But Lute, as he was called, went one step beyond. He learned to make what he needed for doing. During the Depression he needed a hand plane; consequently, he produced one from scraps of a Model-T Ford and had himself a hand-jointer.

Although Lute was a skilled carpenter, his craftsmanship went far beyond making tools. He was a dreamer and thus an inventor. His greatest joy was taking nothing and making something. What was junk to other people was a treasure to Luther Oliver. He stored scrap metal and wood in his shop and knew where every piece was located. One of his more outstanding masterpieces was making a 12 gauge shotgun from pieces of metal salvaged from the rubble of the burned administration building on the campus of ASU. Because all the wood in the building was burned, Oliver confiscated pieces of chestnut wood from an old cabinet in another ASU building. (Oliver was an employee of ASU for 25 years.) Today this gun is displayed in the Appalachian Cultural Museum.

Firearms were not the only thing Oliver made from scraps, although he did hand make 20. One of the more spectacular items he made was an airplane that probably would have flown except his wife grounded any

Luther Oliver was a dreamer and an inventor who liked to make something out of nothing. On the table in this photo are some of his wares, including a 12-gauge shotgun and a combination dulcimer-autoharp. He also made an airplane, but because of his wife's urging, he never tried to fly it. He created a homemade string trimmer to use on the embankments of the campus at ASU before the manufacturers made one you could buy. He was truly a man ahead of his time (photograph furnished by Len Stokes).

efforts he attempted to take to the air. The plane could boast parts from various parts of farm machinery, salvaged wood, cable, sheet metal and an automobile engine. All this from a man with a fifth grade education but who had a natural bent for engineering.

Music was also an important part of Lute's life. He had a beautiful tenor voice and loved to sing, especially in worship. With this talent and a love of hand-crafting, it was only natural his inventive mind would turn to making musical instruments. He fashioned a dulcimer-autoharp. Some of his lovely instruments were made from curly maple.

While Oliver never confessed the things he may have tried but did not master, we certainly applaud the genius he displayed in the items he constructed.

Ernest and Lena Hillard

Council Main

Council Main submitted this profile of the Hillards in 2003.

There are many unsung heroes in this world and I would include Mr. and Mrs. Hillard on such a list if I were making one. Her work and his both contributed much to the quality of life in our region.

Ernest and Lena Hillard came to Cove Creek fresh from Berea College in Kentucky. She was a registered nurse and he an agriculture teacher. I believe the year was 1940. They had both come from humble backgrounds and worked hard to get an education. They had a first-hand knowledge of living below the poverty line and could relate to the problems of poor mountain people.

No one seemed to know just what Lena's job was or whom she worked for. It appeared to be for a foundation and her boss was a Dr. Gamble. What she actually did was to visit homes in the remote sections of our county and try to teach the married women about birth control. She was welcomed by the women, but the men felt she was a threat. Birth control was not a subject for open discussion in the '40s. Her name was often whispered in negative remarks. However, the good she did outlived her reputation. There is no doubt, she was a woman ahead of her time.

I can best tell you about Mr. Hillard by sharing a letter I wrote to him not long before his death. His daughter asked me to read the letter at his memorial service because she felt it expressed the feelings of many of the students he had taught. I did (July 3, 1999).

Dear Mr. Hillard,

I would like to take this opportunity to thank you for remembering me and taking the time to write to me. It meant a lot to me.

I remember the very first time I saw you and Mrs. Hillard. You with your dark curly hair and she with her blonde hair made such a beautiful couple. This chapter in our lives reaches back around sixty years.

Some things I remember about you is when you loaded fifty agriculture students on the back of Ivy Wilson's fertilizer truck and took us to Raleigh to the State Fair. Boyd Wilson was the driver. (None of us took a change of clothes and we slept in the Fair barn on hay. Few, if any, of us had been east of Wilkes County.) This is a story I have shared with my own family many times. Another time you took us to the tobacco market in Johnson City, Tennessee. Every place we stopped that day the juke box was playing Roy Acuff's Wabash Cannon Ball song. That day was in late November and very cold.

I remember going on field trips to farms. You came to Pottertown and checked on my farm projects. My mother would say, "Get the weeds out of those crops and this yard in order, that teacher may come here today." You were certainly an important man in our eyes.

Once you came to Pottertown on Friday and took me to your home in Vilas, and kept me that night. Early on that Saturday morning Floyd Thomas's father brought him over from Mabel to your house. You said we would go to Charlotte to look at farms, cattle, sheep, and hogs. Mrs. Hillard went with us. It took us all day and half of Saturday night to go to Charlotte and back home. We traveled in your 1936 black Ford. Some of the roads between here and Charlotte were gravel. Floyd and I were your live stock judges that day.

I remember when you bought a new 1939 or '40 Plymouth pick-up truck. You would load our class on that truck and we would go on field trips to cut corn, shuck corn, work with cattle, tobacco, chickens, hogs, horses and many more things. You taught us a lot.

The Hillard family moved to Cove Creek in the 1940s. Ernest Hillard came to teach agriculture at Cove Creek High School, and Mrs. Hillard worked as a counselor to families in the community. Mr. Hillard often took his students on field trips to farms in the community. At times they took out-of-town trips to the State Fair in Raleigh, to the tobacco market in Johnson City, to Charlotte for a cattle-judging contest, or for a wood- working contest in Cranberry. He also managed the cannery, a Cove Creek community project (photograph furnished by Catherine Stokes Sheppard).

One cold morning you were taking four of us to Cranberry, N.C. for a wood working contest. The two bigger boys jumped in the cab of the truck. The other boy and me got in the back of the truck up against the cab so we wouldn't be so cold. We got to Vilas and met a car. You had a little shelled corn in your truck bed; we scraped up a little and got a hand full. When we met that old car we sprayed it with corn. The driver, to our surprise, turned around and came back with his old O.Goo horn wide open. You stopped and he jumped out mad! He said we had thrown gravel on his car. We denied it. You told the man you were very sorry. I bet you knew what we had sprayed him with. We never named it and you didn't either. You were so good to us rowdy old ugly boys.

On some field trips you would fill the truck bed full of boys. Some of the bigger boys would stand behind the back window so you couldn't see. We had one big boy we called Pig. He would stand in the middle of the bed and hold each sideboard and get the truck swaying, trying to turn it over. You would have to stop. We would all stand there like no one had done a thing. If one of the little boys like me had told who did it we might have got a beating or pushed off the back of the truck.

Truly, you have been a help in my life. You have taught me so much. I may have been the first in Pottertown to grow tobacco. You were so considerate and never looked down on me because I was from Pottertown.

I have been privileged to talk with your daughters and get to know them. I admire their integrity and intelligence. I thank God for placing you on this planet we call earth. As long as I live you will be dear to my heart. The entire Hillard family has always been a great blessing to me in many ways and I will never forget you and your family.

Sincerely from your student and friend,
Council Lee Main

John Bingham: A Tribute to a Coach

Dan Isaacs

Dan Isaacs wrote and submitted this tribute to John Bingham in 2004.

John Bingham had a short career as a coach (only five years), but it was a dynamic one. The four year record he and his basketball teams compiled was called by some "the dynasty years." It was impressive, and that record was never again equaled at Cove Creek High School. That "dynasty" record reads as follows.

Year	*Wins*	*Losses*	
1951–52	29	4	ended the year with 19 straight wins
1952–53	33	1	lost only in the regional play-offs
1953–54	34	1	lost in the district finals
1954–55	31	4	went all the way to N.C. Class "A" play-offs

As we thought of people who influenced others, we immediately thought of Coach John Bingham. According to school yearbooks and newspaper articles at least twenty-eight boys played on his teams. Some played only one year, others two or three, but only John Banner played all four years. We contacted as many of these players as we could catch up with and asked them if they would like to write a few words about Coach Bingham. These are the responses we received.

"I met Mr. John Bingham at the beginning of the school year 1951, at Cove Creek High School, I was a freshman assigned to the physical education class. I loved sports, especially basketball, and Mr. Bingham encouraged me to set a goal and become a member of the Varsity Basketball team. Under his guidance, coaching abilities, and hours of practice after school, I became part of a team that made

John Bingham enjoyed only five years as a coach and teacher at Cove Creek High School, but they were filled with excitement. Cove Creek became well known for its winning teams. This is his 1952 championship team. First row (left to right): John Banner, Martin Banner, Albert Harmon, Joe McConnell, and Gerald Greene. Second row: Coach John Bingham, Herndon Mast, Charles Henson, Clay Verne Greene, Johnny Horton, and David Elliott (photograph furnished by Clay V. Greene).

basketball history in that area. We won 67 regular games without defeat and entered the State Finals in 1953 & 1954.

"I have many fond memories of my high school years but my fondest memories are from working under Mr. Bingham who not only taught me the game of basketball and baseball; he taught me the values of hard work, dedication, loyalty and teamwork. He inspired me to stay in school and the importance of not only playing sports but academic achievement as well. I was one of nine children and needed at home to work on the farm. My dad, although a loving dad, did not realize the importance of an education. Without Mr. Bingham's encouragement, I probably would have become a high school dropout.

"I recall one of many lessons Mr. Bingham taught me, he was a strict disciplinarian. Everyone knew the rules or you would be disciplined. Mr. Bingham did not have his "favorites" although he had the ability to make each and every one of us feel special. We usually traveled together on the school bus to all games but for one particular game he gave me permission to drive my own vehicle and take another ballplayer with me with the #1 rule—"no girls allowed." We were foolish, as teenage boys will be, and we took our girlfriends. We left early hoping to arrive before Mr. Bingham and not get caught. When we drove into the parking lot, Mr. Bingham was there.

Bingham's 1953 Tri-County championship team of Red Raiders is shown here. First row (left to right): Johnny Horton, Clay Verne Greene, Martin Banner, John Banner, and George Mast. Coach Bingham is on the end. Second row: Jimmy Swift, Jim West, Doug (Hoss). Henson, Ben Fox, and Marvin Combs (photograph furnished by Clay Verne Greene).

"We were both sure we would be sent home immediately or at the very least 'Benched' for the entire game. To our surprise, Mr. Bingham did not say a word. We both played the entire game. Our punishment came the next day; we were called out early not to practice basketball but to listen to a stern lecture on obeying the rules and then we ran 500 laps around the school gym. He allowed us to remain a member of the team. I guess Mr. Bingham really did believe in 'Second Chances.' I realize now that the reason Mr. Bingham let us play the entire game was for the benefit of the whole team. If he had taken two of his Varsity members out of the game we probably would have lost the game and that would have affected the whole team who had nothing to do with our lack of obedience and following the rules.

"Before games, Mr. Bingham often had us meet at his home for the afternoon. He insisted that we rest and relax. He wanted his 'boys,' his 'team,' to be prepared mentally as well as physically before the game.

"After each game, Mr. Bingham took us to a local café for hamburgers and milkshakes; he probably paid for this out of his own budget. I'm not sure, but I doubt the school had funds allocated for this treat.

"I would not want the reader to assume that playing basketball under Mr. Bingham's coaching and leadership was easy. We practiced daily after school — ran laps— and on an occasion when we did not perform as a team we were reminded 'and not gently' that he did not run a 'one man show.' Every player had a responsibility to play for the benefit of the team and nothing less than that would be accepted.

"After graduation I was drafted into the army and served for twenty years. During those years I would often return to that area and occasionally visit with Mr. Bingham. As an adult we not only shared great basketball memories, we had other similar interests. Mr. Bingham served in the navy during World War II and I spent two years in Vietnam. We discovered that war is war regardless of which one; you are never quite the same.

"I have often wondered if Mr. Bingham ever realized what an influence he had on my life. I'm afraid I never told him.

"I keep in touch with my high school companions and former team mates by attending high school reunions and occasional visits. As we reminisce, Mr. Bingham and basketball are usually the topics of conversation. Our coach and friend is missing now but only physically. Mr. Bingham will live forever in our hearts and memories."

(Jim) James B. Swift September 10, 2002

"Coach Bingham inspired every boy who wanted to play basketball to do his very best. One time he told me that my English teacher told him that I was not doing very well in her class. From that time on I made sure I was ready for my English class.

Joe McNeil August 23, 2002

"My senior year (1952–53) at Cove Creek High School looked like it could be like the previous years— driving the school bus, working two part-time jobs after school and on the weekends, plus my work at home. Some of my friends encouraged me to try out for the basketball team of which John Bingham was the coach, but I said I could not because of the jobs I had to do. Roy Clark came to me and said he had someone that would drive his bus and he would drive my bus on the days I had to practice ball. I knew that John Bingham had arranged all of this. To my surprise I made the team and got to play because of John Bingham's help. I loved playing basketball and will never forget John Bingham and my senior year at Cove Creek High School."

Benny Fox August 23, 2002

"Coach Bingham was a person who motivated his players to have a winning attitude through hard work and dedicated effort. He believed in discipline and 'giving your all' whether it was in practice or a game we were involved in. His inspiration and expectation of his players inspired me then and has influenced my life as an adult."

Doug "Hoss" Henson August 23, 2002

"Coach John Bingham came to Cove Creek High School when we were in need of a basketball coach. Although he was a certified teacher, he didn't have a teaching position at that time; basically, he coached our team because of his great love of the game. Coach Bingham knew his basketball fundamentals, but more importantly he could impart these fundamentals to young high school players. He was honest and used fairness in substituting players in and out of the game.

He encouraged us to play 'hard-nosed' ball and to play with strong discipline. He stressed team work and good sportsmanship both off and on the basketball court. Coach Bingham knew how to get his players to play hard and to give their best in every game. I remember one game in particular when we had to start without him. Someone else was filling in for him until he could get there. I don't remember which quarter we were in, but we were losing. When coach Bingham arrived and took over, the game really turned around and we won.

"In my years at Cove Creek High with him we had good teams with outstanding records. He coached our teams to win and we never had a losing season. In fact, we had one of the best fast-break teams in the country. Coach Bingham was a well-respected person and an outstanding coach for a great high school." Albert Harmon August 26, 2002

"John Bingham was a champion of fairness, mutual respect and had constructive solutions with all his players. He was the epitome of success in displaying his knowledge and talent of coaching a sport he had never played. He was a wonderful man and mentor for all his students and players. We played hard for him, for ourselves, our families, our school team (the Red Raiders) and especially for our friends."

Martin Banner September 4, 2002

At the Appalachian gym in Boone, the 1955 Cove Creek High School Red Raiders hoisted Coach John Bingham to take the victory net. This was their fourth straight year as the Tri-County Champions. They defeated Jefferson by a score of 72 to 64. Members of that team were Ted Greene, Bobby Teams, Paul Toby Walsh, Dan Sutherland, Billy Banner, Roy Minton, Houston Younce, John Banner, Dan Isaacs, and Howard Combs (photograph furnished by Dan Isaacs).

"As a 14 year-old lad, I entered Cove Creek High School in August of 1954. I dearly loved sports, especially basketball. While I was in the 8th grade, I had watched the Red Raiders win all their games, and I dreamed about being on a winning team like that some day. But what followed in October of that year changed my life forever. During the 'Raiders' tryouts, I found myself on the roster of the Cove Creek High basketball team coached by John Bingham, who was one of the most highly successful coaches of his time. Cove Creek had already compiled 73 consecutive regular season victories, which included an unprecedented three straight Tri-County (Ashe, Avery, and Watauga) championships. It was my freshman year that our team won its fourth Tri-County championship, a trip to the District tournament, and finally on to the coveted State Tournament in Greensboro. We came in 6th in the state, but we were a happy lot.

"From that year (1954–55), I knew that I wanted to be involved in sports, which eventually happened. I taught and coached for 32 years at the same Cove Creek School that I had attended years ago. I learned all my coaching styles and techniques from Coach John Bingham. And yes, I used his offenses and defenses and the many remembered special plays that made his teams and mine great.

Coach Bingham's total five year career coaching record accomplishment was 146 wins against 18 losses. Not bad for a small rural school of some 350 students in grades 9–12. All throughout these years the fans were many and faithful, trudging through all kinds of weather to see the magic of each basketball game Coach Bingham and his team played.

"A trophy case now stands in the historic Cove Creek High School where you can see many of the trophies won by Cove Creek High School teams."

Dan Isaacs

William Howard Walker

Dr. William Howard Mast

The following was submitted by Dr. William Howard Mast in 2004.

I interviewed Mr. Walker in 1989 in his home. He lived in the house his parents had built when Howard was just a lad. The brick farmhouse reflected a home constructed for comfort and durability. Somehow the house seemed to reflect the personality of the man in overalls who greeted me: William Howard Walker, retired superintendent of schools for Watauga County.

Howard Walker was born December 24, 1906, at Rominger, North Carolina. His parents were John Young and Martha Rominger Walker. He had two brothers, Ralph and Robert. Ralph, who was 18 months older than Howard, was a retired schoolteacher and lived in Boonville, N.C. Robert, the youngest brother, is deceased. Howard grew up on a mountain farm located at Rominger, a remote section of Watauga County. The farm was known as the "Old Walker Place" and was still owned by Howard at the time of his death. He attended a number of elementary schools, called free schools, including Rominger, Johnson, Mountain City, Tennessee, Phillips Branch, Walnut Grove and Valle Crucis. For high school, Howard attended Cove Creek and graduated in 1925. There were 12 students in this class, including his brother Ralph.

Since Howard and Ralph were in the same class it was simple to work out a compromise for doing home chores. Howard did all the morning chores and Ralph did the afternoon chores. This arrangement allowed Howard to stay after school to play and coach basketball, the sport he dearly loved.

The entire Cove Creek School in the '20s consisted of a two-story brick building and a small wood structure that housed the home economics program. Mr. Glenn Greer was the first principal but soon after Howard entered high school, S.F. Horton assumed that position. The high school teaching staff was composed of S.F. Horton (principal and Latin), Mrs. S.F. Horton (French and English), Mr. Will Perry (science and math), and Mr. Ellington (English).

After graduation Howard worked in Detroit, Michigan, where he earned his first year's tuition to attend Berea College in Kentucky. He began his college studies in September of 1925, and graduated four years later with a bachelor of science degree in agriculture. He helped to earn his college expenses by waiting tables and doing janitorial work at the college. His brother Ralph also graduated from Berea.

Upon graduating from college, Howard taught Agriculture and Science at Rockford, Alabama, for one year. In 1930 he returned home and taught agriculture and science at Cove Creek for four years. He coached basketball, and became Cove Creek's first coach. Mr. Walker was instrumental in the construction of a gymnasium at Cove Creek, but it burned in 1939.

In 1934 Howard Walker became superintendent of schools in Watauga County. At age 28 he was probably the youngest person to serve in this responsible position. He served continuously from 1934 to 1943. In 1943 Howard entered the U.S. Navy as a seaman second class. He earned a commission and advanced to the rank of lieutenant. Upon his discharge from the military in 1946 he resumed the responsibilities of superintendent of schools in Watauga County and served until 1954.

Remarkable advances were made in education in Watauga under the leadership of Howard Walker. His job as superintendent of schools began at the height of the Great Depression. This was an era of no jobs, no money, and the worst of conditions for securing funding for education. In retrospect, he was the right man for the job at that time. As a young man, he brought to the office of superintendent a vision of fewer but larger and better schools. He possessed the political savvy and tenacity to accomplish major changes at a time when the probability of such changes were dim.

Education in Watauga County in 1930 consisted of 55 schools, including four high schools; Appalachian, Bethel, Blowing Rock, and Cove Creek. With exception of a few brick buildings, all the schoolhouses were wooden structures. To reduce the level of dust, the teachers often oiled the floors. Transportation for school children was by contract. A private individual who owned a truck would contract his vehicle for conversion to a school bus. These conversions were often crude coverings of the truck bed and adding two benches that ran the length of the truck bed. It is reported that the first contract bus transported children to and from Cove Creek High School in 1925. Mr. Walker realized that if more students were to attain an education beyond 7th grade, they would have to be transported to and from the existing four high schools in the county.

Better transportation would mean more buses and better roads. Walker's first act in 1934 was to purchase 12 contract buses from private ownership and consolidation of the operation of these buses. During the summer when the buses were not in use they were parked in the Cove Creek gymnasium. Unfortunately, a summer lightning storm hit the gymnasium and the buses were destroyed. With the insurance and other monies, the county purchased 26 new buses. Thus began a new era in the transportation of students in Watauga County.

The transporting of more children served as a catalyst to improve the road system. Gradually the roads were improved and new buses were added to the system. When Mr. Walker left office in 1954, with the exception of a few remote areas of the county, every child in the county had access to a consolidated school by one of the more than 50 county and state owned buses.

Perhaps Mr. Walker's most remarkable feat was the consolidation of schools. The county school was the center of community activity. There was much controversy and community protest when it was suggested that these small country schools be abolished in favor of larger consolidated schools. The matter was handled tactfully, and soon new buildings were being constructed. The Works Progress Administration played a major role in this effort. With WPA labor, timber was cut into lumber, sand was dredged from creeks, and rocks were reclaimed from fields. Soon magnificent buildings of stone began to take shape. It became difficult to protest a move that provided so much needed employment for the county residents. Fifty thousand dollars was borrowed from the state to help fund these construction projects. The results were modern stone school buildings at Bethel, Blowing Rock, Boone, Cove Creek, Mabel, and Valle Crucis, in addition to a courthouse annex that housed administrative offices and a school bus garage. With the assistance of the National Youth Administration, wood gymnasiums were built at Cove Creek and Bethel.

With the completion of the modern school buildings, consolidation became an accepted fact and advanced without much controversy. The county now had eight elementary schools and four high schools, rather than about fifty small schools.

Another advancement of Watauga's school system was the implementation of lunchrooms. Watauga County early on recognized the value of a balanced meal to the well being of the student. The meals were reasonable in cost and often a barter system was used for payment of lunch.

During Mr. Walker's tenure as superintendent, teacher certification was raised from 94th place in the state to first place. In reviewing the record of education in Watauga County, there seemed to be a trend for William Howard Walker: he took the worst and made it the best.

Howard returned to full time farming in 1954. In addition to farming, he became a Ford tractor and implement dealer in 1958. He retired in 1972 at the age of 66. He remained in farming until his death in 1998.

S.F. Horton, the Powerhouse of Cove Creek

Nannie Greene

Sam F. Horton touched many lives in the Cove Creek community because of his long tenure with Cove Creek High School. He became principal there in 1923 and, with the exception of three years, he served in that capacity until his retirement 33 years later. He replaced Howard Walker as Watauga County superintendent of schools for three years while Walker served in the U.S. Navy from 1943 to '46.

Sam was born and raised in the Vilas area along with his nine siblings. They lived on a cattle farm owned and operated by his parents, David and Susan Mast Horton. He attended elementary school at Walnut Grover Institute, only a few miles from his home, and he graduated from high school at Appalachian Training School in Boone. Sam earned his B.A. degree at Wake Forest College and studied law at Columbia University. He was admitted to the bar of North Carolina in 1925.

Horton enrolled in the Naval Air Force on December 14, 1917, and after training was shipped to Brest, France. He arrived there on February 28, 1918, where he worked on airplanes and built hangars and airfields until the end of World War I on November 11, 1918.

Sam F. Horton became principal of the newly consolidated school at Cove Creek in 1923. This first physical plant housed both elementary and high school students and had an auditorium. With Mr. Horton's leadership, Cove Creek became the first accredited high school in Watauga County. A home economics program and a vocational agriculture program were added to the curriculum in the late '20s, followed by a business program in 1932. Mr. Horton recruited capable teachers for these new programs.

The first bus service in the county began at Cove Creek in 1925. Buses were actually trucks contracted with private owners and ran from Valle Crucis, Bethel and Amantha. Students rode on benches along the sides of the truck beds. There was no heat, but most beds had a cover.

Growth in enrollment led to a second brick building erected in 1927–28 that would become the Cove Creek High School building. It was beside the first brick building with the white frame home economics building between the two. The first building now became the Cove Creek Elementary School. Since the high school had no auditorium or gymnasium, students in both buildings used the old facilities. In 1933, through the efforts of Mr. Horton and Mr. Howard Walker, who was then a Cove Creek High teacher and coach, a wood frame gymnasium was constructed. In 1934 the county owned buses were stored in the Cove Creek gymnasium during the summer. In 1939 the gym was struck by lightning and burned, destroying all the buses inside.

In 1939, the board of education approved a new high school building that was to be constructed by the Works Progress Administration (WPA) labor about a quarter of a mile away. Help was solicited from the communities in and around Cove Creek. Since this was late Depression years, many people were out of work and welcomed an opportunity to work for wages. Some men gathered native stones from around the area and brought them to the school site, many in wagons or carts. Others worked with the engineer and local contractors, Pete Hagaman and Charlie Hartley. Charlie has a wooden leg, but he would climb those ladders as well as any two-legged man. Local stonemasons also found work here. This project provided a big boost for the local economy. The school was completed in time to begin the 1942–43 school year. Because the new building had no gym or auditorium, the old facilities were still used by all the students.

Mr. Horton recommended that a principal be appointed for the elementary school that was now housed in both brick buildings. With more students being bused from Valle Crucis and Mabel, he felt the new high school needed his full attention. An industrial arts program was added to the curriculum in the new high school.

Cove Creek was always considered one of the finest schools in the county. The many improvements that were made under Mr. Horton's guidance were reasons for its good reputation. The implementation of a good school lunch program, the improvements of the bus system, the additions to the curriculum, along with the introduction of band and a strong sports program is further proof of Mr. Horton's competent leadership. Jennie Love was instrumental in creating a well-equipped and outstanding library. To further assure the success of the school, Mr. Horton continued to hire qualified and innovative teachers.

Through the years that Mr. Horton worked with the school, he had the support of the community. Because of the cooperation between the school and the community, both made tremendous progress. Mr. Horton's personality and communication skills helped the two groups understand each other. He was always looking for things that would make Cove Creek High School a better school, and the students appreciated his efforts. I remember his smile and friendliness, his kindness and fairness to all. I was a student assistant and worked in his office. I never saw him lose his temper or be unkind to anyone — student, parent, or worker. One student said it best this way, "Mr. Horton genuinely cared for his students and could reduce problems to a workable level." What a wonderful trait to possess.

Samuel Ferd Horton married Pearl Fuller in 1926. She taught history, English and French at Cove Creek many years, both before and after the birth of their children. They reared thee children, Fuller, David, and Betty, in their brick home near the school on Cove Creek. Fuller, a graduate of N.C. State College, worked as an engineer with General Electric in North Carolina and Louisiana. David, a West Point graduate, was a pilot in the Air Force and now lives in California. Betty married and still lives in Watauga County.

Mr. and Mrs. Horton were always active in community affairs. Both were dedicated members of Cove Creek Baptist Church. Mr. Horton worked with some local civic groups and Mrs. Horton belonged to the Home Demonstration Club. She loved to decorate with the beautiful flowers that she grew. Both were dedicated educators who spent most of their lives working with children in our community. Cove Creek community was fortunate to have these two talented people living and working there.

Robert G. Shipley

Dr. William Howard Mast

This was submitted by Dr. William Howard Mast in 2004.

Mr. Robert G. Shipley was honored by the Cove Creek High School Class of 1955 when he was presented an Award of Appreciation for his dedicated service as a teacher and his civic contributions to the county and state.

Robert Shipley was born June 23, 1912, in Valle Crucis, North Carolina. His father was William Edwin Shipley and his mother was Minnie Lee Woodie Shipley. He came from a fairly large family, having four sisters and two brothers. He attended Valle Crucis Elementary School. The Shipley family moved from Valle Crucis to Wallace, Virginia, where Robert enrolled in the 4th grade in Wallace Elementary School. He graduated from Wallace High School in 1929.

Robert entered VPI (Virginia Polytechnic Institute) at Blacksburg, Virginia, in September 1929, where he worked his way through college. During his first year, he worked in the dairy department where he hand milked and cared for 17 cows every day. The next year he was promoted to a position in the experimental station where he maintained records. By the time he graduated, he had won local, state, and national dairy judging contests and was highly regarded in his field. He graduated from VPI in June 1933 with a bachelor of science degree in animal husbandry. In addition to this degree, he earned sufficient credits by attending summer sessions and taking course overloads to qualify him for two additional degrees, which included certification to teach vocational agriculture.

Mr. Shipley began a teaching career in 1933 that spanned four decades. His first teaching position was at Patterson School located near Lenoir, North Carolina, where he taught vocational agriculture and was responsible for the dairy operations and assisted in the management of the 1300 acre farm associated with the school. In 1934, he came to Boone High School, later called Appalachian High School, where he started the first vocational agriculture program. He taught at Boone High School for four years. In 1938, he went to Augusta County, Virginia, to teach and continue his education. He was awarded the master of animal husbandry degree from Ohio State University in June 1940.

Upon graduation from Ohio State University, Mr. Shipley accepted a position with the Agricultural Extension Service in Grayson County, Virginia, where he served as a county agent for three years. During this time, in 1942, he married Agnes Davis. In January 1943, he entered the Air Force and served as an instructor teaching tail turret gunnery in the B-24 Bomber. He was later assigned to a mission at the Ascension Island located in the South Atlantic. He was one of 12 researchers conducting experiments in growing vegetables without soil with the expectation that techniques could be developed for vegetables for soldiers in parts of the world where the soil was contaminated.

Mr. Shipley was discharged from the Air Force at the end of World War II and resumed his teaching career. He accepted a position at Cove Creek

High School in January 1946 and taught vocational agriculture at this school until it was consolidated into Watauga High School in 1966. He continued to teach at Watauga High School until his retirement in 1977. He conducted a veteran's training program beginning with World War II veterans and continuing with Korean War and Viet Nam War veterans. At one time, his veteran's training program was among the largest in the state and employed six instructors.

There are many facets to Mr. Shipley's life and work. He was a unique teacher in that he was a practitioner of the agriculture he taught. As a young man in 1929, he became the owner of a beautiful farm located near Vilas, North Carolina. He contributes much of his successful agricultural operations to Mr. Chester Johnson and family, who have been lifelong residents of this farm. The dedicated and faithful service of this family has permitted Mr. Shipley the freedom and flexibility to pursue his teaching career while maintaining the farm.

He raised sheep on his farm for decades and showed them at the state fair for over 25 years. He traveled as far as Madison, Wisconsin, to purchase a ram to improve his stock. He was president for the North Carolina Sheep Breeders Association and one of the first individuals to be inducted into the North Carolina State Fair Hall of Fame.

His livestock activities included beef and dairy cattle, and at one time in his career, he raised horses and ponies. He was active in organizing the Watauga County Hereford Breeders Association and served as the president of this association for over 20 years. He also served as vice president for the State Hereford Breeders Association. He was a pioneer in establishing artificial breeding for dairy cattle in Watauga County and was a participant in the first state sale of artificially bred Holstein heifers conducted in Asheville, North Carolina. Mr. Shipley has been growing Holsteins since 1954 and has supplied this breed of cattle to practically every southeastern state.

In other areas of agriculture, he was instrumental in bringing hybrid corn to Watauga County. He is a former member of the board of directors for the North Carolina Tobacco Growers Association. He is presently one of two North Carolina directors appointed to the Burley Stabilization Board located in Knoxville, Tennessee. This agency administers the government pooling of tobacco for North Carolina, Tennessee, and Virginia. He served as a representative of the Burley Stabilization Board on the Council for Burley Tobacco located in Lexington, Kentucky. In addition to his varied livestock and farming operations, he organized and managed the Cove Creek Horse Show for 18 years.

Mr. Shipley is a member of Henson's Chapel Methodist Church and has been a member of the Boone Rotary Club for 42 years. He led the formation of the Mountaineer Ruritan Club and serves as the secretary of this service organization. He and his wife, Agnes, reared three children: Agnes, Robert, and Janie. They have six grandchildren.

Robert Shipley has led an exemplary life and has touched the lives of those with whom he has come in contact. In his early '90s, he maintains a busy schedule with his farming activities, community functions, and civic responsibilities. With his somewhat unruly shock of silver hair, suntanned features, and pleasant smile, he is always a welcome sight and a reminder of the meaning of dependability and responsibility.

The Music Woman

Catherine Stokes Sheppard

This profile of Vera Byers Church was based on Catherine Stokes Sheppard's interview with her in 2004.

In Silverstone there lives a woman who is so unique that it is difficult to know which of her talents to tell about. She has wonderful stories to tell about growing up. She has wonderful stories to tell about her present day life. How many people who are 94 years old still live alone and still drive a car and express an interest in riding a motorcycle? She also has a computer and looks forward daily to her e-mail. Oh, did I mention that she still teaches piano lessons?

When Vera Byers Church's name is mentioned many of her acquaintances immediately say, "Oh, yes! She taught me piano lessons." Although Vera did not begin to teach until 1957, she was playing the piano long before that, and was always considered a talented musician.

Vera says that although she was an only child, she came from a musical family. Her parents enjoyed music, especially singing. She first learned shaped notes then round notes. Her aunt, Nettie Greer Swift, had had music lessons and taught Vera the basics when she was 8 or 9 years old. Vera loved the piano so much that she taught herself once the basic note reading was mastered. When she started to high school at Cove Creek there was a full time music teacher, Miss Louise Allison, who offered lessons. While Vera learned much from her, she says the best teacher she ever had was Lucy Mast Olsen. "I really bloomed under her," Vera said. Even before high school Vera was playing the pedal organ in church occasionally. "Ethyl Wilson was our organist, but she had a boy friend from some distance away. When he came to visit her she wanted to sit in the congregation with him, so I would

Vera Byers Church learned to play the piano when she was 8 or 9 years old, and she became a talented musician by the time she was in high school. She played the piano and pedal organ in church when she was a teenager. She started teaching piano when she was 47 and has taught every year since then and she is 94 now. She gives private lessons now but taught in four schools, Cove Creek, Mabel, Trade, and Valle Crucis where she had a recital every year. Mrs. Vera could identify most of the students in this photo of one recital group in May 1957. On the first row, left to right, are Linda Donnelly, Brenda Canter, Barbara Perry, Norma Lee Mast, Glenna May, unidentified, Carolyn Sanders, not known, Roxanna May, Sue Miller, Hensel Wallace, and Douglas Bumgarner. Back row: Mrs. Vera Church, Bill Slater, Joyce Roark, Judy Ann Wilson, unidentified, Janet Oliver, Billie Jo Wilson, Elaine Cook, Carolyn Miller, unidentified, and Shirley Wilson (photograph furnished by Vera Church).

play the organ. And I have been playing in church off and on ever since," relates Vera.

At age 18 Vera married her high school sweetheart, Ivan Church. The next 20 years were filled with marriage and child rearing. When World War II came along the county schools were desperate for teachers. (The male teachers were in uniform and lots of the women had gone to better paying jobs.) Vera, along with other ladies in the community, were asked to take some short courses at ASU and teach. Vera taught 6th and 7th grade at Mabel for a while. She says she did not mind teaching, but she hated the courses she had to take.

There was one type course that Vera did want to take. She wanted to learn how to teach music. Her dream was realized when she met a Miss Kent who had moved to Mountain City, Tennessee, from New York. Miss Kent's father was an executive with the railroad and was sent to be in charge of the Mountain City branch. Miss Kent was not a young woman but well educated in music. She had studied in a conservatory in New York. Vera was elated to have the opportunity to study under her and learn how to teach. So at 47 Vera embarked on a new career.

Vera has taught in Cove Creek, Mabel, Valle Crucis and Trade, Tennessee. During these early years of teaching she taught at the school of the respective community. Ten years ago she moved her classes to her home. She says that when she began teaching she charged fifty cents for each 30 minute lesson. Later she raised the fee to one dollar per lesson. Today she limits her students to seven. She says at 94 she still enjoys teaching and the companionship of the students. "I enjoy every minute of it," she says, "but I do not have recitals! That is too much work."

Did she ever have problems with her students? "Oh, yes! I never could teach my own children! I had to hire someone else to teach them." Not surprisingly, two of Vera's children are also very talented musicians. One daughter simply refused music.

Vera says she does not know how many music students she has taught but she has plans for getting out her old roll books and making a count. No matter what the numbers are, I suspect there are several churches that have reaped the benefits of her teaching through the years. Vera Beyers Church has made a difference. Surely, she is the music woman!

Lucille Johnson Hipp: The Flower Lady

Nannie Greene

This profile of Lucille Johnson Hipp was based on Nannie Greene's interview with her in 2005 and personal acquaintance.

Lucille Johnson was born in the Beaver Dam community to Minnie Wilson Johnson and John Grover Johnson. Lucille and her brother, Johnny, grew up on a farm owned and operated by her parents in Beaver Dam, about a mile from Don Hagaman's Country Store. This same farm has been in their family for five generations. Like most families in this area, the Johnsons raised a variety of vegetables in a big garden, usually tended by Mrs. Minnie and the children. On the farm they grew sweet corn, beans, and potatoes for family use, as well as wheat. They grew oats, alfalfa and field corn to be used for feed for the cattle and horses they kept on the farm.

Mr. Grover also had a produce route in the Beech Mountain area and sometimes he was gone overnight. For some of the people he served, he was their only contact with the outside world. He would sell, buy, or trade produce for chickens, eggs, and hams. Later he had a contract with a Mr. Eller in North Wilkesboro who would buy what he had collected. This was a way to supplement his earnings from things grown on his farm. Mrs. Johnson was a teacher. She taught at Beaver Dam School and Forest Grove School in the 1930s, and later as a substitute teacher at Bethel School. For most of her adult life, Mrs. Minnie taught Sunday school at Forest Grove Baptist Church. Following her mother's example, Lucille has been active in church work wherever she has lived. She is currently involved in many activities of the Boone United Methodist Women.

Again Lucille followed in her mother's footsteps and chose education as a career. After she graduated from Bethel High School, she attended Appalachian State Teacher's College, where she earned a bachelor of science degree in elementary education and a minor in music. She began her teaching career in Charlotte, N.C. Throughout her thirty years as a teacher, she remembered Dr. Dougherty's emphasis on teaching "the whole child," and that became her philosophy also.

She met and married Joe Hipp, a native Charlottean. He had graduated from Duke University and coached for a few years before he joined the work force at General Motors. Joe and Lucille have two daughters, Rhesa Lou and Tamra Renee. Rhesa Lou and husband John Rudolph have twins, Nicholas and Mary Noelle. Tamra married Lowell Shaw and they have two sons, Brandon and Collin. Joe and Lucille enjoy being doting grandparents.

After they retired, Lucille and Joe moved back to Beaver Dam in 1990. They built a gorgeous home near her parents. Lucille collects family heirlooms that she displays throughout the house. You will also find some of her personal touches, such as hand-painted borders in every room. All around the house you will find various types of native flowers, as well as cultivated ones. Their home was featured in one of the Home and Garden Tours and many people admired it, both inside and out. She says, "Joe and I have both been surprised at how easy the adjustment has been from city life to living in the country. It's a peacefulness we've never had in the city." She tells us that both daughters and their families have expressed an interest in moving back sometime in the future. Joe and Lucille are contemplating renovating her parent's home place, which was built around 1898, to encourage their return.

It was on that family farm that Lucille first became interested in flowers. Both her mother and her Grandmother Wilson loved growing beautiful flowers, and she remembers how her Mother always stayed busy working with her flowers. So it was only natural that Lucille, too, would develop a genuine interest in flowers. She joined her first Garden Club in 1991 where she worked with her mentor, Ellen Payne. Because of her dedication and commitment to a job she loved, working with flowers, Ellen inspired Lucille to do the same. She has held offices in the local, district, and state levels in garden clubs.

Lucille has served as president of the Blue Ridge Garden Club and as chair of the board of governors of the Daniel Boone Native Gardens for four years. "The gardens are such an asset to Watauga County," she tells us. "Many local people are probably not even aware they exist. Approximately six acres of native plants make up the gardens, many of which are very rare." She spent many hours working in the gardens, replanting, weeding, cultivating, and caring for plants. She has given garden related programs to clubs in Boone and all over the state, and was willing to help anyone who needed her help. Lucille has her own herb garden, and she has also given programs on herbs followed by herbal luncheons in her home.

I like a quote from Sherrie Norris in an article in the *Mountain Times* about Lucille as the April Woman of the Month in 2001. Sherrie said, "Some people just bloom where they're planted, and Lucille Hipp has done that, literally speaking. Known for her love of flowers ... Mrs. Hipp's efforts in the community go far beyond seasonal blooms." She has been president of the Watauga County Council of Garden Clubs; vice-chair of District II Garden Club of North Carolina; served as District II director; and in 2004 was chosen to serve as a member of the board of trustees of the Garden Club of North Carolina.

Lucille is a vivacious, energetic, and capable volunteer who would be an asset to any community in which she lives or works. We are glad she chose to live in our midst. Thank you, Flower Lover, for being "keeper of the gardens" and for your work in the gardens of life which helps to keep our mountains beautiful.

A Pioneer in Nuclear Medicine

Nannie Greene

This profile is based on information shared by Joyce Perry Ragan, daughter of Blanche Perry (1908–1998), in 2003.

Blanche Williams Perry was born in February of 1908 in western Watauga County, where she lived her entire life. In the mid–1940s her doctor detected a goiter in her throat. Her surgeon advised her to have it removed but when he operated he discovered that the enlarged gland was cancerous. He removed as much of it as he could but admitted that since it was wrapped around her trachea it was quite likely that some of it remained.

Fast forward to 1963, when the cancer became active again. Blanche was now under the care of a different doctor who told her that another surgery would destroy her voice-box. However, one of his colleagues, a Doctor George, had been reading about an experimental drug for cancer. After much discussion and prayerful consideration, Blanche decided to try this experimental drug treatment if her case was accepted. Dr. George gathered her medical history and sent it along with an application for participation in the program. Her application was accepted and she was told that the treatment would cost her nothing because it was experimental. The current cost of this treatment was $25,000, quite a hefty sum for 1963.

Blanche Williams Perry lived in Western Watauga County all her life. In 1940 a surgeon discovered her throat cancer. When it became active again in 1963, Blanche chose to participate in a governmental experimental drug treatment in Oak Ridge, Tennessee. After five treatments of what she called "liquid iodine"(cobalt), she came home to await the results. She became cancer free and lived a long, productive life of 90 years. Blanche dedicated her life to working in many church activities at Cove Creek Baptist Church, the Three Forks Baptist Association, and in the Cove Creek community (photograph from Cove Creek Grange collection).

In the summer of 1963 Blanche checked into a governmental medical facility, ORINS (Oak Ridge Institute of Nuclear Studies) in Oak Ridge, Tennessee, for two weeks. They did extensive tests for a week to determine what dosage she should have. Then came the day she had waited for. She was placed alone in a small lead-lined room, probably an ionization chamber which measures the disintegration rate of radioactive materials. The door was closed and a cup of what she called "liquid iodine" (cobalt) was placed on a tray in a door opening and then pushed in to her to drink. As she sat there alone looking at that cup, she wondered if she had made the right decision. Would this kill her, maim her, or cure her? Blanche was a woman of strong spiritual faith and she prayed she had made the right decision. She had lots of time to ponder her decision. She was required to sit there alone until what she called a Geiger counter in her room stopped clicking. This took about six hours.

Blanche stayed in isolation for a week before she could return home, then she went back for four more treatments. The latter treatments required her to stay Monday through Friday each time.

The treatments were successful! Blanche lived a long and fruitful life until her death at age 90. She was a brave pioneer for nuclear medicine. I like to believe that her experience made a difference for the mass of people who since 1963 have successfully undergone treatments with nuclear medicine.

Dr. Frances Farthing

Glenn Farthing

This article, submitted by Glenn Farthing in 2005, includes information from his sister, Mary Hazel Farthing Mast, and from Dixie Huff, sister of Dr. Frances Farthing. Glenn and Ms. Mast are double first cousins of Dr. Farthing.

In terms of the accomplishments of a mountain woman, the story of Frances Farthing, in my opinion, is unexcelled.

One of the most cherished pictures on the wall of our home is of the students and teacher of Room #1 of the 3-room Valle Crucis Elementary School in the fall of 1930. I am there as an 8 year old third grader and Frances is the 19 year old teacher. She had completed two years at Appalachian State Teachers College and was teaching to earn money to continue her education. I soon found that she was to be addressed as "Miss Farthing," not Cousin Frances. I also soon found that she was not only determined to put forth her best effort but that she expected the same level of effort from everybody else. This was one of her strongest attributes and was characteristic of her whole career. She was determined to do the best job possible at every stage of her life. I also found that she could compliment you on a homework assignment but in the same breath chastise you for not having done your best. Her own work ethic was so powerful that she had trouble accepting that others might not have the same fierce desire to excel. When she was working with others toward a goal, her single-mindedness of purpose was so intense that she could not tolerate a differing opinion or a half-hearted effort. This plus her willingness to speak her mind sometimes caused some hard feelings. But her motive was not to injure, but to encourage greater effort and agreement with her viewpoint.

Frances was noted for her frugality. Some even called her stingy. But this was a totally inappropriate word to describe her thrift. In fact, it only applied to her own needs. The school at Valle Crucis had no lunchroom, so everybody brought his own lunch. Many times she shared her lunch with a child that had little or nothing for lunch. Many of her nieces and nephews can speak of her generosity when they needed help in getting an education.

In fact, the key word in Frances' life was *education*. She let nothing interfere with getting her first degree from Appalachian State Teachers College, now Appalachian State University. Then, she taught elementary school for a few years, helping many youngsters get a good start on their education. Next, she decided to further her own education and obtained a degree in nursing from Cornell University's School of Nursing at New York Hospital. I can just see that tall North Carolina girl showing those Yankees something about hard work and dedication, changing their impression of Southerners as slow-moving and not too bright.

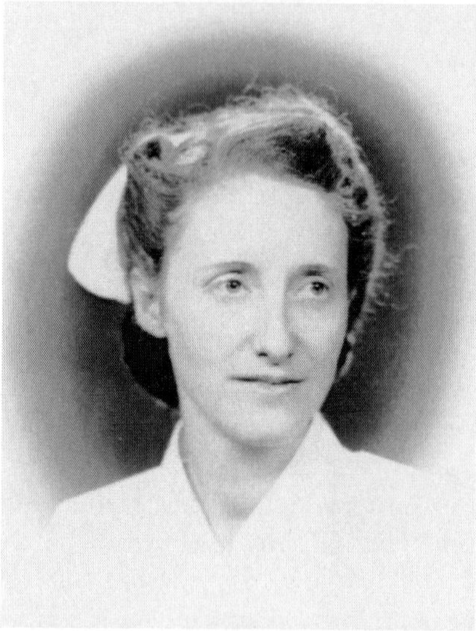

Frances Farthing's life was focussed on education — her own and those around her. She got a teaching certificate from Appalachian State Teachers College, and obtained a degree in nursing from Cornell University in New York. Back in North Carolina she helped establish a four-year baccalaureate degree program in nursing, and earned a master's degree from A.S.T.C. Dr. Farthing was the first North Carolina nurse to earn a Ph.D. in nursing. She became dean of the School of Nursing at Lenoir Rhyne–Grace Hospital, improving the curriculum there until she retired (photograph furnished by Dixie Farthing Huff).

Back home in North Carolina, Frances became the director of nurses at Cabarrus General Hospital in Concord, where she worked to insure the best education of nurses at that institution. In 1961 Frances received a call from Grayson Brothers, the administrative director of Grace Hospital in Morganton. They saw a need to expand their 3-year diploma nurses training program into a 4-year baccalaureate degree program in nursing in partnership with Lenoir Rhyne College in Hickory.

What Frances saw was a chance to improve the educational opportunities for young women in Western North Carolina. She undertook the task with complete dedication, vision, foresight, hard work, persistence and enthusiasm. She also saw the need to further her own education and obtained her master of arts degree from Appalachian in 1962. Following that she took courses from Florida State College in Tallahassee, Florida, culminating in their conferring on her a doctoral degree in education. She was the first nurse to be so honored by Florida State. (Frances was the first North Carolina nurse to receive a doctorate and at that time there were fewer than 200 nurses in the USA who held a Ph.D.) Dr. Frances Farthing then became the dean of the School of Nursing at Lenoir Rhyne–Grace Hospital. By the time that the first class graduated in 1964 the school had won accreditation by the North Carolina Board of Nursing. She continued to expand and improve the curriculum until her retirement in 1978.

As an example of her frugality in terms of her own needs, this tall, over 6-foot woman drove a Volkswagen bug while she was developing the nursing school, commuting to Florida State, and visiting high schools in Western North Carolina to recruit students for her nursing school. She never did allow herself the luxury of a full size sedan, though she could well afford it and most certainly deserved it.

Frances drew her strength from her love of the mountains, especially the village of Valle Crucis. When developers threatened to destroy the charm of Valle Crucis as a place where time stood still, Frances spearheaded the effort to limit development by winning for the community the designation as a National Historic District, the first place so honored in North Carolina.

In retirement, Frances could not sit idle and take it easy. She was driven to be accomplishing something worthwhile. She modernized the home and other buildings at the family farm on the Watauga River, she established a grant program called "Learning Links" for the Avery and Mitchell County Schools to promote creative teaching, learning and motivation; she has endowed scholarships at Lenoir Rhyne, Appalachian State University, Caldwell Community College and Mayland Community College. These are not just a single scholarship per college, but multiple funds to serve various purposes. She led many of her friends to join her in establishing these programs. Her friend, Dr. Virginia Foxx, formerly head of Mayland Community College and now a U.S. Representative, speaks eloquently of Frances' love for helping young people get an education. Even during the last few years of her life when she was battling a malignancy, she found time to volunteer at the local elementary school as a tutor for 2nd graders who needed additional help.

Education was not the only interest of Frances, she was also an environmentalist. She donated a 57 acre farm, valued at $295,000, to the National Committee for the New River, a nature conservancy group. The committee was to use the money from the sale of the farm to procure easements along the New River and Watauga River, seeking to prevent development and keep these rivers in their natural state.

Dr. Frances Farthing never sought praise for all she accomplished, but she had many honors, awards and citations, including those from Appalachian State University, Lenoir Rhyne College, and Cornell University, who designated her a Distinguished Alumnus for her service to the nursing profession.

Although Frances never married and never had children, she had a wealth of experience with them. As the oldest of eight children, she had much to do with helping rear her younger siblings. Her brother Baxter still remembers her skill at preparing meals. When her mother died an untimely death, Frances became grandmother to her nieces and nephews. Their pet name for her was "Frankie Mom," and she never tired of being with them at every opportunity and encouraging them to get a good education.

The pioneer spirit of her forefathers lived on in Frances. She was willing to travel uncharted paths and blaze new trails. The words *I can* epitomize the approach Frances took to the many challenges she faced in her long, productive life. She was truly a role model for not only her younger siblings and their progeny, but also for the many students she taught throughout her long career.

Part 5: You Can Get There from Here

There is an anecdote often told in the mountain counties that certainly applies to Western Watauga County:

It seems that once a real estate agent and a client were riding on the back roads of our area and became confused as to where they were. They noticed a man near the road who was chopping wood. Obviously he was at home and would know the area well. They pulled over and posed a question. "Mister, please tell us, can we get to Boone from here?" The fellow removed his cap, scratched his head and replied, "Why, sonny, you can get to anywhere in the world from here!"

As we have interviewed people for this book we have come to realize how true that answer is. We have found that our mountains have gaps, and those who desire to go far and wide have been able to do so. Our vision has not been limited by our view.

A few generations ago mountain people tended to live and die within a short distance from their birth place. Education, war, limited job opportunities, and ambition have led young people to follow their dreams, even the dreams that took them all over the world. Yet many of those who left also have chosen to come back.

Many of those who stayed in Watauga have been very successful. Almost every community has citizens that have been successful in a career that might be classified as unusual or at least interesting. For example, Eugene Wilson from Silverstone has served his county twelve years as a county commissioner and since has served 15 years as a member of the North Carolina House of Representatives. From Vilas is Velma Burnley, who was elected in 1991 as Boone's first female mayor. She is now serving in her 14th year in that capacity.

Ned Trivette from Timbered Ridge became a vice-chancelor at Appalachian State University.

Dr. Sandra Main Anderson is director of Watauga County Division of Caldwell Community College. She is from Vilas. David Horton from Cove Creek graduated from West Point and has an exciting career in the military. We might add that while at West Point he was once a roommate of a cadet named Norman Schwarzkopf. Not by a long shot are the people named in this section the only ones who have had wonderful careers; these are simply the ones we know about. Western Watauga has given our county, state and nation many professional people. We have not produced a U.S. president … yet! But we do abound in good citizens.

Since we were aware of several individuals whom we considered to have had exciting careers away from Watauga, we insisted (just short of force sometimes) that they tell us where they had been and what they had done. We believe our readers will enjoy knowing their stories.

Dr. Shelton Dugger

Gene Blair

Gene Blair submitted this profile of Dr. Shelton Dugger in 2002.

Dr. Gordon Shelton Dugger was a native of the Vilas community. He was born to John G. and Ruth (Combs) Dugger on July 17, 1921. Shelton attended school at Cove Creek and graduated from Cove Creek High School in 1937 at the age of 15 with one of the highest grade averages ever recorded at that time. He left Vilas in the fall of that year.

When he was 16, he entered the University of North Carolina at Chapel Hill, where he graduated with a pre-medical degree. He was an honor student and was inducted into Phi Beta Kappa. After a year of medical school there, he transferred to Johns Hopkins Medical School as a member of the Army Special Training Group. Upon graduation, he was sent to Panama Canal Zone where he served for two years. He spent some time at the VA Hospital in American Lake, Washington, and then went into private practice in St. Helena, Oregon. Later he entered the McGill School of the Montreal Neurological Institute.

Shelton Dugger was born in Vilas in 1921 and graduated from Cove Creek High School sixteen years later. He spent three years in medical school, two years in the U.S. Army, and then completed his medical training at the Montreal Neurological Institute in Canada. He returned to the University of North Carolina where he served as the chief of neurosurgery until he retired in 1978 (photograph furnished by James Dugger).

Upon completion of his training in Montreal, Canada, Dr. Dugger returned to the University of North Carolina in 1954 as an associate professor of neurosurgery. Within two years he became the chief of neurosurgery and served in that capacity until his retirement in 1978. At Chapel Hill he established a graduate program for medical students that became renowned throughout the Southeast.

Among his many achievements, Dr. Dugger developed a surgical procedure called the pituitary stalk section used to treat certain types of malignant tumors. Because of his long and distinguished service, the School of Medicine named its neurology library in his honor.

Dr. Dugger was also interested in history and he served on the executive board of the N.C. Department of Archives and History.

Although Dr. Dugger never returned to Vilas to live, he did come back for visits. Family members and friends were aware of his accomplishments as a neurosurgeon, and they followed his success in the field of neurology closely. He died at the age of 59. He was a brilliant doctor who left his legacy in the medical profession.

Carlock "Carl" Greene: Mid-Atlantic Scouts Hall of Famer

Carlock "Carl" Greene

In 1998 at Camden Yards, home of the Baltimore Orioles, Carlock "Carl" Greene was inducted into the Mid-Atlantic Scouts Hall of Fame. He has played baseball, coached baseball, and scouted for baseball and he knows baseball. Hanging on the wall in the Scouts Hall of Fame is a bronze plaque with his name on it that proves you can get there from here! Below is Carl Greene's story as told to Nannie Greene in January 2002.

My name is Carlock Greene but I have always been called just Carl. My parents were Herman and Pearl Greene. Mama was a school teacher and Dad was a carpenter and house mover. I lived in a place called Henson Hollow at Amantha, N.C., about three-quarters of a mile from Henson Chapel Methodist Church. My two brothers, Pat and Jimmy, and I all went to Cove Creek Elementary School and I graduated from Cove Creek High School in 1949. I remember when we would walk down close to the church to wait for the school bus. It seemed to me like we had a lot more snow then. I thought snow stayed on the ground about all winter. My brother, Pat, was just a little feller, and he would just about freeze to death waiting for the bus. If the snow was very deep, our Daddy would ride us out to the road on a horse. Sometimes Omar Swift would come down riding on a horse and he would let me ride to school behind him. It was good to get a ride and not have to wait for that bus in the cold. On these snowy mornings, the bus was always late. It had to come from the Tennessee line and back in mountainous areas. We were lucky if it came by 10 o'clock. We would hardly get to school when they would let us out to go back home about 12 o'clock. We were lucky. Mr. Don Swift was the janitor at the school. Sometimes he would have to stay there all night to keep the school furnace going.

On less hectic days there would be about fifteen to twenty of us kids waitin' for the bus. We would play ball out in the highway. There was very little traffic and as far as I know none of us ever got hit by a car or anything. We were always playing ball of some kind. Somebody always seemed to have a ball or if we were at school, there were always balls there. But if we didn't have balls we would throw rocks. I remember that I would throw rocks at our barn with a metal roof. My Daddy would wear me out. Sometimes I would throw rocks at electrical poles trying to hit the electrical insulators and break them. Then my Dad would wear me out again. I was always throwing something.

I guess I became interested in playing ball when I was about eleven years old after my Mother took me to visit a cousin, Claude Trivette. He played pro ball on several different baseball teams and finally ended up as a manager of a team in Johnson City, Tennessee. He gave me my first baseball and glove, which really sparked my interest in baseball. My parents and grandparents were always interested in sports and we went to a lot of ball games. One time they took me to Hickory to see the Brooklyn Dodgers play Cleveland. Bob Feller pitched for Cleveland and Bob Porterfield pitched for Brooklyn. I thought Porterfield pitched about as hard as Feller. That game really got me interested in pitching.

My grandparents, Ed and Essie Henson, like my parents always enjoyed going to ball games. Course there wasn't much else to do but go to ball games back then. In high school I played on any kind of ball team. I was on the basketball team for four years. Our school started a football team in 1947 and I played on it. But my senior year I didn't play because I had already decided that I wanted to play baseball and the scouts didn't want me to play football. I guess they were afraid I would get hurt somehow. We had a pitcher on our high school team who had been in World War II. He was a good pitcher who threw real hard. I watched him and tried to learn from him. His name was Dexter Rominger. I admired him and I guess he had as much influence on me as anybody. Mr. Sam Osborne was our coach at Cove Creek and he taught me how to become a team player. I always got along fine with my teammates and there wasn't much rivalry between us. We just wanted the team to win. My whole family supported me in my decision to try to play baseball. My daddy, my brother Pat, and even my mother used to catch my pitches. I throwed and throwed and throwed.

The scouts never did talk to me. They might come by and shake hands with me ever now and then, but mostly they talked to others about me and my love for baseball. They talked to my parents, my grandparents and I guess my coach. Anyhow, I signed with the Braves in 1949 for a salary of $4,999.99. My first assignment as a pro player was with the Hi-Toms in High Point. I played with them for a year before I joined the Navy. I had planned to go into the Army, but a high school classmate of mine, Richard Minton, had joined the Army and the week before I was supposed to go, Richard was killed in the parachute division, so I decided right then to take my chances in the Navy. I served in the Navy for three years, mostly in Norfolk, Virginia. I became a barber and played a lot of ball. We played a lot of teams with well-known players at that time, Pete Rose and Kent Harrison and Louie Aparichio.

Carlock "Carl" Greene, a talented baseball pitcher, graduated from Cove Creek High School in 1949. He signed on with the Braves immediately after graduation. He served three years in the Navy and again became a pitcher for the Braves. Carl ended his pitching career in 1970 after 15 years in the pro circuit. In 1970 he became a scout for the Braves teams and continued that career for 29 years. In 1998 he was inducted into the Scouts Hall of Fame (photograph furnished by Carl Greene).

I married Mary Sue Love in 1953. I thought she was the prettiest girl in high school. We have had a great life together. We've lived all over the U.S. and in Mexico City, Vancouver, Toronto, Canada, and in Caracas, Venezuela. She had to be ready to move at any time, sometimes with only 24 hours' notice. After the children came along it was a little harder to find the right places to live. Mary was always there for the children and for me. We now have two boys and twin girls and two grandsons. Our 50th anniversary is just around the corner. Mary spent a lot of her spare time collecting newspaper articles compiling a scrapbook of my pro-ball days. She did a good job on it.

I never did want to go to college. It wasn't that I didn't have an option. I could have gone to Duke and I had other offers, but I just never considered college.

After the Navy I signed with the Braves in Evansville, Indiana. They later became the Boston Braves, the Milwaukee Braves and finally the

Atlanta Braves. In the 1950s I played with the Corpus Christi Clippers, where I had my best season in 1956. That year I won 25 games, 21 in regular season and four in the playoffs. Then I went to the Coastal League in San Francisco where I had a bone spur and had to have an operation on it. I never did pitch the same after that. I had only one losing record while I played Triple A ball. I played with the Louisville and Sacramento teams, the Vancouver Mounties, and the Toronto Maple Leafs, where I was chosen for the International All-Star Team. That game was played in Baltimore, Maryland. In 1964 I played with the Denver Bears, with the Atlanta Braves in 1965, and ended my pitching career at the Braves Farm Club in 1967 where I was a player and a pitching coach. I enjoyed 15 years in the pro-ball circuit in both the minor and major leagues. I was a competitive player. I thought there was a difference between winning and losing. That's just the way I was brought up. My most memorable game was played in 1965 in Austin, Texas. I went in as a relief pitcher and pitched 15 innings. I told the other boys that they might as well make some runs because I wasn't going to let the other team win that game. I play to win.

We had a home in the Vilas area where we moved after I retired. I used my Navy training and became a barber and worked in Boone. But I was pretty restless and not used to staying in one place very long. So in 1970 when I received a call from Montreal offering me a deal to scout for them, I told them I was interested. Now I didn't even know what I was supposed to do exactly, but I was excited about getting back into baseball. With the help of three veteran scouts who took me under their wings, I learned how to line up my prospects, set up a schedule and all that. My salary for that first year was $10,000 and I thought I was rich. Of course gas was just 32¢ a gallon and a good motel room was only $10 a night. Now you're lucky to find a good motel room for $100 a night and gas is out of sight.

I signed up my first three players in one week. I thought that scouting was going to be a breeze. Barry Foote was the first player I signed on. We offered him $68,000. Now everybody playing ball makes at least one million dollars. The other two players were Sam Ewing and Phil Garner. They all did pretty well, and I thought I had the easiest job in the world. As I learned later, it wasn't always that way. From Montreal I went with the Philadelphia Phillies for nine years, then to Houston Astros for thirteen years, and then completed my 29 years as a scout with the Dodgers. It was nothing for me to drive 300 to 400 miles a day. I was in a motel room about 200 nights a year. It was a challenge, but I liked what I was doing.

My scouting teachers must have trained me right or I wouldn't have stayed with it for all those years. Looking for new talent is exciting. I always get asked what you look for in a young player. I would look for their arm speed, bat speed, power, how fast they could run, how they could field the ball, and their instincts. I always looked for a plus of some sort in each player and then I would just hope that I made the right decision about that player. Scouting has been enjoyable, but it has changed a lot since that first year. I have lived and breathed baseball most of my life, but I wouldn't trade any of it for anything.

Financial Aide to J. Willard and Alice S. Marriott

Kathryn Clay Bodeen

Kathryn Clay Bodeen submitted this text in 2003. Today she and her husband have retired and live in Sparta, N.C.

When I was asked to contribute to this section of the book, my initial reaction was that I didn't qualify, feeling that I was not in the same league with others whom I knew had excelled in their careers. But, I reasoned if one criterion for inclusion was being in an unusual occupation, then perhaps I did fall within the parameters.

One of the authors asked if I had always dreamed of a particular vocation or if I just lucked out. It was an intriguing question and one which I had never really thought about, so it inspired me to reconstruct how I arrived at where I am today. Predestination has always been a rather depressing concept to me, but in retrospect, I wonder if there may have been an overall plan, with the confluence of faith (more my mother's than my own), education, and what appeared at times to be sheer luck bringing it to fruition.

I graduated from Cove Creek High School in 1952 and my goal was to attend Woman's College (now UNC-G), obtain a degree in business education, and return to the mountains to teach high school business subjects. Though I had been accepted for admission, the money for college simply was not there. At the end of a summer's waitressing job, I had accumulated about $500 in savings, which would get me through one semester, but not the next. I had sought scholarship assistance but had heard nothing. So my thought was to forget it all, but Mother, Allie Clay, would not give up. She said, "Do you *want* to go to college?" I answered, " Yes, of course, but…." In her matter-of-fact way, she said, "Well then, where there is a will there is a way!" This sounded like pure foolishness to me, but with her persuasion I boarded the Greyhound bus, bound for Greensboro.

When I arrived at my dorm, the house counselor said, "Your mother wants you to call her." In those days we didn't place long-distance calls except for emergencies, or extreme cases. So in panic, I thought, "Something terrible must have happened." With my heart thumping, I called to get the bad news. Mother said calmly, as if she had known it all along, "You received a letter from the college this morning. I just thought you'd like to know that you got the scholarship." So year one was covered.

By the second year another small scholarship appeared, along with jobs in the student aid office and college library. Combining those windfalls with summer jobs in Greensboro (living rent-free with an older sister) and some loving "egg money" checks from home, I was able to finish the next three years. Mother's undaunting faith had started the whole process and kept it alive during some down periods.

Two months before graduation, I had not yet looked into teaching possibilities and after my student teaching experiences, I wasn't really sure I was ready to face a classroom of rowdy teenagers. Then either predestination or sheer luck intervened. The chancellor's office was near the student aid office where I worked, and I knew the chancellor only to say "Hello." One morning he appeared at my door and said, "I have a good friend who has a law firm in Washington. He is looking for a secretary to work with three young lawyers. Would you be interested in going up for an interview?"

Enough said! The next morning I was on a train to D.C., with instructions to take a cab to the firm's Mayflower Hotel apartment, then to report for an interview the following day. The train ride, the stay in such plush surroundings, the interview — there was such a rush from all the new experiences that I could hardly take it in. I remember buying a postcard showing a picture of the hotel, putting a pillow in one of the apartment windows, then running outside to identify which window on the photo had a pillow in the window. I circled that window and sent the card to Mother with a note, "This is where I am staying!" I got the job and found the smattering of business law which had been a part of my curriculum served me well.

Four years later a friend advised that a new research firm was opening in town and it was advertising for a bookkeeper. Though I was perfectly happy in the work I was doing, I had enjoyed my college accounting courses more than any of the others. So the allure of the financial work, combined with an increase in salary and benefits, led me to a new job for the next 12 years. Again those college courses which had been designed for another profession worked to my benefit.

The commute to downtown had become increasingly difficult over the years, and I had married during the interim and had the added responsibilities of a home. So I began watching the ads for a job closer to where we lived. One which especially intrigued me, and in which I could combine the accounting and secretarial skills, was to work for an investment adviser specializing in growth stocks and who needed someone to do performance calculations for his managed accounts. This was during the heady market of 1972 when growth was king and it was a very exciting time to watch the stocks of promising young companies surge upward. Then came the plunge in the market in 1974, and especially hard hit were the growth stocks. Though I loved the work and wanted to stay in the investments field, I decided it would be wise to look for a job covering a broader spectrum of investments than the so-called growth stocks. So it was back to the "Help Wanted" pages.

This is perhaps where sheer luck surfaced again, or simply being at the right place at the right time. A tiny, intriguing ad had appeared in the old *Washington Star.* It was for a secretary/bookkeeper to an investment adviser, but there was no name of employer, only a box number to which to send one's resume. It was enough of a come on to entice me, so I responded. Two days later I received a call. The caller identified himself as the investment adviser who had placed the ad. He said he liked my resume and asked if I could join him for an interview at J. Willard Marriott, Sr.'s office the next day. I gulped. The name of the founder and chairman of the board of Marriott Corporation was by then well known across the world, and especially in the D.C. area where he had his humble beginnings with a 9-stool root beer stand. A dedicated Mormon, he epitomized the American Dream, having harvested the fruits of honesty, vision and hard work. Based on what I already knew from reading about the Marriott family, there was no question in my mind that I wanted that interview!

Mr. M. told me, with that wonderful twinkle in his eye, that it was the way I walked that made him decide to hire me. He said, "You walked in here that day like you meant business." But I believe it was the combination of teaching skills, all of which would prove useful in the work I did for him, which landed me the job. He was looking for someone who could combine into one accounting system his investments in stocks, bonds, and real estate and then track their performance. He was delighted with the fact that I also took shorthand and could thus record his discussions with various advisers.

I started on a self-employed basis, part time for Mr. Marriott and part time for the adviser. But Mr. M. was always looking at the bottom line. Six months later he decided he didn't need both an in-house adviser and bookkeeper. He asked me to work full time on his and Mrs. Marriott's investments and to become administrator of his family's foundation and several family trusts. This was a fascinating combination of duties and over the next 25 years provided the opportunity also to work with his two sons and their families.

This is not to say there was always smooth sailing. There were frustrations voiced by advisers and even a few corporate employees that this upstart woman was keeping notes on their conversations and reducing their lengthy reports to shortened formats for the chairman's review. (His opinion was that everything worth saying could be said on one page.) The complaints bothered me, but with the charisma he applied so deftly to ruffled feathers, Mr. M. would say that I was being too sensitive, reminding me that, "You are working for me, not them."

Ever the negotiator, in 1980 Mr. Marriott said, "I met a young lady out West who said she could do the same work for me that you're doing, and for half the price." I had become quite comfortable in the job and it was a jolt to realize I was not indispensable. I feigned confidence and said, "Then I guess you should hire her and I'll look for another job." He looked surprised, studied my expression and said, "Oh, you will, will you?" I was shaking inside but managed to keep calm and simply replied, "Yes, Sir." I've never forgotten the way he closed one eye and squinted at me and said, with utmost admiration, "Boy, you're tough!" He never mentioned hiring someone else again, but as back-up insurance I went to night school to receive financial planning certification in case I found myself out the door and needing a new vocation.

Mr. M. and I had a common interest in music. He had sung in a quartet in college, The Hum-Drummers. Forty years later I sang with a quartet in D.C., The Dixie Doodles. So we compiled a songbook for group singing. Starting with about 70 Hum-Drummers' favorites, we added more recent ones, ending with the lyrics for 166 songs. I can still see him leaning back in his easy chair, eyes closed, and quietly singing the ones he wanted to add but for which I didn't know the words. Meanwhile, I was frantically writing the lyrics in shorthand. His favorite, by the way, was "Who's in the Strawberry Patch with Sally?"

Mr. M. loved the corporate farm in Virginia and delighted in socializing at the annual company picnics held there. He had had a couple of heart attacks and worried his family by taking his Jeep off-road on the farm's steep hills. I remember one such ride which was great fun for me but a terrifying experience for my husband and three women employees. At the annual picnic Mr. M. said to the five of us, "Let's go for a Jeep ride. Kay, you sit in front with me, you can open the gates, and we'll sing." The other four sat on narrow benches along each side of the back, with no rails or grab bars. So we went flying over hill and dale, only stopping long enough occasionally for me to open a gate to another pasture full of cows and their deposits. The two of us sang lustily, drowning out the shouts from the back of the Jeep.

When we returned to the picnic, I should have noticed the relief and exhaustion on the faces of the other four riders as they practically fell out of the back of the Jeep. I said to my husband, Bill, "Wasn't that *fun*!" He exploded. "Maybe it was fun for you! but you had a windshield in front of you and a seat! We were grabbing everything we could hang on to, including legs, arms and whatever, and ducking all the cow sh__ flying through the air!" We still laugh at the memory.

After Mr. M. died in 1985, I continued working for Mrs. Marriott, the foundation, and trusts. Over the years I became very fond of Mrs. Marriott. She was called Allie, as was my mother, so maybe that was part of the bond I felt with her. It was evident that she was indeed an exceptional woman, gentle, quiet, and unassuming, but as much of a businesswoman as Mr. M. was a businessman.

She was a director and vice president of the company and was very intuitive, with a tremendous knowledge of the working of the company she helped to build. She died in 2000, and those who knew them both, as well as many who did not, were infinitely blessed by their friendship and the contributions they made during their lives and which continue through funds they established for countless schools and charities.

Maybe there is such a thing as predestination, after all. When I review the past 50 years, I realize there must have been a grand scheme which allowed faith, work, and sheer luck to come together. And yes, "You can get there from here," but there will always be a corner of my heart which stays in those beautiful

For Kathryn Clay Bodeen money for college was not readily available, but with college assistant jobs, scholarships, and a mother who never gave up on her and wouldn't let her give up on herself, she graduated from Woman's College at Greensboro. She worked her way up through the ranks from a secretary for three young lawyers to a bookkeeper with a new research firm, then as a secretary-bookkeeper for an investment adviser, and finally as the administrator for the founder and chairman of the Marriott Corporation for 25 years. She says faith, work, and sheer luck came together to make her successful (photograph furnished by Kathryn Bodeen).

mountains and with the families and friends who sustained me throughout.

My Career in the CIA

Carlton H. Swift

Carlton H. Swift contributed this text in September 2002. He lives in McLean, Virginia.

On December 10, 1951, I walked into the building at 2430 E Street N.W., Washington, D.C. At that moment, I left behind life as I had known it and became an employee of the Central Intelligence Agency. I never looked back.

What brought me to this place at this time? From high school onward I thought of a career in government at some level, state or federal. I was also interested in a possible career in engineering or architecture. I made some false starts in pre-engineering courses at Appalachian State Teachers College, then dropped out and signed up for a two year hitch in the Navy. When discharged from the military, I re-enrolled at Appalachian. Upon completing two years study at ASTC, I transferred to the University of North Carolina, Chapel Hill, and switched my major to political science. I received a BA degree from UNC in June of 1951 and immediately headed for Washington to look for a federal job. Congressman Robert L. Doughton was most helpful. He arranged interviews for me at the young CIA (then only four years old) and at other federal agencies. I hung around D.C. for a while waiting for action on my applications, but nothing visible seemed to be happening. Low on funds (i.e., flat broke) I returned home somewhat dejected. Some months later there came a letter from 2430 E Street directing me to report there on 10 December, if interested in working for the CIA. Needless to say, I was elated.

But what was the CIA all about? I knew next to nothing about what it really did, and that's the way it was planned. In those days, no outsider knew. Once inside the CIA, I was informed that I would need security clearances up to the top secret level and that it would take some time to complete my background investigation, which had begun shortly after my earlier interview and application. Meanwhile, I would be on the payroll and sit in a pool with others awaiting clearance. And there I sat, and sat, and sat. Some four months later, after extensive physical and mental examinations, as well as polygraph (lie detector) tests, I was cleared and ready to begin secretive work, or so I thought. Instead, I was sent out of town for some intensive training. What did I learn? Well, I learned the tradecraft of the specific job for which I had been hired. And I deduced that the CIA was about defining itself as the premier intelligence organization in the world. Over time, most domestic and foreign observers acknowledged it achieved that objective, despite some flubs and flaps along the way.

In July 1952, I was posted (under military cover) to West Germany, the front line of the Cold War with the Soviet Bloc. When I retired I signed a "Secrecy Oath" which precludes me from revealing CIA sources and methods. But I can assure you the agency played a crucial role in bringing about the downfall of Communism. I am particularly proud to have been a part of that effort.

When I arrived in Frankfurt, Germany was still under military occupation and evidence of World War II was everywhere to be seen. Rubble still filled the streets of Old Town Frankfurt and refugees from Iron Curtain countries roamed all about. The scene was much the same in other major cities. We Americans had to park our cars in guarded parking lots. Little did I know then that I would spend the next ten years in Europe. This period saw astounding economic recovery, a steady deterioration in East/West relations, the creation of the Federal Republic of Germany, great unrest in Communist East Germany, the Hungarian revolution, the building of the Berlin Wall and daily incidents along the West German border with East Germany and Czechoslovakia. But I doubt the reader is much interested in this political and military muck of a half century ago.

Together with exciting employment, I was determined to soak up some European history, culture and cuisine. With friends I visited many, many historic cathedrals, castles and cities, including most of the capitals of Western Europe and Scandinavia.

Over the 1953 New Year Holiday, I traveled with two friends via military train through the Soviet Zone of East Germany to Berlin. Our orders, typed in Russian, were scrutinized (together with our persons) by the Russian military at the border crossing. Blinds on the train were drawn and had to remain so as we traveled through Soviet occupied East Germany. While in West Berlin, we hired a car with driver (who worked for American Express) and crossed from the American Sector into East Berlin as tourists. As soon as we crossed the sector border, a surveillance car fell in behind and stayed with us the entire time. We drove by Hitler's bunker where he committed suicide at war's end and visited the Russian War Memorial where some 2,800 Soviet troops, killed in the battle of Berlin, are buried. It was all very exciting but on our return to Frankfurt my friends and I were roundly reprimanded for crossing into East Berlin. It was worth it. We were lucky that we did not receive more that a tongue lashing for that caper.

After receiving his bachelor's degree in political science from the University of North Carolina in 1951, Carlton Swift became interested in working for the government. The CIA and other agencies in Washington, D.C., interviewed him, and after months of background investigation, he got security clearance and received intensive training. He served most of his time from 1952 to 1961 based in Germany. From 1962 until his retirement in 1986, he worked in Washington with Senior Intelligence Service and managed many computer personnel. He served the CIA for 40 years (photograph furnished by Carlton Swift).

After about a year I was transferred to a small operational base between Frankfurt and Heidelberg. While I was there largely in a support role, I did accompany base operational officers from time to time to the Czech border. There we would lie on our bellies at the edge of the woods, looking across the ploughed (and carefully harrowed) ground into Communist Czechoslovakia. The ground was ploughed by Czechs and Soviets to detect footprints of any agents we might be attempting to infiltrate through the Iron Curtain. Guards constantly patrolled the border looking for evidence of crossings. These exercises were very interesting and sometimes we came up with a new and creative ways to get people across. Some of the schemes were flatly harebrained. For example, a colleague once proposed using stilts to cross the ploughed strip to avoid leaving large, easily detected footprints. Needless to say this idea was promptly rejected. Somewhere in this time frame I visited Vienna. Like Germany, Austria was occupied by the four Allied powers: the Soviets, British, French, and Americans. Vienna, however, unlike Berlin, was divided into five sectors. The fifth one was designated the International Sector and the occupying powers rotated patrol and guard duty each month. It was Ok for us to visit the International Sector. When I was there, the Soviets had responsibility for the sector. I moved about freely taking photos of sites of interest and of Soviet troops. They did not view this kindly and a sawed-off, half-pint soldier with a big machine gun trained on me confiscated the film in my camera. I did not challenge the legality of his actions.

In 1954 I transferred to Munich, from which many of our East Bloc Operations were conducted. There I finished my first tour. After brief home leave, I returned to Munich. In 1956 the Hungarians revolted against the Soviet domination and were brutally suppressed. I worked about 20 hours a day as Hungarian refugees streamed into Austria and were sent to Munich. There they were debriefed and processed for settlement in the U.S. and other Western countries. Hearing their terrible experiences made me angry, ready and willing to take up arms against the Soviets. While there was some discussion of invading Hungary, the U.S. military did nothing more than assist the refugees.

I ended my second tour in Munich in the spring of 1957, came on Home Leave, married my wife, Diane, and returned to Frankfurt. Diane was also a CIA employee whom I had met a couple of years earlier while back at headquarters between tours. We ultimately had four children, the first of whom was born in Germany. At the beginning of my third assignment I switched to the technical arenas and pursued the agency's early efforts to apply automation (IBM Electrical Accounting Machines) to intelligence processing overseas. This was before we brought the first computers into the agency. Both my third and fourth tours were served in Frankfurt.

Between Christmas and New Year's, 1961, I made my last trip to Berlin. The infamous Berlin Wall had just been built. A lady friend who was stationed there and I trekked along the West side of the wall for a mile or so near midnight in bitter cold and snow. I did not want to leave Germany without seeing it. Before it was finally torn down, many unfortunate East Germans were killed trying to escape to the West through, over or under The Wall.

Today a small section of the demolished wall stands just outside the headquarters building on the CIA campus. When it was brought here in the 1990s, I wanted to think it was a section that I had looked at on that bitter night thirty some years earlier. The probability is low.

In early 1962 I came to our beautiful new headquarters building in the Virginia countryside. The remainder of my career was spent at headquarters working on computer solutions to intelligence problems. I climbed through the ranks one grade level at a time to reach Senior Intelligence Service (SIS). When I retired in 1986 I was chief of the Clandestine Service's System's group, managing a large number of computer personnel.

Several years later I returned to the agency as an independent contractor and worked in that capacity for four more years. In the year 2000 I finally hung it all up, having served an aggregate of 40 years. I could not have wished for a more satisfying career.

Ray Hicks

Catherine Stokes Sheppard

This profile of the well-known Ray Hicks is based on an April 21, 2003, article in the Watauga Democrat *and on his performances.*

Surely there is no one in Watauga County who has been photographed more or whose picture has been published more often, appeared on public television more or whose company has been sought more than Ray Hicks. Not even university presidents or local politicians have gained the celebrity status that Ray Hicks has.

Who is this tall, thin man that attracts so much attention? This man who always wears bib overalls and a cocked hat, and rolls his own cigarettes from a tin of Prince Albert smoking tobacco?

Leonard Ray Hicks was born in 1922 on the side of Beech Mountain, an eighth generation American. The land on which the Hicks ancestors settled is beautiful beyond belief, but not conducive to farming. As a matter of fact it is a harsh land, steep and rocky. Yet the Hicks families have clung to it through the years with an unyielding tenacity. They grew cabbage, corn, beans and whatever they could but never enough to accumulate more than a meager living. In 1914 Ray's father built a large two-storied house for his family. The humble, unpainted, un-insulated house still stands and it was here that Ray was born and spent most of his life. It is here that the TV cameras and newspaper reporters have come. It is here that the college professors and students have come. It is here that people from across America and some from Europe have come. Why? Because Ray Hicks was a storyteller.

Miss Jennie Love was a teacher at Cove Creek High School. She knew many of the mountain families and she knew their stories. She knew the storytelling tradition of the Hicks families as well as that of the Wards and Harmons and others. In the early 1950s she invited Ray Hicks to her class to tell stories as a part of her American literature class. He was so popular that soon other teachers were inviting him to their classes. Ray has said that Miss Love gave him money for gasoline to come to the school. Thus he gave credit to Jennie Love for introducing him to the world of storytelling for hire as well as for entertainment. However, most of Ray's stories through the years have been told not for money, but for his own pleasure and that of his friends and admirers. He was invited to the first Storytelling Festival in Jonesboro, Tennessee. After that the world began to beat a path to his door.

Of the multitude of storytellers in this area, what made Ray unique? To sit and listen to Ray tell a story was like turning time back several hundred years. He not only told the stories he learned from his grandfather, who in turn had learned them from his grandfather, he tells them in the voice of his English and Scottish forefathers. His facial expressions, his hand gestures, the raising and lowering of his voice, the leaning forward to his audience in a hoarse whisper all combined to hold the listener spellbound. He could tell you a bar (bear) clim (climbed) a tree and that haints (ghosts) lit out (ran). These expressions are not affectations; this is how Ray spoke in everyday language. But when Ray used these words in a story the listener was transported to another time period. In order not to frighten children Ray told them the stories are not true, but the listener must believe them while he is telling the story. And for a few moments the listener really did believe. Ray had quite a repertoire of material to draw from. His stories were about haints, witches, magic, haunted woods, bears, bats, thieves, or unrequited love that causes young men to risk great peril for the hand of a beautiful girl. Sometimes he admitted not all of them were old stories. Sometimes he made them up. Nevertheless, all were entertaining.

In 1983 the National Endowment for the Arts invited Ray and his wife Rosa to Washington, D.C., and named him a National Heritage Fellow. Not only was he classified as a national treasure, he was given an award of $5000. This was the most money he had ever had at one time and certainly the farthest he had ever been from his home.

In 2001 Ray was diagnosed with terminal cancer. This humble man who had lived in the same house most of his life without central heat, running water or a telephone became a rich man — rich in friends. Friends came from far and near to lend a hand. Fundraisers were held. Contributions were made for his personal care. Ray survived another couple of years, still in his home facing the mountain he knew so well, still attended by his loving wife Rosa. He felt well enough some days to spin a yarn or two and greet friends who came to call and help out. No matter what circumstances could have been, this is the way Ray chose to live out his days. He died at his home in 2003.

Wayne Tester Follows His Dream

Joyce P. Ragan

This profile of Wayne Tester was submitted by Joyce P. Ragan in 2003.

From a small rural community in northwestern North Carolina comes one of the brightest talents in the music world. Wayne Tester has written songs for some very well known country artists, such as Tracy Byrd and Garth Brooks. How did this boy get from here to there? Talent and hard work!

Wayne Tester grew up in Vilas with his parents and two brothers, one of them his twin. Wayne had a natural talent for music so it was no surprise when he received a degree in music from Appalachian State University. He moved to Nashville, Tennessee, the perfect place for a songwriter to pursue a career in music. Wayne has written songs for stars, scores for movies, choruses for Christian programs, and an opening rendition for the Olympics. That's pretty good for a piano player from Western Watauga County (photograph furnished by Bina Tester).

Wayne and his twin brother Duane were born in Watauga County to Arlis and Bina Tester. He has an older brother, Larry. From their earliest days, their parents took the children to Cove Creek Baptist Church where Wayne began his musical career. At the age of five Wayne began taking piano lessons and his teacher noticed his natural talent for music. When he was a young teenager, he began playing for the youth groups at church, and in a short time he was playing for church services. Later he became the music director for the church while he was still a student at Appalachian State University, where he earned a degree in music.

After graduating from ASU, Wayne packed up and moved to Nashville in 1988. Having no job and knowing no one, he began to follow his dream of a career in music. Gradually he made contacts and got to know people in the music industry. He became the music leader on Opryland's *General Jackson* showboat.

Wayne's first break came as a jingle writer for commercials. His first attempt at jingle writing was for a women's fashion commercial and the company liked what they heard. So he was on his way! The next break came for Wayne when he met David Briggs, who had played keyboards for Elvis Presley. Briggs brought Wayne on board on the production end, where he worked as a composer, programmer and keyboardist. Wayne contributed underscore to the 1992 Country Music Association awards show.

Following his work on the awards show, Wayne met and worked with movie scores writer David Foster. Foster introduced him to Leeds Levy, a former president of MCA Music. Song writer Dave Loggins, who was also with MCA, was in need of a keyboardist and someone who could write songs. This was the final break that Wayne needed. Using the piano skills he had learned back home in Vilas, Wayne began working as a staff writer with Dave Loggins. He signed a contract with MCA in 1992, where he worked on several Country Music award shows, as well as other productions. Wayne has several film and TV credits, such as "Get Out of My Dreams" for *SunsetBeach* and "Could It Be Me" for Dreamworks' *Prince of Egypt* soundtrack. Another milestone for Wayne was working as a staff writer on different projects for Disney Music Publishing in Burbank, California. He wrote seven songs for the MGM film *Tom Sawyer* and was associate producer for that soundtrack, working with Tony Brown and Mark Wright.

Some of Wayne's work includes "Love By Grace" recorded by Wynonna Judd, "Let Me Live Another Day" by Lisa Bishop, and "Lonely Only Goes So Far" by the Sky Kings. "Lifestyles of the Not So Rich and Famous" became a country smash for Tracy Byrd. Wayne says that song had its roots in Vilas, where Wayne's dad owned and operated a service station. Every morning a group of men in the community would gather to drink coffee, gossip and wait for the rural mail carrier. He told a friend that after listening to those men talk, he had an idea for some of the lyrics for the song. (Could this have been about drinking RC Colas and eating moon pies?)

One of Wayne's biggest hits, co-written with Tony Arata, was sung by Garth Brooks. "The Change" was written about having faith in oneself, but Brooks gave it a new meaning on his video when he used it to pay tribute to the victims and families of the Oklahoma City bombing tragedy.

Wayne also co-wrote several songs for the Christian market. "Freedom Rings" was one of his first, written to celebrate our nation's freedom. Cove Creek Baptist Church choir chose this song for their special Fourth-of-July freedom celebration. They invited Wayne, who was at home for the holiday, to accompany them as they sang his song. That performance received a standing ovation from his hometown crowd.

Probably Wayne's most prestigious project was co-writing the song "Dare to Dream," one of three theme songs used for the Sydney Olympic Games in 2000. This song was performed by Olivia Newton-John and the Australian sensation John Farnham. It was featured on the album *The Official Soundtrack: The Games of the XXVII Olympian — Music from the Official Opening Ceremony*." Tester was quoted as saying, "This is the biggest thing I've done so far because it is international.... I'm truly excited about this and thank God for the opportunity."

Recently Wayne has formed a private company which should offer more career opportunities for him. He will serve on a contract basis and is currently working with Lifeway Christian Resources. He provides, integrates and implements music into curriculum, events and ministry areas of their programs. He still lives in Nashville as do his three children, Bradley and twins Brandon and Shannon. His parents and brother Larry's family still reside in Vilas, N.C. Twin brother Duane's family lives in Cary, N.C. Wayne's family, relatives and lots of friends scattered around the country encourage him in his songwriting efforts and wish him well as he continues to follow his dream. What a talent!

Tuning In on the World

Ben Mast

Ben Mast submitted his story in 2004.

I was born two days before Christmas in 1932, in the depths of the Great Depression. Times were hard, my parents had to scrape to make ends meet, and the virtue of thrift was deeply ingrained in me for the rest of my life. Yet some of my most cherished recollections date to those austere days.

Such memories are now writ large as rural legends. There was excitement year-round as neighbor Papaw Mast plied his many farm enterprises: lambing and calving in the spring; gathering hay in high summer; filling the cellar and granary with harvested apples and salted hams in the fall; cranking the hit-and-miss engine to grind cattle fodder and saw logs for winter fires in the fall; and stoking the blacksmith bellows to craft new wagon rims in the winter. Another memory is the summer idyll of Grandma Shell's in the forested Bethel uplands where I took breaks from hoeing tobacco to search out rhododendron thickets for ginseng and teaberry; more importantly, I learned from Uncle Don Shell cabinet and chair making at the century-old, foot-cranked lathe of that artisan family. The historic Cove Creek gristmill, founded by Joseph Harrison Mast and then thriving as a prime community institution under the ownership of Don Stokes, spawned wistful memories of skating and swimming on the mill pond and daring other youths to "walk the wheel" when miller Hensel Stokes had the mill running full blast.

Some of the most poignant memories centered on an early fascination for electronics, radio, and broadcasting. When neighbor Junior Simpson, who had a genius-level IQ, more than once troubleshot the circuitry of our

1932-vintage Majestic console, I admiringly followed his logic in tracing the source (usually a shorted capacitor). I was spellbound from earliest childhood by the radio broadcasts I picked up on crystal sets or on radios, none more so than Orson Welles' "War of the Worlds" in 1938, which prompted my brothers and sister to search the heavens for Martian invaders and consult our learned neighbor, the legendary Mr. Grant, for advice. The elderly sage, who had helped my father carry on the South's first cheese factory he'd pioneered in 1916, had this to say: "Ai yoi-yoi, you should beware invaders from Europe, not Mars." I'll never forget tweaking radio sets to catch fiery speeches by Adolf Hitler and Benito Mussolini as the Second World War was raging. Eldest brother Harold, back from signal corps duty once the war ended, passed along many superheterodyne tips, so that I was able to coax out of our old Crosley model 138 "cathedral" set a strong signal of Joe Lewis boxing bouts and World Series baseball. Just as exciting was success in pulling in, very late at night, WQXR in New York, which broadcast continuous classical music. Radio sparked my childhood imagination and opened up for me a world I was ready to join.

After enrolling at Appalachian State Teachers College in 1951 just as the Korean War broke out, I received a student deferment; however, I always felt bad that former classmates were being shot at in Korea while I sat in the classroom. I worked my way through college at Boone radio station WATA, serving as music host, interviewer and sportscaster. One of the talent shows hosted on weekends featured a brilliant young guitarist and singer named Doc Watson. I also originated one of the first nation-wide broadcasts of the Appalachian choir, then directed by Virginia Wary Linney.

Just before graduating from ASTC I was awarded a Morehead Scholarship for postgraduate study in communications and political science at the University of North Carolina. While at Chapel Hill I served as news director of WUNC-TV, narrated an award-winning NBC radio series (in which Charles Kuralt participated as an actor), and worked part-time at radio station WPTF in Raleigh.

On completion of the Morehead program I served two years in the army as a broadcast specialist. The first assignment was principal newscaster at Armed Forces Radio and Television Headquarters, New York City, and also interviewer of many celebrities at movie and theater premieres on Broadway. Late in 1958, the scene changed to the center of U.S. military broadcasting in Europe, the American Forces Network in Frankfurt, Germany. There I continued in the newscasting role and also was special events reporter throughout Europe, including Berlin during the East-West crisis of 1959, and originated special commemorative broadcasts from American cemeteries in Europe on Memorial Day. The final AFN assignment was an interview with Edward R. Murrow in San Moritz, Switzerland. After discharge, I applied for and received a commission in the U.S. Navy. I served with the Office of Naval Intelligence for over 25 years, on active and reserve duty, retiring at the rank of captain. The final post was executive officer of the nationwide naval attaché unit supporting the Defense Intelligence Agency. Very interesting active duty assignments were with the joint chiefs of staff, and as intelligence debriefer of returned Viet Nam prisoners of war, including then–Captain James Stockdale.

After military discharge, a Japan Society Scholarship at Duke University made possible preparation for Ph.D. study. With Air Force sponsorship, I also traveled to six Latin American countries to research the U.S. military assistance program.

Career employment began with the Voice of America headquarters in Washington, D.C., as producer, news broadcaster, and later, as features editor. At the same time, I was asked to provide "live" worldwide broadcasts as a radio commentator at United Nations Headquarters in New York during the historic 1960 General Assembly Meeting, attended by the greatest gathering of world leaders since the coronation of Edward VI. I was on hand to broadcast Ambassador Henry Cabot Lodge's exposé of the Soviet "bugging" of the U.S. embassy "eagle" in Moscow; also, the spectacle of Soviet Premier Nikita Khrushchev banging his shoe on the table in contempt of the proceedings; and later, U.S. delegate Adlai Stevenson's angry UN confrontation with the Soviets and Cubans during the Cuban missile crisis.

Ben Mast worked at the Boone radio station early in the 1950s. He worked his way through Appalachian State Teachers College serving as music host, interviewer, and sportscaster for station WATA. From there, a brilliant career in communications was launched. It skyrocketed from Boone to Chapel Hill, N.C., to Washington, D.C., to Switzerland for an interview with Edward R. Murrow, and worldwide commitments. He was a newscaster, producer of films and TV documentaries; a news writer and feature editor; a radio commentator; an interviewer; and a Navy debriefer of prisoners of war. He is still busy at home and overseas since his retirement (photograph furnished by Ben Mast).

There were also brief assignments with national American networks. In the early 1960s, I was hired by ABC news chief James Hagerty, former press secretary to President Dwight Eisenhower, as TV documentary and news writer. Later John Ehle, a former professor at UNC and then advisor to Governor Terry Sanford, persuaded me to return to N.C. and head up the North Carolina Film Board, the first state documentary film unit in America. Together with Canadian filmmaker Jim Beveridge, I produced several award-winning films in a short time, including *The Road to Carolina* (early N.C. history), *Tryon Palace*, *The Ayes Have It* (the N.C. state legislature), *The Vanishing Frontier* (the N.C. mountains), and *The Piedmont Crescent*. Following the assassination of JFK, and amid growing tensions over civil rights protests, I was authorized by the governor to work with administration counselor John Brooks (also a Morehead scholar) to negotiate an end to student demonstrations, which were then being led by Jesse Jackson. Despite many difficulties, I persuaded Jackson and the students to express their grievances in a film series that would be co-sponsored by the N.C. Film Board and private TV stations, so that "protests would be taken off the street and into the TV set." This plan was successfully carried out, the students quietly discontinued their demonstrations, and tensions were defused. Although never publicly credited, I believe this intervention helped spare North Carolina the destructive race relations experienced in other areas of the South during sorely troubled times.

Returning to Washington, I joined the Naval Photographic Center as a writer and narrator of film and TV/video documentaries for the Navy, Department of Defense, and the White House. Later I served as an administrator of the Navy's media training and education program. There were commendations from the U.S. president, the secretary of defense's office, and the chief of naval operations for several career achievements. In off-duty spare time, I worked at television stations in Washington, D.C., and hosted and narrated for such clients as Foster Parents Plan, the Library of Congress' Books for the Blind, the National Security Industrial Association, and religious and charity organizations.

After retirement a new set of activities has kept me busy both at home and overseas. Volunteer work in Washington has involved casework in the White House Agency Liaison Office, docent and research assistance for the White House Preservation Office, and Congressional lobbying for the League of Women Voters Headquarters. For the past eight years I have been recruited by the State Department for election observation missions with the Organization for Security and Cooperation in Europe in the Balkan region (Bosnia, Croatia, Serbia, Macedonia, and Romania), and also in countries formerly within the Soviet Union, including Armenia and Belarus. I also served as public affairs officer for the United Nations Development

Programme office in Skopje, Macedonia, in 1998 following the Kosovo crisis. These assignments have been challenging but also rewarding and fulfilling.

My current memberships include the White House Docents Group; DACOR, the Organization of U.S. Diplomatic and Consular Officers, retired; the German Research Association; the Finlandia Foundation; and the Georgetown Citizens Association. I have been captain of the local voting precinct in local elections in Georgetown, Washington, D.C.

I met my wife Ingrid in Germany at one of the diplomatic missions in Frankfurt, Germany, while on military duty, and we have been married for 42 years. Son Chris is a scientist with the Merck Corporation in Philadelphia, daughter Dorothea is an artist and lives in Scranton, Pennsylvania, and we have three grandchildren.

The superannuated life would not be complete without occasional stays in the Watauga homeland where it all began. The unfolding decades have wrought poignant change, and time has taken its toll. Many colorful personalities have slipped into the shadows, as have landmarks such as the old gristmill, "lost and by the river mourned," to quote Thomas Wolfe. The Will Moody farmhouse and outbuildings, where I spent many happy hours as a youth, have been restored to serve as a modest mountain retreat to enjoy latter-day pursuits—renewing old ties and researching and writing local history, which I hope to turn into a book. The cobwebbed recesses of the old barns and springhouse have yielded Uncle Will's and Aunt Laura's hand-crank telephone and 1931 Philco table radio, and the restoration of these artifacts has rekindled an early hobby—bringing back to life vintage electronic sets. Preservation of these and other treasures has also united past and present and brought a deeper appreciation of a uniquely rich heritage.

California, Here I Come!

Odenia Miller Rowe

Odenia Miller Rowe submitted her recollections of her 1938 trip to California in 2000.

My early years on Cove Creek—the area, the church, school, friends, neighbors and so many precious relatives—were such an important influence in my choices as I struck out on my own "to conquer the world and its challenges."

I was working for Bonnie Jean Lewis Rivers and her husband Rob who owned the *Watauga Democrat*. It was the summer of 1938 when Rob came home for dinner and said, "Odenia, how'd you like to go to California?" With little or no hesitation, I said, "How do I do that? I'd love to go, but...." Although my dad, Jim Miller, had worked out my first year's tuition at Appalachian, I was all ears.

Odenia Miller left Cove Creek on a Greyhound bus shortly after graduating from Cove Creek High School. Her destination was California. She returned to her home several times, taking family members back with her one by one. In this photo, a Cove Creek friend and neighbor, Lester Deal, was on leave when he visited Odenia and her husband, Howard Rowe, at their home in California in 1949. She loves living in California (photograph furnished by Odenia Miller Rowe).

That same evening we all drove to Cove Creek along with Mary Leslie Marshall, whom Rob knew and who had placed an ad with Rob for a "dependable housekeeper and companion for her two children, aged seven and 10, in exchange for room and board and $36 per month, plus going to the Junior College." After a conference with Sam Horton, Tom Moody, Rev. Fletcher, and Mr. and Mrs. Rivers, I was allowed to go. The trip was long and interesting as we were traveling on a sleeper Greyhound bus from Kansas City to Los Angeles, and then on a smaller bus to Santa Maria where I lived for the next two years.

The Marshalls were very nice and generous to me. We traveled in the summer. I was able to go to the World's Fairs in New York and San Francisco, as well as to Callender, Ontario, Canada, to see the Dionne quintuplets. I went to the Ballet Ruse in Los

Angeles, and also saw many shows at the Shrine Auditorium in L.A. There I attended Paderewski's concert on his last tour.

After I graduated from the junior college, I went to San Jose State College near San Francisco. There I worked for families, usually college professors, as cook and housekeeper in exchange for room and board. I also worked as assistant to college professors in various capacities and was paid by the government under a program instigated by Franklin D. Roosevelt. I worked hard, graduated with honors, and had ten cents left, but I was debt free.

Howard Rowe and I had been high school sweethearts, in fact, he and Dad were the ones who saw me off on the bus in '38. We had corresponded for four years. He came home on leave after losing his ship *The West Virginia* at Pearl Harbor. (Six months later he would lose *The Lexington.*) He asked me to marry him on June 18, one day before graduation. I did not hesitate to say "Yes!" We were married on June 22, 1942. We have had 57 years of good times filled with travel while in the military. We have been in many states and in Guam and the Philippines, where I taught. We have four children: Suzanne, a retired teacher; Chuck, a retired fireman; Rick, who owns a pool business; and Lena, who is a good wife and mom.

Part 6: Preserving Our Heritage

Western Watauga County has such a rich heritage from both nature and our forefathers that we often tend to overlook its provenance. Nature gave us beauty beyond measure. Our trees are lush and green in summer and weave a tapestry of colors in the fall, only to become shimmering diamonds in the snow and ice. Our streams are abundant and provide us with the babbling sounds that lull our tired spirits. Our meadows provide us with cultivated crops and feed for cattle. Our summer temperatures are perfect for the escape from city heat. Our snow covered slopes and fields give an ethereal beauty that allows us to slow down and reflect. Yes, nature has been good to our region. But what did our forefathers do?

The pioneers who came to Western Watauga with their handcarts and teams of oxen were not seeking beauty. They were looking for land that was productive and for safe home sites. Those big trees had to be cut by manpower. The rocky streams were not navigable; the meadow lands were full of stones that had to be removed by muscle and sweat. Pretty or not, the winters had to be survived. Yet the pioneers stayed. They fought the climate, the Indians, the hardships, and sometimes each other. Certainly there were those who decided for one reason or another that this place was not for them and they moved on to places like Kentucky, or Texas, or Tennessee. By the early 1800s these hardy souls who had remained had sturdy homes and barns. They had built meetinghouses that could be used for worship or education. They had Masonic lodges. They built community.

Each generation passed its values to the next. One has only to ride along the countryside and view the lovely little churches (some large ones, too) and comfortable homes to get a glimpse of our past. It is no accident that we sit in the shadow of a university that had its origin 100 years ago. The Dougherty brothers knew that mountain people were eager for an education. They knew that if they could get the school started the students would appear. They came and then went back to their home communities and taught others. Good schools became a priority.

How can it be that in only two hundred years our land has gone from a wilderness to a prosperous area? Perhaps the traits that have been most common in our culture are hard work and thrift. We have been taught to be self-reliant, to work hard, and to be thrifty. Who of us, as children, has not been quoted the old adage, "waste not, want not?" This is why we preserve our old family homes, we rebel at losing our community identity, and we treasure an architectural gem that once was our school. We do not worship our past but we do revere it. We pay tribute to our forefathers by preserving the culture they worked so hard to form. They built community, we organize to keep it.

Building Community in Foscoe

Catherine Stokes Sheppard

The following was compiled from interviews with Carmalee Ellis, Verlene Roark and Bernice Byrd in 2004.

Traditionally people in Western Watauga have helped each other when the need arose. Today is no different from the days of barn raisings and hog killings. Helping hands still come to the rescue in Foscoe.

Several years ago the citizens of Foscoe realized the need for a community building. They were able to purchase a former campground located in the heart of their community. They enlisted the help of Senator Virginia Foxx, who was instrumental in getting a grant. The locals came together, organized, rolled up their sleeves and went to work. Soon they had paid for their property which included 6.5 acres of land and a nice building, suitable for community events.

What did they do? They used whatever talents became available. Rosa Ellis Auton planned and organized breakfasts to be served to the public. Ber-

Foscoe needed a community building. Interested people found a campground for sale and they wanted to buy that land. Many fundraisers were planned and organized. One successful venture was cooking breakfasts to be served to the public. Soon people far and wide were coming there for breakfast. Together they paid off the mortgage and built a Foscoe Community Center suitable for many events (photograph by Catherine Stokes Sheppard).

nice Byrd made her mouthwatering biscuits, Carmelee Ellis made gravy in the old mountain tradition, Verlene Roark fried bacon, served up jelly, and visited the tables, as she claims, entertained the guests. Blanche Byrd put her spin on good old country ham and Marvin Auton made the just right coffee. Ralph Neilles washed the dishes, ran errands, and kept the grounds.

Others, too numerous to mention, have given generously of their time and talents to make these projects a success.

The breakfasts became so popular that people from all over the county began to show up for the fine vittles.

After the mortgage was paid the breakfasts and barbecue dinners continued for other worthwhile projects. If someone in the community has medical bills beyond their means, a benefit is almost sure to be held. Relay for Life is another cause that has benefited from the good cooks of Foscoe.

Perhaps the greatest benefit of all this has been the bringing together of the people of Foscoe into a united, active community. While many of the workers were born in Foscoe, others are the so-called transplants who have proved that they, too, belong in the Foscoe community.

Community Preservationists

Nannie Greene

Retirement for some means finding a place in a warm climate where one can lounge around and read or pursue a hobby or just chill out. Not so for James (Andy) and Alice Andrews. They came to Western Watauga to put down roots. As they approached retirement they looked around a bit and chose Sugar Grove as their general location, then a property off Mast Gap Road led them to the head of Hicks Hollar where they established their new home. There is more to the story than just two mid-westerners finding a new location.

Andy was born in Rhode Island. After a stint in the U.S. Navy he enrolled in Joplin Junior College in Missouri, where he met Alice. Education and employment combined to take the Andrews family to several homes. Actually, their four children were each born in a different state. After earning his Ph.D. in Iowa, Andy taught at the University of Cincinnati in Ohio. So how did they end up in Hicks Hollar? I asked Andy why they chose this area and he said that Alice thought Boone was a lot like her hometown in Missouri, with a peaceful countryside and natural beauty. Andy grinned and admitted that he just liked the people, and Andy himself is a likable guy.

James and Alice Andrews chose to buy land and build a home between Valle Crucis and Sugar Grove on Mast Gap Road. They soon became involved in the restoration of the old Cove Creek High School building. They share their time, talents and work to make good things happen in the community they call home (photograph furnished by James Andrews).

By the time the paint was dry on their new home they had involved themselves in community affairs. Andy joined the lunch bunch at Western Watauga Community Center, where he began to learn about the needs in the community, as well as to make a wider circle of friends.

I got to know Andy when I started working with the Cove Creek Preservation and Development, Inc., at the old Cove Creek High School building. Andy was always there and ready to help anyone who wanted to work on restoring the building. Nothing was ever too hard or too easy for him to do. He just wanted to help save that beautiful old building. He worked with groups, individuals, or alone. He ripped up carpets, replaced flooring, painted, and cleaned out spaces that no one else would attempt. He cleared out rooms and got them ready for use. He simply did what needed to be done. Personally, I have called on Andy many times for help in the museum. He always responded, with his sleeves rolled up and with a smile added, "Anything else I can do for you?"

Truly, Andy is an idea person and lots of his ideas will fly. One of his brilliant suggestions was to have the Cove Creek Farm Heritage Days. In 1997 Andy coordinated the two-day festival that continues as an annual event of information, fun, music, and fellowship. Andy has the gift of visualizing the overall program that will involve many people in the community. Another invaluable service to his community has been working with Tommy Walsh to get the Doc Watson Musicfest off the ground. Andy worked tirelessly year after year to help make that event a success.

When it comes to community service, we must not overlook Alice Andrews. She retired several years after Andy did, but like her husband she joined right in to work on community projects. She always did her share on Farm Heritage Days, and she soon became a member of the board of directors of the CCP&D. She, too, is always available to help with cleaning, preparing for and assisting with any program that will help the community. A recent endeavor in which both Alice and Andy have been actively involved was the opening of the Sugar Grove Developmental Day School that is located in the stone building the community has strived to rescue.

It is fortunate for us that Andy and Alice Andrews adopted our heritage as theirs. They have shown that they care about their community and willingly work hard and long hours to make good things come about. They have shared their time, talents, and diligence to make good things happen and the Cove Creek community is reaping the fruits of their labor. They have set a fine example for those of us whose forefathers forged a community from the wilderness.

Saving a Community Landmark

Nannie Greene

The community surrounding the Cove Creek High School was referred to as Cove Creek, but the Sherwood Post Office and the Sugar Grove Post Office served the residents in this area. There was a Cove Creek Post Office in the Asheville area. This often caused a bit of identity crisis.

Sherwood Post Office closed in the mid–1950s and in 1957 Highway 421 moved to a new location. In 1965 Cove Creek High School, along with other area high schools, consolidated into a central high school located in Boone. The Cove Creek Elementary School moved into the stone school building. The villages of Sugar Grove, Cove Creek, Amantha, Mast, Mabel, Silverstone, and Zionville were all concerned when the Cove Creek Elementary School moved to a new site several miles away in 1995, but Cove Creek was devastated. As a result of these changes, people began to move away, and the area began to decline. More people moved away than those who moved in. Young people who had gone away to school did not return because job opportunities were limited.

In 1990 the U.S. Postal Service held a meeting with the local citizens and announced that the Sugar Grove Post Office would close and it would be impossible for the citizens to countermand this decree. This was the death knell for community identity at Sugar Grove. What the U.S. Postal Service did not understand was the psyche of the mountain people. They did not know about the "cooperative spirit of all public enterprise." When the meeting adjourned, Jerry Adams, a soft-spoken, gentle man took the bull by the horns. He stood outside the door and invited each citizen to attend the Grange meeting the next week. He declared that no business other than saving the post office would be discussed until this matter was resolved.

The people who loved their community, both those from the old families of the region and those who had chosen to move here from afar, rallied to Jerry's call. They organized a committee to save the post office. The local chapter of the Grange provided

Top: **Nannie Greene, a retired teacher, volunteers to work with activities that benefit the preservation and sustainability of her alma mater, Cove Creek High School. *Bottom:* Cove Creek and surrounding communities were thrilled when Cove Creek High School was built in the early 1940s. When the school was abandoned in 1995, several community groups recognized the need to save that beautiful structure. Together they organized Cove Creek Preservation and Development to help the Community Council preserve the community and to make Cove Creek High School a usable space that would be able to sustain itself. It is still a work in progress (photograph by Jerry Adams).**

seed money and the action began. Jerry and Carolyn Adams, Leo and Shirley Mast, Jack and Marian Simpson, Hugh and Peggy Hagaman, John Mast, Dorothy Mast Harrigan, David Lassiter, Andy and Alice Andrews, Paul and Evelyn Shepherd, Faith Wright, Nora Wilson, Robert Shipley, and other locals began to work. People outside the community worked also. Robert and Elizabeth Atkiss and Ben Mast were a few of several who lent a hand. Letter writing campaigns and articles published in newspapers across the state gained the attention of elected officials, both locally and nationally. Committee members went to Washington, D.C., and knocked on doors and leaned heavily on our representatives. It worked! In the year 2005, the Sugar Grove Post Office is alive and well. So is the community, but the lines have expanded to include the people living in areas such as Mast Gap, Watauga River, Rush Branch, and on toward the Tennessee state line.

A Community Council

One might say that saving the post office was a wake-up call to the Sugar Grove community. The citizens realized that there were other local concerns that needed to be addressed. Upon investigation they learned that they could form a community council, but two boards, the Watauga County Planning Board and the Watauga County Commissioners, must approve any projects they proposed. No longer would they have to be an isolated group. Many of the people who had served on the Post Office Committee became involved in the Cove Creek Community Council. Others joined in.

The first project of the council was to survey the community to find what the populace wanted. The results showed there was a tremendous agreement that the area wanted to save the now threatened stone school building that had become vacant. The stone building was built in the early forties as a WPA project and it is truly an architectural gem. It has been the focal point of the community since that time. The people felt it must be saved from the wrecking crew. However, it would require expensive repairs. Questions began to arise. Where would the money come from? How could the building be used? Could it be self-supporting? Was it insurable? At that stage the building belonged to the Watauga County Board of Education, which could not afford to maintain it. Who should have the responsibility of the building? Someone must answer these questions.

Cove Creek Preservation & Development, Inc.

The next step was to form a committee to address these questions. In October of 1995 the Cove Creek Grange appropriated $250 to incorporate Cove Creek Preservation and Development, Inc. Jerry Adams was chosen as president and Leo Mast as vice-president, and seven directors were elected to serve on the board. Nan Greene served as treasurer.

Marian and Jack Simpson and Hugh Hagaman were already gathering information necessary to apply for Cove Creek High School to be put on the North Carolina Register of Historic Places, and they did the same for the National Register. They worked tirelessly until both were awarded. A plaque of proof hangs on the building beside the front door.

In July of 1996 the county accepted the school property from the Board of Education. The commissioners agreed to replace the leaking roof before turning the building over to CCP&D for $1 a year and the responsibility of its upkeep. The organization applied for and received non-profit status, receiving a 501-c tax number.

Because the Cove Creek High School alumni needed to become involved, a school reunion was planned in 1996. Information was gathered for the alumni. Names and addresses of CCHS graduates, a list of the teachers, history of the school, and pictures of some of the school activities were collected and compiled into a book called *Memories of Cove Creek High School.* In June over 400 alumni met at CCHS, where they were told about hopes for saving the school. Most were thrilled at the idea and offered their support, and more than 700 of the books have been sold.

Tommy Walsh, an employee of ASU in the Sustainable Development program, was working in the Cove Creek area. He incorporated the school efforts into his work and moved his office into the stone building. Tommy's expertise in promoting projects such as CCP&D has been invaluable, and his ability to work with people is uncanny. It was his initial guidance that led us to find the answers to many of our questions.

Other local organizations were asked to support our efforts. The Watauga Historical Society sponsored a yard sale. The Cove Creek Grange and the N.C. Grange donated the first $3,000 to our cause. The Community Council conducted the survey and got a walking trail put on the school grounds. Cove Creek Ruitians donated funds and services. Skyline Telephone Membership added their financial assistance. Bricca Sweet and others searched for and applied for available grants. It was a cooperative effort.

Tommy Walsh and James (Andy) Andrews, coordinator of Cove Creek Farm Heritage Days, along with some of the CCP&D directors, came up with an idea of sponsoring a concert to honor Doc Watson, a musician well known in this area. That idea became a reality in July of 1997 with a Doc Watson Appreciation Day held on the school grounds. Seven similar events have been held annually since then. From that idea came a brighter picture. Why not create a Doc Watson Museum and house it inside the historic Cove Creek High School? To make this happen more money was needed. Representative Gene Wilson secured CCP&D's first substantial donation from the North Carolina General Assembly. With that $25,000, a clean-up process was begun and the floors of the school became the first priority. The original floors proved to be beautiful when they were cleaned and finished.

Doc and Merle Watson Museum

To create a museum, another committee was needed. Tommy Walsh contacted a professor from Appalachian State University, Dr. Charles Watkins, who agreed to steer the Museum Committee. Nine other members joined him and Tommy to lay the groundwork for a museum. One important member of the committee, Rachel Rivers-Coffey, was an admirer and good friend of Doc Watson. She gave the first individual gift to be used to begin this task. Individuals or groups could become founders or sponsors of the museum by making a donation.

In 1998 the front entrance hall was opened to the public. It was billed as the future home of the Doc and Merle Watson Museum. The committee had done its job. With the help of Dr. Watkins, Tommy Walsh, Rachel Rivers-Coffey, Marian Simpson, Peggy Hagaman, Nan Greene, Frank Payne, Brenda Shepherd, Phil Minor, and Jon Townsend, seven wall posters depicting the life and success of Doc and Merle Watson graced the hallways. A display case filled with Doc and Merle's guitars and banjos stood in the middle of the hall. Doc and Merle had won the Emmy and Grammy awards which were displayed. More than one hundred visitors came to that first opening.

Two additional wall posters have been placed in the hall, and an additional case was made especially for Merle's huge, beautiful harp. Four original sketches by Willard Gayhart are beautifully framed and hanging down the hall with other pictures and posters. Two large rooms are open to house information of Doc's roots and a large array of pictures furnished by the Watson family. To honor Doc in 2004, CCP&D commissioned Dale Tucker to design and build an eight-foot shadowbox replica of Doc's guitar with a CD to furnish music. It is a wonderful showpiece. One room is dedicated to friends of MusicFest. Pictures and musical instruments are usually on display there. The Museum Committee members are a faithful group of volunteers who spend many hours in planning, laboring, and strategizing to make the museum a place of honor for two wonderfully talented musicians.

The first and second year performances at Doc Watson Appreciation Day drew big crowds of fans. With Doc's permission, the MusicFest has continued. The interest has been great and the rain has been scarce over the years. One year guests from seven countries, thirty states, and D.C. attended. This past year a group from Japan, a family from Australia, and visitors from Canada came by and were fascinated by what they saw and heard. Performers come from everywhere. Doc and his grandson Richard are the featured artists, but many of Doc's friends and colleagues, such as Tut Taylor, T. Michael Coleman, and David Holt, perform every year. They and local bands have been very supportive of this extravaganza and give freely of their time and talents. A portion of the proceeds goes to fund the museum and sustain the building where it is located.

Revitalizing Cove Creek High School

Old buildings have many problems. A major problem at Cove Creek School was no heating system. The CCP&D Board asked Jack Simpson to look for options and bring a suggested plan to the board. Because of its historic status, an architect and engineers were brought in to inspect the building before their recommendation was made. Their choice was a geothermal system because it would not detract from the exterior of the building, it was environmentally friendly, and in the long run it would be cheaper to operate. That heating and cooling system is now installed.

Many people wanted the windows to look like they did when Cove Creek High School was built. To save heat, thermal replacement windows would be more practical. Betty Boyd came up with a plan to help pay for these. Each class graduating from Cove Creek High School from 1943 through 1965 was contacted about the windows. Many classes and several individuals purchased windows. Most windows have now been paid for.

Another improvement was made while the windows were being replaced. Some stones had become discolored and grout needed to be cleaned out. Repairing was done and the building looks much cleaner now.

Karen James, a loyal volunteer, and Amy Shelton, CCP&D's present chairperson, are always looking for available grant monies to help with improvement projects. They applied for grants for an improved water system, and another for the start-up expenses for the Sugar Grove Developmental Day School. To dig a new well and build new bathrooms, a grant of $25,000 was received, and the day school received a $45,000 grant. Other grants will be sought from time to time in areas where they are needed.

CCP&D strives to preserve the community heritage by having an annual Farm Heritage Day Festival, and by keeping Cove Creek alumni involved. Work has begun on the final unfinished area of the building. There a space will be dedicated to the history of the communities around Cove Creek High School, and a space will be made suitable for class reunions or a variety of programs. A filled trophy case is already there, but more items and pictures will be added. Plans for this area have not been completed.

A community that was near death has been revived and again could be called "progressive and cooperative in all public enterprise." Cove Creek High School, a big part of our community heritage, has been saved, and we did it together. I believe our forefathers would be very proud of us!

Rescuing the Wilson-Vines House

Catherine Stokes Sheppard

It is not unusual for an individual to restore an old family dwelling. After all, the house may hold dear memories or honor the family. But it is a true love of history that causes a person to simply buy a stranger's house and lovingly restore it to comply with the National Historic Registry guidelines. That is exactly what Robert and Marilyn Prejean did.

In 2003, Marilyn Prejean told me that when she and her husband

Marilyn and Robert Prejean moved from Texas to Bethel, North Carolina, to find her dream house — a big farmhouse begging to be restored. They bought the property and went to work on this 1895 home. It took several years of hard labor to restore the house and grounds to the beautiful homestead you see today, in a community who welcomed them and where they became good neighbors (photograph by Karen James).

moved from Texas to North Carolina, they first purchased a log cabin. She enjoyed the rustic living but she still had that long-time yearning for an old farmhouse to restore. She and her real estate agent rode many miles looking for her dream house. One day as they drove along the Bethel School Road from Hwy. 321, Marilyn looked over toward the Rush Branch Road and said, "There is my house!" She also noted that it had a *For Sale* sign. An inspection showed that the 1895 home needed lots of work both in the house and on the grounds. But Marilyn was not to be dissuaded. The Prejeans bought the property and went to work. After several years of hard labor that was interrupted by Marilyn's cancer treatments, the house was fully restored and the grounds were beautiful. Marilyn loved to show the photo on her wall of the original owners. She pointed out details that honored those first owners. In fact, she invited former occupants to visit the home. When the house was included on a garden club house and garden tour, it was hard to believe that this house had not always been in the Prejean family. The house and owners seemed to fit.

The Prejeans did not just move to Bethel to renovate a house. While they did turn a white elephant into a community gem they did not stop there. They became active members of the Bethel Baptist Church, and enjoyed being good community citizens. Marilyn became active in the Daniel Boone Garden Club and the Home Demonstration Club. It was a sad loss to the community when Marilyn lost her life to cancer in 2004. What a legacy she left to her community. The Wilson-Vines house shines now as a showplace in Bethel.

Valle Crucis Conserves for the Future

Nannie Greene and Catherine Stokes Sheppard

This text is based on a June 25, 2005, Watauga Democrat *article.*

Valle Crucis has been noted throughout the history of Watauga County as being a progressive community. The historic district they have created there is evidence of this. As the population of the area in recent years began to increase and building expanded, the citizens became concerned that the character of the community could be lost in this growth spurt.

"How can we save our natural beauty, protect our environment, save our recreational areas, and continue to grow?" This was the question facing the concerned citizens. It was at this point that the High Country Conservancy, a local land trust, became involved. They had solutions for the citizens.

Several families in the Valle Crucis community donated easements on land to help protect their environment and save the natural beauty of their community. Mast General Store owners gave an easement on the land adjacent to the store and the Valle Crucis Community Park, securing a portion of the past to be enjoyed in the future (photograph courtesy of Mast General Store, photograph by J.D. Dooley).

Through the High Country Conservancy, the land placed in the conservancy is still owned by the individual, but it cannot be developed. Several families in the area had already donated easements, and in 2005 others joined this effort. John and Faye Cooper, owners of the Mast General Store, gave an easement of 22 acres of land adjacent to their store and the Valle Crucis Community Park. This property will contribute to the area's scenic quality.

Jim and Mary Neal Henson and the Pressley family have given easements on privately owned land. The Henson land may be used as a working farm. The Pressley property adjoins the Watauga River and provides a natural buffer along the river, reducing erosion.

Sometimes community members get together and decide that a certain property can be important to the region's history. For instance, the purchase of the Taylor Farm conserved 66 acres. It was a farm that had been passed down through the family for 150 years. About 50 community members joined forces to raise $30,000 for the easements.

Money from the U.S. Department of Agriculture, the N.C. Natural Heritage Trust Fund, and the Cannon Foundation has been used to buy easements on 73 acres of the Episcopal Church historic mission school property, which once featured working agriculture. Participation in the easement program is entirely voluntary.

Valle Crucis has set an example for all of Western Watauga County. By saving forest lands, farms, and streams, the community is securing a past to be waiting for the enjoyment of the future.

Stone School Buildings

Catherine Stokes Sheppard

While the Works Progress Administration (WPA) was a much criticized endeavor in many corridors, it was a truly great boost to Western

Top: **Stone buildings such as Bethel School were work projects in Watauga County during the Depression years. Bethel is still used as an elementary school.** ***Bottom:*** **Valle Crucis School was a WPA project that helped provide employment and a school for the community. It still stands and serves elementary students.**

Top: Mabel School was vacated several years ago, but the new Charter School hopes to have its classes there. _Bottom:_ Historic Cove Creek High School is now home to the Sugar Grove Day Care School and Jung Tao School, an alternative school of medicine. A museum was created there to honor Doc Watson, a Watauga native and nationally recognized musician. Offices are located there, and space is being readied for historical artifacts and community activities (photographs furnished by Jerry Adams).

Watauga County. Perhaps the greatest windfall to our county was the erection of much needed school buildings.

We have said a good deal about the beautiful high school building at Cove Creek, but we must not overlook the stone schools at Bethel, Mabel, and Valle Crucis. All the buildings became more than an edifice for teaching children. Each builder put his heart and soul into the construction. Men in the late 1930s were desperate for employment, especially those in the building trades. Not only was this an opportunity for employment, but also a vision of the future for their children. Most of the stone came from the surrounding community, as did the stonemasons. That gave special meaning to the structure.

As the school populations grew, new space was required for the schools. Bethel and Valle Crucis were successful in incorporating the stone buildings into their new structures. How wonderful that those buildings could be saved! Unfortunately Mabel and Cove Creek did not have suitable land available to retain their stone buildings and new, larger schools were built in different locations. These beautiful stone structures should last a long, long time, and as long as they exist, so will a poignant bit of our heritage.

Opinions on Heritage

Jack and Marian Simpson

Jack and Marian Simpson submitted the following in 2002. Marian passed away June 14, 2005.

Heritage may be defined as the sum total of everything tangible and intangible that has been passed down to us by our ancestors. Consequently, there is validity in the statement "There is nothing new on the face of the earth." Whether we talk about natural resources that have been set aside for public use, architectural examples, religious and/or moral principles, art, science, or any other field of endeavor or knowledge, heritage is a major part of the existing information related to it.

It is hard to imagine any area of our personal lives not affected and influenced by heritage. It is just as hard for many of us to remain conscious of that influence. In our busy, work-a-day world, we are so focused on the "quantity" of life that we frequently sacrifice quality. Much quality can be added to our lives with the development of a greater appreciation of our heritage.

The tragedy of September 11, 2001, has been a wake-up call to many of us. It has resulted in a great outpouring of national pride — a reminder to many of us why our American heritage is so special. Many of us were taking that part of our heritage for granted prior to September 11. Today we are more aware than we have been for a long time of the sacrifices made by our forefathers and the contemporary heroes of September 11 to make and keep this country great.

National pride is but one example of how an increased awareness of our heritage can add quality to our daily lives.

Knowledge of local and family heritage can be significant in our understanding of who we are and how we came to have certain attitudes, prejudices, value systems, etc., and may even help us to decide to change some of them (for the better, hopefully).

We are all leaving a legacy that will become a part of the heritage of our descendants, whether we like it or not. Perhaps our legacy will not be known outside a small family group, but it will still be there. Preserving unique art work or architecture that provides insight into the lives of previous generations and communities can be a valuable contribution to the heritage of future generations with a family or community link to that which is preserved.

Marian and I became involved in the preservation of the Historic Cove Creek High School Building for the obvious reasons that we both graduated from high school there and it is a beautiful piece of architecture that we'd hate to see destroyed. As Marian got more involved with the research that was required to get the building on the National Historic Register, we both started to realize there were a lot more and better reasons to preserve the building for posterity.

The building has so many stories to tell about the people of this area that paint a far different picture of rural Appalachia in the late Depression era than the stereotypical "ignorant hillbillies" image that is so often conveyed. It is not surprising to see that many of the people who attended school in this building have gone on to highly successful careers in many walks of life after examining some of the characteristics of their ancestors reflected in this building.

The building was completed in 1941 as a WPA project and was the product of local materials and local craftsmen. That in itself is a tribute to the American spirit of overcoming the Great Depression by having the federal government provide jobs to local residents in depressed areas that improved the infrastructure for future economic growth.

The architect for the building was Clarence Coffee from Caldwell County. The workmen were virtually all from Watauga County and most were from the Cove Creek Community. The quality of the workmanship in the building is immediately evident. From the beautiful stone work to the lack of settlement cracks after 60 plus years to the beautiful oak hardwood floors that still look new, the pride in workmanship is obvious.

Careful examination of the building itself reveals a tremendous amount of information about the area, the community, and the character of the people who constructed it. The masonry is truly a work of art and speaks volumes about the skills of those particular craftsmen. The design is simple but elegant, and it will have aesthetic appeal for generations to come. The local materials used reflect many of the natural beauties of this area and remind us of why the area continues to attract so many. The picturesque rural setting is a reminder not only of the beauty of the area but of the hardship many of the local residents endured to attend school in all types of weather in this rather remote spot.

Stories of the vision of the local officials and the obstacles they had to overcome to get approval for the construction, individual accomplishments of the workers themselves, and the impact of World War II on the project were all part of the research on getting the building on the National Register for Historic Places.

For Marian and me, being a small part of a community-minded group effort to preserve this piece of local heritage has been extremely fulfilling. Perhaps one's most important personal legacy can sometimes be realized by proactive efforts to preserve a legacy others have left that may otherwise be destroyed.

Community Interaction

Sarah Joslin and Nannie Greene

The dictionary defines sustainable development as "a practice that sustains a given condition, such as economic growth, without destroying or depleting natural resources, or polluting the environment." Appalachian State University has a unique program through the Sustainable Development Department. The goal of the Sustainable Development Outreach Program is to "find workable solutions to public issues." The current trend in Appalachian Studies agrees that grassroots agencies are the most successful way to promote sustainable development in economically depressed regions. The Appalachian Studies Association provides a connection between academic communities and local grassroots organizations that work together to impact the success of projects.

There are a variety of positive outcomes from service-learning and community development projects. Benefits can be seen both inside and outside the academic institution involved. From within the university, community development projects allow for departmental interactions, which can result in a greater understanding of surrounding communities. This relationship can create a positive experience for both surrounding community members and future students, and a basis for future projects is constructed. Communities surrounding the university stand to gain further insight, economic resources, and volunteers to implement positive change for their grassroots development projects.

Cove Creek is a community in the midst of change. Affordable housing and livable wages are hard to come by countywide. Residents find it more difficult to remain in the community due to the cost of living increase, the property tax increases, and poor growth planning.

After an assessment study conducted by the Sustainable Development Outreach Program in 1997, it was found that most community members were concerned with losing the rural feel of their community as well as losing their identity. They also felt that planning needed to occur and that the community should have a voice in such planning. In order to ensure a community voice in such development, Cove Creek Preservation and Development, Inc., was formed.

ASU Sustainable Development became involved with CCP&D while it was still forming. A sustainable development coordinator was hired to maintain an office located within the now historic Cove Creek High School building. This position provides a meditative buffer between community members and the university. The coordinator is a local area resident who has familial ties to the community. In this respect, the coordinator understands the social dynamics of the community and presents a management style with which most community members are comfortable dealing. The coordinator is a major asset to CCP&D because of his ability to mobilize residents and his fundraising and social networking abilities.

The CCP&D board is composed of community members and the sustainable development outreach coordinator. The board is a mix of native community members, returning native community members, and outside newcomers, which affords the board a wide-ranging pool of human capital resources. Board members are subject to an election process and a term limit of three years. The board opens meetings to the community to continually gain insight.

Through the relationship with ASU, CCP&D has been successful in retaining their goal of preserving the historic stone school building. Cove Creek High School was a social centerpiece for the community, and the opportunities afforded by CCP&D have helped to reestablish lost identity for many members of the community. In addition, CCP&D has gained university support through non-monetary resources. The ASU Sustainable Outreach Program has provided CCP&D with research pertaining to community perceived assets and priorities, which affirms aforementioned anticipated results.

Community involvement within CCP&D does not seem to be limited to a few individuals. The outpouring of volunteer support during major events is an indicator of widespread community support of CCP&D projects. All professionals who work with community development groups should realize the potential of local area community members. Once communal assets are recognized, community groups can begin to strengthen weaknesses.

CCP&D generates income in four ways. First, building tenants rent space to accommodate their businesses. The Chinese School of Medicine brings professionals from all over the nation to attend this accredited alternative school. Second, CCP&D hosts festivals annually to raise funds. Third, personal donations account for a lot of building maintenance. The windows throughout the building have all been replaced through honorariums and memorial gifts. In renovating certain sections of the building, volunteers play a key role. A recent example would be the new Sugar Grove Day Care Center's renovated space, where community volunteers did a bulk of the remodeling. Fourth, CCP&D gains support for certain projects through grants. Some examples of project grant work would be the geothermal heating system and the new water system. Both projects required thousands of dollars that would have been difficult through current fundraising strategies.

Tommy Walsh is employed by Appalachian State University and serves as a sustainable development outreach coordinator. He works closely with Cove Creek Preservation and Development on community development projects and is especially helpful in coordinating community resources and fundraising projects. Together they strive to meet the needs of the community and preserve the heritage of rural Cove Creek (photograph furnished by Tommy Walsh).

Together CCP&D and ASU Sustainable Development strive to meet the needs of the community. Through this partnership, it appears through research that both university and community members want to preserve the heritage and rural community atmosphere of Sugar Grove, while providing economic opportunity. It seems as though the relationship between the community and the university is positive in attaining this goal.

Appendix: Backward Glances

Catherine Stokes Sheppard

Most of us have photos that show various aspects of everyday life from our past. Not everything is so visible. As I reflect on memories of things in my childhood just maybe you, the reader, will recall mental pictures of similar incidents in your own life. If you are too young for such memories perhaps your grandparents can enlighten you about their childhood.

Recycling

I was born in 1929 in the heart of the Depression and my family used everything until there was little usefulness left in it. One example that comes to my mind is bed sheets. They were usually homemade of a coarse muslin that we called domestic. The fabric came in the correct width and my mother, Winnie Taylor Stokes, hemmed the top and bottom ends. The fabric would bleach out as it was washed until it would eventually be white and no longer coarse. When the center part of the sheet began to be thin, Mama would sew together the outside edges, rip the middle open, hem those ragged edges, and the sheet was put back into service with a seam down the middle. When that sheet became thin in the middle or developed holes it was not cast aside. It would then be torn into strips and used as bandages. I might add that we also had "good" sheets on the guest bed which eventually worked their way to every day use and were reincarnated. Sheets and pillow cases were always ironed, with the pillow cases being heavily starched.

Newspapers were another item that found second and third uses. My family always had a newspaper, even in hard times. After we read them from cover to cover, we might pass them on to neighbors who read them and sometimes used them for wallpaper. Their last journey was often to the little house behind the house. They were not in the race with Charmin but they served the same purpose.

The coarse, tightly woven cotton bags that feed came in also had many uses. In our family they were hemmed, a tab was sewed on one corner (to accommodate a nail) and they became an every day hand towel to be shared by every member of the family. The flour bags were not as rough in texture but they, too, found many second uses.

I have heard other families tell about making garments from men's worn wool pants. If the man in the family wore his woolen pants until they had a shine, the wife would take the good parts of the legs and make pants for a small boy or a skirt for a girl. Also, parts from wool pants would often be used as scraps for a quilt. One must remember that during the Depression only cotton and wool were available for men's clothes. Synthetics were yet to come.

Home Health Care

Going to the doctor did not become a common practice until after World War II. A broken bone or an attack of appendicitis, or maybe pneumonia would be deemed bad enough to warrant the services of a doctor. A severe cold or sore throat, a rash, scabies, or toothache would have been treated at home. After all, if it was not life threatening, why go? Most of the medicines we take for granted today were unheard of then, including penicillin and the sulfas. Then too, there was the ever present fact that it took cash to go to the doctor and most of our population did not have it. Most homes had a stash of castor oil, Vick's salve, cod liver oil, Epsom salts, rubbing alcohol, iodine, Mercurochrome, turpentine, sulfur and lard, paregoric and of course there was whiskey for snakebites! These items were basic, their uses and combinations were varied. A severe burn might be treated with a mixture of castor oil and honey. Sassafras tea was often used to treat measles or any disease causing a high fever.

I recall how embarrassed I was when I was filling out an application for college and I was requested to list a family doctor. I had not been to the doctor since I was a small child and that doctor was then dead. I finally listed one whose name I had heard and prayed on one ever knew the truth.

My elderly grandmother had high blood pressure and her legs would swell and open sores would drain. In the mid-thirties the medical world did not know there was a connection between blood pressure and diet, or if they did the word had not yet reached my grandmother. There was not even a simple diuretic. Every night Mama would bathe Grandma's legs and wrap them in bandages made from the sheets. She would repeat the process in the morning. The soiled bandages would be rinsed, put in a pot and boiled to be reused. This pot was used for nothing but boiling bandages and it seems to me it boiled constantly.

Intimate Apparel

When I was a little girl Mama always made my clothes from the skin out. When I was very small my little cotton underpants fastened with a button. I do not know if elastic was not in common use or if Mama did not have the money to buy it. I do know that babies wore long stockings that buttoned to their underpants. By the time I was 7 or 8 years old my underpants were a rayon knit that had legs to the knees with elastic bands. We called them bloomers. All underwear that was "store bought" for ladies or children was the same color, sort of a sick pink. I suppose it was rayon, I do know the texture was pretty much the same as nylon. White underclothes came into use in the early '40s, about the same time that nylon was available.

My slips were also homemade until I was high school age. Adjustable straps were unheard of also. Some girls wore underwear that reflected the kind of flour from which the family biscuits were made. I do not remember that I ever owned flour sack clothes but I wouldn't be surprised to know mine were recycled from something.

The older ladies in my acquaintance all wore corsets. When I was young I thought it was because they wanted to look thin. As an adult I have come to realize it was for back comfort. The corset must have been terribly hot in summer, difficult to put on and lace up every day, and uncomfortable to wear. However, one should not take the importance of the corset for granted. The 1936 Sears Roebuck Catalog (a book of utmost importance in every household) devoted seventeen pages to nothing but corsets! Now that is a lot of intimate apparel.

Did I mention that the corset also held up the stockings? That reminds me to tell you about garters and garter belts. Stockings, both cotton and silk, and later nylon, simply could not stand alone. Something had to hold them in place. The garter was an elastic band slipped over the top of the stocking and rolled down to the knee. It could be adjusted in tightness to fit the leg. I do not know why ladies did not die from blood clots because surely the circulation was disturbed! Later the garter belt was invented and was a popular part of every lady's wardrobe (except those who wore a corset) until panty hose came along.

Hosiery

Thank God for nylon! When I was a child not only children wore cotton stockings, so did our mothers. When a lady owned a pair of silk hose she was really well-off. These, by the way, had a seam up the back that must be kept straight. Even the early nylon hose had a seam. How well I remember the last thing required before I left the house (dressed up) was to stand in front of the mirror and look over my shoulder to see if those blasted seams were straight.

I have no idea who invented nylon panty hose but that person has my undying gratitude.

Milk and Bread and Other Goodies

In the mountain counties almost everyone who lived in the rural areas had a milk cow. (The same was true for small towns.) Since this time period was before the rural electrification we were sadly in need of refrigeration. In order to keep the milk fresh, my relatives had a system of putting the drinking milk in glass containers which were put into a stoneware crock that was then placed in water that ran continuously from a cool mountain spring. Butter was handled in the same manner.

Milk was such a staple in the diet of the mountain people that if the cow ate wild onions we felt lost till the milk cleared up. Even worse was if the cow died or the family fell on such hard times they had to sell the cow. As a rule the entire family drank milk with meals. Iced tea was unheard of at our house because first, we had no ice and second, tea had to be purchased from the store. Many times in my years growing up our supper menu was a cake of cornbread, sweet milk, and cooked apples. Could anything taste better!

I weep at the demise of the cherry trees. Some wonderful childhood memories are built around eating cherries. The red ones were tasty but could not compare to the big black cherries. For those who never had the privilege of eating the big black cherry, it was smaller than the Bing, sweeter, and about the same color. They usually ripened around the end of June and some churches would plan an outing to picnic at somebody's cherry orchard. Of course the dessert was cherries … the aftermath may have been a stomach ache.

Gypsies

I am not sure that I ever actually saw a Gypsy or if I just heard so much about them that I thought I had actually seen them. I do know that from time to time they came through the country and were greatly feared by my grandmother Taylor. They would travel in bands and stop at farmhouses and while one was telling your fortune another would relieve your chicken house of a bird or two. I don't know if they did great damage or mostly just frightened people. I do remember that parents would tell children, "If you misbehave I will sell you to the Gypsies." That was enough to make me wary!

Thieves!

Today it is not unusual for a home to be broken into and electronic equipment or silver to be stolen. I remember in the late '30s someone broke into our smokehouse and stole our cured hams. This happened two different years. More than once our clothes had been left on the clothesline overnight and were not there the next morning. In particular, I remember an adult cousin lived with us and his long knit underwear was stolen off the clothesline and other items were not bothered. Once just the sheets were removed from the line.

For Barter or Worse

Money was as scarce as hen's teeth during the Great Depression. People who could have a garden and a hog or two usually had plenty to eat, but there was little money in circulation. We used the barter system for more than shopping at the local store.

We had a neighbor whom I adored. Dove Day was an older teenager who often came to visit our home. She would take me for a piggyback ride, or play a game with me. She enjoyed reading our old magazines. She begged for chores of any kind and expected little in return. She often came and helped with the washing. Our washing technology at that time consisted of a wash pot, tin tubs and a washboard. Her pay may have been vegetables from the garden or clothes that were no longer useful for our family. Sometimes Mama could pay her with cash and Dove would be so happy.

My aunt was a teacher who had a passion for nice clothes. When she discarded something Dove was waiting for it. Once she brought Dove a really nice black silk dress that no longer fit. Dove was ecstatic! She tried it on and it was almost too tight, but Dove thought it was perfect. My aunt explained to Dove that silk was rather fragile and she could not wash it. Dove was cautioned to save it for church and not get it soiled. Dove would not take the dress off and insisted on wearing it home.

Mama noticed that she never saw Dove wear the dress, and one day asked her why she did not wear it. Dove dropped her head and confessed that on the way home the day she got the dress, someone dared her to jump across the gate and she did. She tore the silk dress beyond repair. Maybe we could declare this as a day's work for a moment of glory.

Desperation

When I was very young, maybe six years old, we lived in Wilkes County with my grandparents, Sally and Adolphus Taylor. I had no brothers or sisters and was a very lonely little girl. I always needed a playmate. My grandfather's house was a large (for that time) white house beside Highway 421. I suppose it must have looked prosperous to the people who walked by because during the mid–30s there were few days that someone did not stop and ask for food or a place to sleep. My grandmother had a big heart and always cooked more than she knew her family could eat and at day's end she never threw out any leftovers. I can still hear her say, "You never know who will come here hungry." They came and she fed them on the back porch. Some would ask if they could sleep in the barn. Before Grandpa said "yes" he always asked if they had any matches. He did not want any matches in his barn. (How did he think they could buy smokes?) Sometimes the people traveled in singles and sometimes in groups.

One group that made a lasting impression on me stopped by on a hot summer day in mid-afternoon and asked for food and water. A young woman carried a large pasteboard box and led a beautiful little girl who looked to be about four years old. The child had long brown curls and big brown eyes. I thought she was beautiful. Anyway, the mother asked my mother if she would take the little girl and keep her until she (the mother) could improve her life. I thought God had answered my prayers until my begging to keep her proved to be in vain. Mama was trying to keep soul and body together and could not take on any more. Besides, there were too many unanswered questions. I know now that Mama was probably right but had it been left to Grandma and me I expect I would have had a playmate.

Another traveler who made a lasting impression on me was a man who stopped after our supper, just before dark, and asked to sleep in the barn. He had big sores on his arms. He did not ask for food but Grandma asked him if he would like some supper. She brought him a big plate of vegetables and he ate almost like an animal. I am sure he was starved. He retired to the barn and as was usually the case we never saw the guest again. But sometime before our family got up he had chopped a big pile of stove wood.

That was his payment for hospitality. Apparently, this man had lost everything but his pride.

Once in a while a beggar would identify himself as a relative of someone our family knew and Grandpa would invite him to sleep in our house. I do recall that Grandpa said that he never turned away a beggar and none ever brought him any harm.

The Joy of Recess!

I was privileged to have been born before the days of lawsuits concerning school activities. Otherwise I might never have experienced a snowball fight. I am sure these also took place at private homes but since I was an only child this was not an at-home memory. At school, when there was a big snow on the ground, we would choose teams, without the knowledge of the teacher, and at recess we would roll up a long bank of snow to duck behind. The better pitchers got to throw the missiles. Since I had absolutely no athletic ability I was one of the makers. I would make a mean snowball and hand it to a thrower. It was considered illegal to make a snowball with a piece of coal or a stone in the middle. This was punishable. No one could imagine my consternation when I went to Eastern North Carolina to teach and we had one of the rare snowfalls (maybe a whole inch). The principal came on the intercom to warn the teachers that no students would be allowed on the playground that day because of the snow.

Another school memory that I joyfully recall was playing in the creek at recess. When I was in seventh grade I attended school in Wilkes County. The school had four teachers for grades one through seven. Lewis Fork Creek bordered our playground and when the weather was really hot the teachers allowed us to wade in the creek. I bet the teachers wished they could too!

The Freshet

For those who do not know what a freshet is, let me explain. A freshet occurs following heavy rains that cause the creeks to flood. When I was a child my Stokes grandmother's house sat maybe a hundred yards from the Cove Creek. I recall several times when the creek would flood and water would back up in her basement where she had her kitchen. I thought this was so exciting because she would put on her boots and wade in the water and bring utensils upstairs and cook cornmeal mush on the wood heater. Also, we would sit on the front porch and watch the chicken coops and other farm items float down the creek. We would speculate on what certain items were as they went by. One of my teenage cousins, Roger Stokes, was a rather enterprising youth. He would get out of Grandma's sight and fish things out of the water. (Grandma was so afraid of water she would have forbidden him to do that. He pretty much lived by the philosophy that it was easier to get forgiveness than permission.) If he fished out something metal he would sell it to the junk man, who sold it to the Japanese. Ironically, this metal was, in all probability, used in ammunition that later was shot at him in the South Pacific!

Child's Play

Before the days of the Mickey Mouse Club and Howdy Doodie, children did something called creative play. The number of children that gathered in the neighborhood determined the game. Several children would warrant a ball game, which required a ball and bat. If no one had the equipment it was not too hard to improvise. A piece of scrap lumber with a small amount of whittling to form a handle would serve for a bat. A ball could be made of string with a small stone in the center. Of course a flat bat and a string ball never made the big leagues, but it could make for a fun afternoon. Another fun game was ante-over. This complex game required a soft ball and a one story building. Children would divide into two teams, one team on either side of the building. The ball was thrown over the roof and if anyone caught it he could run to the other side, tag a player and take him to help the other team. The side with the most players in the end was declared the winner. Kick the can was another favorite game. Hide and seek was also popular.

Two or three little girls would make a playhouse by drawing rooms on the ground and naming them bedroom, kitchen, etc. Horseshoes was a popular game for both boys and girls. It would have been rare for a mother to tell a child to go outside and play. Children knew if they stayed inside soon there would be a chore for them to do and the outside was a haven.

As the Depression began to fade and children had a few coins, the comic books became quite popular, especially for adolescents. One family would read their comic books and exchange them with another family so that there would be lots of reading for small amounts of money. A little later the county bookmobile became very popular. Most of us lived too far from a library to use their resources, but in the mid-thirties the bookmobile came into being. This was a bus equipped with books that came to designated locations every two weeks. For children who liked to read this traveling library was a godsend. Parents often enjoyed the books as much as the children.

Entertainment for the Grown-Ups

I have discussed how children entertained themselves during the '30s and '40s, but what of the adults? Before the days of television, entertainment was simple and inexpensive. In the Cove Creek community men regularly gathered at Clyde Mast's croquet court. Mr. Mast had built a regulation clay croquet court between his store and his residence. Many young people played croquet on their lawns but their papa played a more serious game.

Another popular sport at Cove Creek was checkers. The roller mill near the school was the gathering place for checkers. Hensel Stokes was the miller but he could usually find time to take a checker break. The big competition was often between David Bingham and one of the Stokes boys. Ed Stokes had eight sons, and six of them were outstanding checker players. Ed was the champion and he handed his skills down to his sons, who to this day carry on the tradition. Most country stores had a checker board which was usually busy, but for a serious game one had to go to the mill.

Some families were musical and every weekend the entire family would go to another musician's home and they would play music. Banjos, guitars, mandolins and fiddles were popular instruments for the home musicians. There were no drums or amplifiers or other accoutrements that we feel vital today. That is not to say their music was not enhanced. For sound effects they used washboards, spoons, pie pans, kettles and even paper bags.

Bicycle riding was another popular form of entertainment that could be shared by the whole family. James Mast, his son Jimmy and daughter Marjorie rode their bikes every Sunday afternoon from their home at Mast to Boone. Well, that is how it started. There were many bikers along the way who would fall in with them and by the time they got to Boone the road was full! One must remember this was before the days of mountain bikes or even speed bikes; just plain old two wheelers. I might add, helmets for bikers were unheard of also. However, the traffic was light.

Then there was baseball! Guys who did not wish to play (or who were not good enough for the team) could go to Ben Ward's field and be a spectator. In the late '40s Ben Ward leveled a mountain top and built a baseball field to the exact dimensions of the Municipal Stadium in Cleveland, Ohio. High school boys usually had their own teams that parents enjoyed. Or if this was not feasible they could usually catch a game on the radio. Many adults followed the success of their children's school basketball teams and were regular in attendance.

What about the women? Most farm wives did not have time for entertainment, but now and then there would be a quilting. The churches had Missionary Societies which were an outlet for the ladies. For the non-farm women there was the game of Bridge. Nell Collins, Rena Billings, Lucy Watson and Mattie Lane Walsh kept a running game going. Several women who worked outside the home played once a week.

Of all the entertainments, nothing could top plain old visiting. Sunday afternoon was sure to find friends and relatives calling on each other. News and gossip were shared while the children played. In summer a family could count on their kinfolk from below the mountains coming to visit for at least a week. Sometimes kinfolk came that one did not know he was related to. (May I be forgiven for that thought!) Western Watauga enjoyed about the same entertainment as the rest of our rural South. We did what we could afford to do.

Vacation was just a word in a book to many of us. Few people were affluent enough to go on a vacation. Tom and Eude Moody along with Hensel and Pearle Stokes made an annual pilgrimage to the beach. I recall thinking how wonderful it must be to take such a trip. We always knew of people from Florida who came to Mrs. Taylor's home in Valle Crucis or other homes for the summer. Few of us related that to ourselves.

Today we hear so much about "family togetherness." That was unnecessary in the '30s and '40s. Most families were together so much that we yearned for some aloneness. However, I am sure strong family bonds were formed. We might conclude that, as families, we entertained each other.

Skaters on the Pond

We old-timers like to tell how much hotter the summers used to be and how much cooler the winters were. I can attest to some truth in that. When I was a little girl in the late thirties, I saw ice skates for the first time. That time the milldam was frozen, and a young man named Gordon Spainhour from the Mast community came to Cove Creek and skated with real ice skates. Most of us would wear our rubber over-shoes and slide on the ice, but no one thought of owning a pair of skates. Also, I do not recall seeing the millpond frozen hard enough to be safe for skaters since that time. Today I am amazed that the ice was so solid, but then I was in total awe of the skates and the skater. The image is still with me.

I do have a photo of my cousin and me skating (actually sliding) on Cove Creek. I think the year was 1940 but I am not absolutely sure. The water in front of our house was not deep and I suppose it was not unusual for it to freeze, but it was unusual for it to be solid enough for children to slide on it.

The Linoleum Rug

There was a time in Western Watauga County when many mountain homes had bare wooden floors. Hooked rugs and braided rugs may have enhanced the living room and bedrooms but, alas, the kitchen floor was naked. In order to keep this room clean, a Saturday ritual in most houses was to scrub the floor with hot water and homemade soap.

Then came the great day in the '30s when the linoleum rug salesman began to show up on doorsteps. No product could have been more welcomed by the housewife, or no more unappreciated by the husbands. These salesmen went from door to door hawking their product. I remember the day that the salesman came to my grandfather's house. When he explained the fine points of linoleum I could see that Granny was almost salivating, but Grandpa was clutching his pocketbook tightly. (Fort Knox was not more secure than Grandpa Taylor's pocketbook.) A rug to cover their large kitchen would cost eight dollars! The first time the salesman came he was sent away with no sale. Grandpa must have been threatened with no cooking or some other ill treatment because before long the salesman was back and delivering a rug. In a short time more rugs were added to other downstairs rooms.

The linoleum salesman hauled the rugs on the back of his truck, but before long the rugs had become so popular that the larger country stores as well as the hardware stores carried quite an inventory of rugs. It is not unusual today for my husband or me to refer to our vinyl floor as linoleum. The term became truly a household word.

The Electric Light

Not long after the linoleum rug, the electric light came to the homes of the country people. It was 1937 when electricity came to our house. We lived in a typical 1900s house that had an L shape with four rooms downstairs and two bedrooms on the second floor. Each room and the front hall had one overhead light that was turned on or off with a pull cord. There was a wall switch for both front and back porch. There was a wall receptacle in the sitting room so that we could have a radio. Another receptacle was in the dining room so that maybe sometime we could have a refrigerator. All this came at the astronomical price of forty dollars. Sure enough, we got the radio and later a refrigerator that had the motor on top. For all of her life I never saw my mother get as excited over a possession as she did over an electric churn. That was the moment she felt she had arrived. As I reflect on changes I have seen in my life, I think none has impressed me more than seeing electricity come to my family. It opened a new world to us, as I am sure it did to others.

The Sewing Machine

I dare to say a bride today would not give a hoot about owning a sewing machine. That has not always been true. In past generations no home was considered complete without a sewing machine. Few women worked outside the home and a vital part of the housewife's duties was to sew. Even if the woman did not have the skills for making clothing, there were always repairs to be made. (Remember, nothing was destroyed until every shred of usefulness had been consumed.) Mothers made the shirts for sons and husbands and sometimes the pants were homemade. Few girls knew the joy of a "store bought" dress.

In the '30s, '40s and '50s home economics was taught in the public schools and sewing was an integral part of the course. My mother had gone to Appalachian Training School in the '20s and I have often heard her say that one of the most beneficial lessons (beyond Latin) was learning to take a newspaper and making a dress pattern from it. This skill was no longer taught when I took home ec and I regret it. I cannot imagine not knowing how to do simple sewing. I still rate the usefulness of my sewing machine right along with my washing machine.

The College Girl in the 1940s

Any university woman today should be amused to see how her life differs from that of her grandmother. For starters, in the 1940s she would have been a college girl or a coed if she went to a co-educational school. Forget coed dorms. No matter if she went to a coed or all woman's school there was a strict rule: no guys past the parlor door. In freshmen dorms the doors were locked (probably barred) at 9:00 P.M. A girl could walk to town but not ride in a car without special permission. This was not much of an inconvenience because none of the students had cars anyhow. Anytime a girl left the campus she had to sign out, stating her name and where she could be found. If she left with a date, information about him had to be on file.

When I transferred from Appalachian State Teachers College to Radford College I found rules more severe. This was at a time when guys were coming home from the military service and wanted to meet girls. Blind dates were usually the way. Of course our parents had not met him; of

REQUEST FOR CALLER at Radford College

I, ______________, ______________, ☐ Sr. ☐ Jr. ☐ Soph. ☐ Fresh. ______________
(Surname first) (Check) (Date)
Dormitory ______________ Room Number______________
Request permission to receive as a caller

Mr. ______________ of ______________

Where did you meet him?______________

How long have you known him?______________

Have your parents met him? ______________

Has he called at your home?______________

What does he do?______________
Name of person who can give further information if necessary:

Name ______________ address______________

Girls attending Radford College in Virginia were required to have written permission to receive callers. They could not ride in cars, but they could walk. If they left the campus with a date, information about him must be on file. This is the form they filled out for their visitors. (Courtesy Catherine Stokes Sheppard.)

course he had not called at our home. There were ways around that rule! Once a guy was approved it was ok to go out with him as long as we walked. Do I need to confess that if a guy was approved his name might show up on the sign-out book with several girls on the same night? Then, as now, we figured that rules were made to be broken. The one unpardonable offense was use of alcohol. If a girl was seen drinking even a beer, she was immediately suspended.

At Radford College we were admonished to always be ladies. We were given demerits if we appeared on campus with our hair in curlers. The same was true if we went to the dining hall less than fully dressed. (No such thing as a raincoat over pajamas.) If we went to Roanoke shopping or to a concert we were expected to wear a hat and gloves. This was true even if we went to a football game. Looking back, I can see that was not all bad.

Remember, the 1940s was the era of the Big Bands. This brings wonderful memories to me. Radford was a small school, but we were the Women's Division of Virginia Polytechnic Institute and only 18 miles away. Once each semester V.P.I. would host a Big Band dance. Here was where the logistics figured in favor of the all-women's school. After all, V.P.I. had several thousand males, most of whom where single, and Radford had eight hundred girls. Go figure! A chartered bus would take us to Blacksburg where we met our dates at the bus stop. It was lots of fun. We could ride with our dates after we became seniors. The great thing was that we had the opportunity to go to a Big Band dance, even if it might be with a blind date. Ladies, we have come a long way.

I Remember the Words of My Father

My father, Don Stokes, was a small man who was full of big tales. He loved to sit by the fire on a cold night and spin yarns in which he was always the hero. A neighbor, Mr. Andy Greer, often came over after supper and he, too, enjoyed telling tales. As a child I was enthralled by the stories they told. Looking back I remember few of the stories but I vividly recall their language, their expressions. At the time, it never occurred to me that everybody in the English-speaking world did not use the same vocabulary as Dad and Mr. Greer, because their idioms were so commonplace. Now I like to think that their language was pure Western Watauga as handed down from many generations. Since people from many locales have chosen to move into Western Watauga, our speech is bound to become more diverse. Below are some of the words and phrases and modern translations that can give the reader a glimpse of a language that well may be dying.

He *lawed* me. (took me to court)
He was *churched* for playing the fiddle and dancing. (excommunicated)
We sat around and *spun yarns.* (told stories)
He was a *stout* man. (very strong)
We ate *leather britches* for supper. (dried string beans)
She is *plumb* crazy. (completely)
The cake is *awful* good. (delicious)
She was *petted* to death. (spoiled child)
She *retch upon the manuel.* (reached on the mantel)
The matches are on the *fireboard.* (mantel)
Put the sugar in a *poke.* (paper bag)
Would you like a *mess of salet greens?* (enough salad greens for a meal)
She was the *awfulest case ever I saw.* (unique person)
We boys hung around the store *just gassing.* (telling lies)
The child is a *woods colt.* (born out of wedlock)
I don't have any *currency*. (money)
He is old enough to go *sparking.* (courting)
She has *set her cap for that boy.* (trying to get a boyfriend)
He is sparking a *grass widow.* (abandoned wife)
I need to go to town and do a little *trading.* (shopping)
She sits around *wool gathering.* (day dreaming)
I am *afixin'* to go. (preparing)

How are you? *Oh, I'm fair to middlin'.* (OK)
How are you? *I'm common, common, awful common.* (not very well)
I need a cup and *sasser.* (saucer)
She was burned while *sassering* her coffee. (drinking hot beverage from the saucer)
She is as hard to fool as slipping daylight past a rooster. (no explanation needed on this one)
My dad always made dog, log, and hog rhyme: dawg, lawg, hawg.

Sometimes in rare moments I will hear myself use one of the words of my father. It always puts a smile on my face and a glow in my heart. However, I believe I have never said lawg or hawg! But my husband reminds, it is not too late.

Flies and Fleas

Today I tried to make war on a single fly in my kitchen but the fly was more cunning than I. In a state of sheer aggravation I gave up with the promise to give chase another day. Then in a moment of déjà vu, I recalled that in my childhood one little old fly was hardly a matter for concern.

Almost everyone had animals and if one family did not, their neighbors did. Where there were animals there were sure to be flies. Many homes did not have screens, so flies were all over the place in warm weather. To make our meals palatable we used a fly-broom. This was constructed from a straight stick or old broom-handle with a newspaper hung across the wood. The newspaper was cut into vertical ribbons and the cook would stand by the table and sway the fly-broom over the table to chase away the flies. This was especially useful at church dinners on the grounds.

Another item found in most homes was the flypaper. This paper was covered with a substance that had the consistency of honey with some type of pesticide. The paper came in a roll that resembled a shotgun shell. When it was opened, it would spiral down about two feet. This was attached to the ceiling of the room. The fly was attracted to the honey-like substance but when he landed, he would stick to the paper. Then the fly ate enough poison to die. After that came the fly gun. This was a hand sprayer filled with some sort of sweet smelling liquid that would invite the fly into the room, as though there were not enough already. The person attacking the flies would close the doors and windows, spray the room and hurriedly leave the room, only to return in about thirty minutes to sweep up the dead bodies. We referred to the spray as flit because the first brand of spray was

Flit. Soon all spray, regardless of brand name, was called simply "fly flit." It was not unusual to hear someone say, "It is time to flit the flies."

Actually, killing flies was a sport of sorts. Schoolboys who became bored with lessons would endeavor to kill flies with their bare hands. Some even moved up to using rubber bands as weapons. The contest was to see who could kill the most. Anyone who has never killed a fly with his bare hands has no idea of the skill required. The sport continued with the older folk who often sat on the porch with a fly-swatter in hand. I doubt that they counted the dead, but they could make life unpleasant for the buzzing flies.

A favorite fly story in our family was about my Uncle Ed Stokes and the Picture Making Man. My grandmother took her three children to have their picture made when the traveling photographer came around. After the children were put in place, I am sure this was Grandmother's positioning, Grandmother admonished the children to not move. The three Stokes children knew from experience that their life depended on not moving if that was what Ma said. To this day, we have a nice family photo with Uncle Ed's nose in a twitch supporting a fly. He dared not swat the fly.

With reference to the window screens, in the few houses that had them, the screens were not permanently attached to the windows. They were purchased in varying heights and the width expanded to fit the window. Should a family move they took the screens along. However, those who owned their own homes often nailed the screen wire directly to the window frame. Storm windows had not yet come into being. By the mid-forties, most people had aspired to having window screens and some had even moved on to having screened porches. While this made our homes both more sanitary and comfortable, it certainly did not rid the world of flies!

Another pest that could drive one to distraction was the flea. Like the fly, the flea enjoyed the company of animals, though the biological association was different. The flea jumped on the animal to eat, not to rest. He did his resting on hay or the wool of a sheep.

My dad's hayloft was the greatest place to play and also the best place to become flea infested. Wherever the dogs, sheep, horses and cows went, the fleas were sure to follow. I remember getting flea bites and the itchy knots that resulted. Dad had a vat filled with a terrible smelling liquid that he ran the sheep and dogs through to kill fleas but I had to tough it out on my own. Thank goodness for Deet!

The Traveling Salesman

Through the years, we have all heard many jokes and stories about the traveling salesman who went from one residence to another peddling his wares. My father always referred to that person as a drummer. In my era he was the traveling salesman. One such was the man who sold lightning rods.

The lightning rod salesman was usually a pretty slick talker. He convinced the entire family that if your house did not have lightning rods it would probably burn to the ground within a week and all of the family would die from having been hit by lightning. The guilt trip was so heavy that most fathers would fork over the money. It almost became a status symbol to have lightning rods on your house. In my limited realm of acquaintances, I never knew anyone whose house actually was hit by lightning, with or without the rods.

Hot on the heels of the lightning rod salesman came the magazine salesman, then the Bible salesman (usually a young man who claimed to be working his way through college). Then there was the encyclopedia salesman and soon the peddlers of vacuum cleaners, after that the Rawleigh man, and later the Blair products salesman. In the case of the Blair products, the salesperson was a lady. Much later came the Avon lady. There was seldom a week that one salesperson or another did not show up on our steps.

My father was an avid reader but he hated to cope with salesmen. Once my mother was not at home when the *Progressive Farmer* agent came. As soon as he made his spiel my dad told him, "I cannot read." Dad thought this would send him on his way. The persistent salesman said, "Maybe your wife would enjoy this." Of course, one lie always leads to another, so Dad added, "No, she can't read either." The salesman then lamented, "Oh, how unfortunate!"

Mama returned about the time the salesman reached his car. When she learned what Dad had told the man, she was furious. Not because Dad did not subscribe to the magazine, but because he had told someone that she, a Duke University graduate, could not read. My Dad had a strange sense of humor and could make a joke of even serious matters. It was no surprise that soon "Oh, how unfortunate!" became a household expression.

Traveling salesmen called so often that we had a special chair by the door that we invited them to sit in. The chair had a very straight back and was so uncomfortable that the salesman would not stay long. Actually, we also invited itinerate preachers to sit there too.

Church Services

Sunday morning worship services have changed very little since my childhood. We still sing the same hymns and the order of the service is pretty much as I remember it, and certainly, the message is the same. Unfortunately, there are still dissents in the church.

I often hear people complain about the sameness of church. I think it is wonderful! It provides continuity to my faith heritage. (If it ain't broke, don't fix it!) Oh, yes, there are some changes and I would like to think that they are very significant. I do not recall that social justice was a sermon topic in the '30s and '40s. I admit it has been a long time since I heard an elderly worshiper call out "Amen!" in the middle of a sermon but I bet there are still silent "amens" being felt. The amenities are more modern and female ministers are being accepted in most denominations. But, I believe the sameness is more than the differences.

Revivals were an entirely different thing! They were usually held in August and often referred to as the August meeting rather than a revival. Since August was our warmest month, a church filled with people became rather warm. The local funeral parlors had a quick remedy for managing the heat. Every country church had handheld fans with a spiritual picture on one side and large advertisements of the funeral home on the back. Needless to say, a hell-fire sermon and a reminder from the funeral home were great incentives to get people in the right frame of mind for soul-searching.

In some churches, a revival meeting took on the atmosphere of a carnival. I must have been about twelve years old when I went to such a service with my grandfather. It was a real hell-fire and brimstone sermon (totally different from anything I had ever heard before). Then there was an altar call. Several men and women from the church went up and down the aisles begging sinners to repent, long and loud. I was terrified! I had no idea what to expect next. Soon I realized that there was a long row of people kneeling in front of the pulpit, moaning and groaning loudly. The person next to me explained that was the "mourner's bench" where people confessed their sins and then got saved. Later I learned that was a pretty typical revival service in many mountain churches. The churches I had attended were far more sedate.

The revival was usually followed by a baptizing. Through the 1930s few rural churches had indoor baptisteries (except the Methodist and Episcopal, who used fonts). So down to the creek or river we went. The baptizing was often followed by a big "dinner on the grounds."

Weddings today are a far cry from those of my childhood. I was a college student when I first attended a formal church wedding (mid–'40s). The bride was from a rather affluent family. Prior to World War II most people in Western Watauga simply could not afford an expensive wedding. Most of the time the couple was married in the bride's home with her family present, or they went to a justice of the peace somewhere. For a wedding dress, the bride usually chose a dress that would be her Sunday dress for a while to come. When World War II came along, young couples often made spur of the moment decisions to marry before the groom went off to war. There was seldom time for making elaborate preparations. I recall one couple who were college students at Appalachian. He was about to be drafted and they wanted to marry immediately. The bride borrowed her roommate's dress for the ceremony. Later she asked to buy the dress but the roommate did not want to sell!

I was six years old when my mother's sister got married. The ceremony was in the parlor of my grandfather's home. The bride's immediate family was there. The bride wore a suit that would be suitable for traveling. Mama played the pedal organ and I was the ring bearer. I thought that was pretty exciting. I just could not understand why my grandmother cried and cried. Moving to Wyoming sounded pretty grand to me, not that I had a clue where Wyoming was. To me the grandest part was that I got a new dress: factory made too! Looking back, I guess that was a fairly typical wedding for that time. Some couples did marry in the church, but usually without the trappings of today.

Funerals have also undergone much change. Unlike weddings which have moved into the church, funerals have more or less moved out. In the '30s and '40s most funerals were in the church to which the deceased belonged. If the deceased did not have a church, the service was usually at the home. Those gathered for the service would stand in the yard or around the grave. I do not recall ever hearing of a service being at a funeral home. Friends were always received at home. Funeral home services became popular in the late '40s and early '50s.

I recall attending an "at home" funeral in the 1950s. The home was large and the weather was rather chilly. Most of the women went inside the house and the men stood in the yard. I was standing in a bedroom and some older ladies sat on the bed. We had to be very quiet to hear the minister, who was in another room. Suddenly, Wham! The bed in front of me crashed to the floor. No one was injured, the service proceeded, but most ladies near me had difficulty paying attention to the minister.

Len Stokes recalls that he and his brother Edward were asked to be pallbearers at the funeral of an older friend. The service was well attended but few elected to go to the gravesite. This occurred in the dead of winter and the old family cemetery was on top of a mountain. The road conditions were so poor that a hearse could not make the steep incline. However, a 4-wheel farm truck was brought in. By now, the pallbearers were on foot. As they neared the top of the ridge, the casket began to slide and soon it came off the truck and headed down the mountain. Len vows that it passed him doing 50 miles per hour. Len and Edward exchanged glances and without a word, they took off behind the casket. They probably passed the casket but they kept on going. They had had all the burial rites they could handle for one day.

The Country Store

Man is by nature a gregarious creature and from time immemorial it appears that he has enjoyed meeting with his acquaintances anywhere from an open campfire to the exclusive English gentleman's club. It was only logical that in the rural south the gathering place would be the country store. So it was in Western Watauga County.

The country store was a unique institution. The range of merchandise went from horse collars to chamber pots and from groceries to yard goods. Some even carried caskets for the dead. In the 1930s and '40s the barter system was alive and well. If one did not have cash or credit, a live chicken would do! (An egg would get a kid a package of Kool-Aid.) If a trusted customer did not have cash, he simply said to the clerk, "Set it down." With such a varied selection of goods and simple payment plans, it is no wonder the local men could easily find an excuse to go to the store.

Many such stores had a pot-bellied stove in the middle of the floor embellished by a circle of nail kegs. Often one keg was reserved for a checkerboard. It was a good idea to arrive early if one wanted to get in the game. The range of topics of conversation was as varied as the merchandise on the shelves. Sometimes the arguments became so heated it was necessary for the storekeeper to intercede. Most of the talk, however, concerned the weather, politics, or just local gossip.

Some stores were also the site of the local post office. During World War II a worried father might go to the store to await the delivery of the mail, praying that he could have news of a son on the front line or of family who had gone north to work in a war factory. If no news came, he did not have to tell the others. They knew instinctively; they were his friends and they asked no questions.

Each store seemed to have a personality of its own. Some seemed to be somber or even downright grumpy. The conversation was usually rather negative. Other stores rang with laughter from the jokes being told or the jokes men played on each other. Some groups had a reputation of playing harmless jokes on each other. From the Great Depression through World War II there was not much to laugh about and no doubt, these tricks were tension relievers.

In Clyde Mast's store, there was a sign that told its message and left the customer smiling, maybe. It was large and the first thing one saw when he entered the store. It went something like this: Old man credit is dead.

He lingered long and suffered much. Bad pay killed him. He died last week ... by this time he stinketh.

The country store did not offer gourmet food but it could provide a lunch that would sustain those too far from home to get a hot meal. A meal of fast food in the '30s and '40s might have been a hunk cut from a hoop of cheese sitting on the counter and soda crackers from an open barrel. Sardines and crackers were also favored lunch foods.

Although it was the male population that enjoyed the country store as their social life, that is not to say the women and children did not shop also. For them it was strictly for shopping. Sometimes the storekeeper's wife worked in the store, but it was primarily the men's domain.

In the mid to late '30s, when cars and trucks began to be commonplace, many country stores added gasoline pumps to their inventory. Perhaps this was the handwriting on the wall. With the coming of the auto, people could travel farther from home to larger shopping centers where there was a greater variety of merchandise. The 1950s and '60s saw the beginning of the end for the country store. Mast's Store in Valle Crucis has survived successfully because of its tourist appeal. Some owners have converted to a different type business, but many simply closed their doors. The 1970s gasoline crunch pretty much finished the rural gasoline pumps. The few stores in the rural parts of Western Watauga today are quite different from the markets of the 1930s and '40s. Only the older people can recall the heydays of places like Jim Mast's, Sherwood's, Don Hagaman's, Tom Moody's, Clyde Perry's, Clyde Mast's, Aubyn Farthing's and Doc Mast's. Time moves on!

INDEX